TOP PERFORMANCE

The book that picks up where the perennial bestseller *See You at the Top* leaves off...

"He will undoubtedly go down in history as the number one salesman of our time!"

> —Mary Kay Ash
> Founder and President
> Mary Kay Cosmetics

"Zig Ziglar is the Will Rogers of this generation."
> —Hal Krouse
> Republican National Committee, Colorado

"If anyone ever wanted a blueprint for success and leadership, *Top Performance* will be the book to read."
> —Dave Liniger
> Chief Executive Officer
> RE/MAX International, Inc.

"If they want the competitive edge, managers and doctors...in any industry ... had better read *Top Performance* ... no, I mean they'd better learn to live *Top Performance*!"
> —David M. Hunter
> Executive Vice President
> M. Bostin Associates

ABOUT THE AUTHOR

Zig Ziglar is the author of the nationwide bestsellers *Zig Ziglar's Secrets of Closing the Sale* and *See You at the Top*. He has been featured in *The Washington Post* and *The New York Times* and has appeared on *The Today Show*, *60 Minutes*, *The Donahue Show*, and *20/20*.

An internationally known authority on high-level performance, Zig Ziglar has spoken at thousands of motivational seminars across the country. His I CAN course is taught in more than 3000 schools, and hundreds of companies use his books, tapes, films, and videos to train their employees. He is recognized as one of the most dynamic speakers in America and has appeared on the same platform with such outstanding personalities as President Ronald Reagan, Dr. Norman Vincent Peale, Art Linkletter, and Dr. Robert Schuller.

To P. C. Merrill
A Top Performer
whose leadership by example
had a lifetime impact on my performance

ZIG ZIGLAR

Top Performance

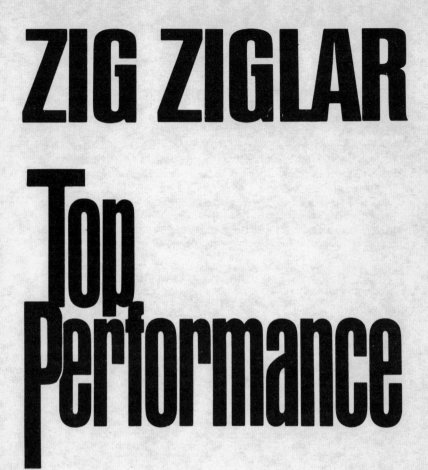

BERKLEY BOOKS, NEW YORK

This Berkley book contains the complete
text of the original hardcover edition.

TOP PERFORMANCE

A Berkley Book / published by arrangement with
Fleming H. Revell Company

PRINTING HISTORY
Fleming H. Revell Company edition published 1986
Berkley edition / April 1987

ISBN: 0-425-09973-3

A BERKLEY BOOK ® TM 757,375
Berkley Books are published by The Berkley Publishing Group,
200 Madison Avenue, New York, NY 10016.
The name "BERKLEY" and the stylized "B" with design
are trademarks belonging to Berkley Publishing Corporation.

PRINTED IN CANADA

Acknowledgments

In many ways, this is the most unusual and exciting book I have written. *Unusual* because for the first time, I worked with a coauthor. As a matter of fact, without the contribution and assistance of Jim Savage, our vice-president of Corporate Training, this book would not have been written. *Exciting* because this book makes practical tools out of the motivational principles I have shared for many years and which Jim has tested and applied in his career. He truly is the classic example of the axiom "If you do more than you are paid to do, you will eventually be paid more for what you do." He exemplifies the principles *Top Performance* teaches.

When Jim Savage joined our organization in January of 1981, it marked the end of his three-year pursuit of an opportunity to work with us. Initially, because we had no other opening, we hired him in a capacity which was considerably below his experience and capabilities. He had served as both a teacher and coach for eleven years, had worked as a scout with the Washington Redskins (two governors of the State of Texas and the Dallas mayor have issued proclamations forgiving him for that), and had functioned in an executive capacity with another human resource development company.

Initially, Jim traveled with me and was responsible for on-site activities, including sales of our products wherever I spoke around the country. Jim handled every assignment with complete commitment and with great enthusiasm. It was obvious to us that we had to utilize his talents and energies in other areas. For the last five years Jim has, among other things, authored training materials and manuals to enhance our product line and developed and implemented a comprehensive recognition-and-incentive program for our corporate staff. In addition, his abilities as a speaker and consultant have led to well over three hundred speaking and training opportunities with corporations of all sizes over the last three years. Thank you, Jim, for a job well done.

As always, Laurie Magers, my ever-faithful, always dependable administrative assistant, did a magnificent job; when called upon, Kay Lynn Westervelt, who works so closely with Laurie, also did a beautiful job. I owe a particularly heavy debt of gratitude to my friend Fred Smith, whom I hold in such high regard, for his willingness to contribute thoughts and ideas throughout the book. A very special thank you to Leo Presley, assistant state director of Business and Industry Services, Oklahoma State Department of Vocational Education, who encouraged us and gave important direction on getting involved on a larger scale in corporate America. Leo is one of the brightest young men I have ever known.

Also, to the president of the Zig Ziglar Corporation, Ron Ezinga, whose steady hand at the helm and encouraging guidance has kept us at least partially on course in meeting our guidelines. Then, of course, there's my wife, "the Redhead," whose willingness to tolerate some intolerable demands on our time together, combined with her loving support, has made the book not only possible but an exciting experience. To the other members of our staff and to the numerous authors who contributed through your articles, thank you.

Zig Ziglar

Contents

CONTENTS

PART II
The Science of Top Performance

PART III
Motivating the Top Performer

Foreword

Fifteen percent of the reason you get a job, keep that job, and move ahead in that job, is determined by your technical skills and knowledge—regardless of your profession! That's what human engineer Cavett Robert says. What about the other 85 percent? Cavett quotes Stanford Research Institute, Harvard University, and the Carnegie Foundation (which spent one million dollars and five years in the research) as having *proved* that 85 percent of the reason you get a job, will keep that job, and move ahead in that job has to do with your *people skills and people knowledge!*

I'm completely convinced he's right. As I travel around the country sharing ideas on personal growth, sales training, and the corporate concepts we teach at the Zig Ziglar Corporation, I become more and more aware of the critical need for specialized instruction on how we can *manage* ourselves and others for maximum effectiveness. As I visit with professionals from all walks of life, I see common problems in many—if not all—of the different situations men and women are facing . . . and the common denominator in these problems is always the same: people.

So obviously, "managing people" (starting with yourself) becomes a high priority if we are to be successful. In this book, we have three primary goals relating to understanding people management skills:

1. We will identify the key factors in people management, including helping managers to identify potential sources of conflict.
2. We will offer solutions to help overcome these potential sources of conflict.
3. We will share how you can apply the principles and ideas other managers have used successfully, thereby taking this book out of the realm of "theory" and making it applicable in the "real world."

According to *Megatrends* author John Naisbitt, "For the reinvented, information-age corporation of 1985 and beyond, the challenge is retraining *managers*, not retraining workers." With this in mind, the ultimate goal of *Top Performance* is to develop excellence in managers and to provide management with teaching procedures and inspiration to effectively develop and utilize team members.

MAKE THEM WANT YOUR LEADERSHIP

The foundation for developing yourself and others is wrapped up in this principle:

You can have everything in life
you want if you will just help
enough other people get what they want!

I have used this statement for nearly thirty years as a foundational truth, and never is the concept more accurate than when managing yourself and others. However, it is important for you to understand that I'm talking about a *principle* and not a *tactic*. As a tactic the words would be crass and ineffective. As a principle the concept works because it makes others *want* your leadership.

The great managers from all fields *know* that when they put people first, their effectiveness and efficiency improve. Zoltan Merszel, who left Dow Chemical to become president of Occidental Petroleum, said, "My philosophy is that *people* make business; technology is a distant second."

USE *ALL* YOUR STRENGTH

Chances are excellent you agree that one basic definition of *management* is "getting things done through people." The story is told of a little guy valiantly but futilely trying to move a heavy log to clear a pathway to his favorite hideout. His dad stood nearby and finally asked him why he wasn't using all his strength. The little guy assured his dad he was straining with all his might. His dad quietly told him he was not using all his strength, because he hadn't asked him (his dad) to help. Successful managers use *all* their strength by recognizing, developing, and utilizing the physical, mental, and spiritual talents of their subordinates. They learn what makes people tick, and they transfer their own feelings of excitement and enthusiasm to those who follow their leadership.

That last sentence is true whether you are a sales manager, a supervisor, a trainer, a corporate executive, a parent, a doctor, a teacher, a coach, or any number of other professionals "on the grow"! Chances are good that if you are not already doing well in your chosen career, you are on the verge of a breakthrough to becoming more successful. Regardless of your chosen profession in life, *Top Performance: How to Develop Excellence in Yourself and Others* is written specifically for *you!*

By now you should be ready to go, so hold on to your hat and grab your marking pen, because you and I are headed for the most action- and information-packed book you have ever *worked* through!

Introduction

―――――――――――――――――――――

Several years ago, this old boy down home won a bass fiddle in a drawing. It came complete with an instruction book, but unfortunately every page—except the first one—had been torn out. All that was left was a single picture showing the left hand in one position at the top of the fiddle and the other hand with the bow in a position across the strings near the middle of the bass fiddle. The old boy thought that was *the* position for playing the bass fiddle, so he carefully noted the position of each hand and started pulling the bow back and forth. Obviously, he was "Old Johnny One Note." Back and forth he drew the bow and the gruesome sound came forth. He was diligent in his practice and did it every single day.

Needless to say, his wife was soon climbing the walls. Then one day she went to a concert and, as it happened, sat next to the orchestra within a few feet of the bass fiddle. She was intrigued with the way the fellow moved his left hand up and down the strings while repeatedly changing the bow position. He made fast strokes and slow strokes and he pulled the bow all over those strings. The music was beautiful, so the wife returned home all excited about what she had seen and found old Johnny One Note playing his fiddle.

Knowing his nature and not wanting to upset him, she gently said, "Honey, can I ask you a question?" Without breaking stride or slowing down, he said, "Sure." Wife: "At the concert I noticed that the bass fiddle player kept moving his left hand up and down and left and right, while his right hand moved slowly on occasion and rapidly on occasion, and he moved it in a number of different spots. I'm just curious as to why he was moving his hands and the bow in so many different ways and places, while you hold both your hands and the bow in the same spot." The old boy never broke stride; continuing to play, he simply said, "The answer's easy. That old boy's still lookin' for his place and I done found mine!"

Now, my friends, obviously this story never happened, but I do fear it happens many times in life and in the business world, where many people "find their places" and don't want to make any changes. I know that's not your attitude in and about life or you wouldn't be reading this book! I share the story because you will have to deal with those who do have that kind of attitude. Hopefully, the suggestions we offer will help you in your own career, as well as give you some guidelines to help others open their minds to develop and use their abilities.

PART I

THE ART OF TOP PERFORMANCE

The object of art is to crystallize emotion into thoughts and then fix it in form.

Delsarte

Choosing to
Be a Top Performer

We are free up to the point of choice, then the choice controls the chooser.

Mary Crowley

1 Our success in life is determined by the choices we make. You are going to be making choices that will determine your success as you learn to manage yourself and others. To be effective in making proper choices, you must understand the difference between *reacting* and *responding*.

On January 23, 1981, I was in Kansas City, Missouri. It had been one of those weeks. As we'd say down home, "I'd been drove hard and hung up wet!" I wasn't just whipped—I was *whupped!* And there is a difference. That particular morning I had a lengthy recording session—four solid hours. When I record, of necessity I must turn my volume and tempo up a couple of notches. The only means of communication I have on a recording is my voice, so I must utilize it to the fullest or the people who listen to the recording might let their minds drift and miss the message.

That morning for four solid hours the session was wide-open, full-speed ahead, no holds barred. (I speak at about 280 words a minute with gusts up to 450.) I finished at exactly one o'clock and since we had a three o'clock departure time for Dallas, we had to hurry. The airline had told us to get to the airport at least an hour early to secure our recording equipment, which is very heavy and bulky. My son-in-law, Chad Witmeyer, who is the general manager for At the Top, our recording and cassette-duplication corporation, packed our gear as quickly as possible and the two of us made a mad dash for the airport, which is a thirty-minute trip from downtown Kansas City.

We pulled into the airport at exactly two o'clock. There were two long lines and we selected the shortest of the two. I noticed almost immediately that one of the ticket agents was walking around behind the counter and I saw a POSITION CLOSED sign at one end. My experience told me she would remove POSITION CLOSED and replace it with POSITION OPEN, so I mentally and physically got ready to make a quick dash to the counter when she opened the other line. In a matter of minutes she walked over the POSITION CLOSED sign, flipped it to POSITION OPEN, and smilingly announced to the group, "Those of you who have a seat on the three o'clock flight to Dallas come over here."

SURPRISE, SURPRISE!

Quick as a flash, I ran to her position and was first in line. The ticket agent looked at me, smiled, and said, "The three o'clock flight to Dallas has been canceled." To this I enthusiastically responded, "Fantastic!" When I said that, the ticket agent, with a puzzled expression on her face, asked, "Now, why in the world would you say 'fantastic' when I've just told you the three o'clock flight to Dallas has been canceled?" I smiled back at her and said, "Ma'am, there are only three reasons why anybody would cancel a flight to Dallas, Texas. Number one, something must be wrong with that airplane; number two, something must be wrong with the person who is going to fly that airplane; number three, something must be wrong with the weather they're going to fly that airplane in. Now, ma'am, if any one of those three situations exists, I don't want to be up there. I want to be right down here! Fantastic!"

HOT DOG, I'VE GOT SOME BAD NEWS FOR YOU!

Have you ever noticed how some people seem to delight in delivering bad news? It's as if they just can't wait to let you know that life is tough and you're in for a tough time. To my response, the ticket agent put her hands on her hips in an authoritative, "I'm not through with you yet" kind of position and said, "Yes, but the next flight doesn't leave until 6:05." To that I responded, "Fantastic!"

By now the other two lines of people were looking in my direction and undoubtedly wondering, *Who is that nut who says everything is fantastic?* The lady herself looked at me in complete shock and said, "Now I'm really puzzled. Why in the world would you say 'fantastic' when I've just told you that you've got a four-hour wait in the airport in Kansas City?" I smilingly said, "Ma'am, it's really very simple. I'm fifty-four years old and never before in my entire life have I had a chance to spend four hours in the airport in Kansas City, Missouri. Why," I said, "do you realize that at this moment there are literally tens of millions of people on the face of this earth who not only are cold, but who also are hungry? Here I am in a beautiful facility and even though it's cold outside, it's comfortable inside. Down the corridor is a nice little coffee shop. I'm going to go down there, relax for a few minutes, and enjoy a cup of coffee. Then I've got some extremely important work which I need to do and here I am in one of the nicest buildings in the whole area. It is easily the biggest, most comfortable, rent-free office I've ever had at my disposal. Fantastic!"

THAT'S PRETTY STRONG—EVEN FOR POSITIVE THINKERS

Now, I'm reasonably confident you may be saying to yourself, "Ziglar, I'll go along with a lot of this 'positive thinking' stuff, but man, that's a little strong!" You might even be saying to yourself, "I wonder if he *really* did say that?" As we'd say down home, "On my scout's honor, that's exactly what I said."

To this you might well say, "Okay, Ziglar, you said it. But now tell me the truth—did you *really* feel that way?" To this I respond, "Of course not!" At least initially I didn't really feel that way. Like most travelers who've had a tough week on the road, I would have preferred to have been on my way home, but for the next four hours I did not have that option. However, I did have two other options to choose from. I could have chosen to *respond*—which is positive—or I could have chosen to *react*—which is negative. I chose to respond.

If *react* and *respond* sound like the same things to you, let me explain the difference. You go to the doctor, who gives you a prescription and tells you to come back the next day. When you go back, if he looks worried and tells you he needs to change the prescription because your body is "reacting" to the medicine, you're probably going to be concerned. On the other hand, if he tells you your body is "responding" to the medicine, you're going to smile because you know you're on your way to recovery. So, to react is negative and to respond is positive—the choice is yours! It's a fact that *you can't tailor-make the situations in life, but you can tailor-make the attitudes to fit those situations before they arise.*

When the ticket agent told me my flight had been canceled, I could have reacted sarcastically and said, "That's great! That's just great! I've had reservations for this flight for over a month and I've had the ticket for two weeks. I've done everything you've told me to do, including nearly breaking my neck to get here an hour early. All I need is my boarding pass and my seat assignment, but without explanation and without apology you tell me some dodo has canceled my flight! Well, I want to know why the flight was canceled! As I drove up I saw several of your airplanes sitting out on the runway, not doing a cotton-pickin' thing. Why can't you take one of them and fly us to Dallas like you are supposed to? What are they doing out there, anyhow? Who made the dumdum decision to cancel my flight to Dallas, Texas?" I could have reacted in that sarcastic manner. *And the next flight still leaves at 6:05!*

RESPOND—FOR A BETTER TOMORROW

Now, my reading friend, there are some things you simply are not going to change. If you were born white, you're going to stay white. If you were born black, you're going to stay black. I don't care how much thought you give it, you're not going to add a single cubit to your height. You're not going to change when you were born, where you were born, how you were born, or to whom you were born. As a matter of fact, you're not going to change one single whisper that's taken place in the *yesterdays* of your life.

Tomorrow is a different subject. Regardless of your past, your tomorrow is a clean slate. You can choose what you want to write on that slate. You make that choice each time you decide to *respond* to negative events or *react* to those negative events. As a manager, when your employees act in a rude, thoughtless, and inconsiderate manner and are impossible to deal with, please understand you can still *choose* to respond or react. Your choice will play a major role in your relationship with your employee. Obviously, this doesn't mean that to lead others you, the manager, must be "perfect" and never blow your cool. That's not only unrealistic, it is impossible—and maybe even undesirable. After all, managers are people, too, and our employees need to know we are human and have feelings. On balance, however, we need to be careful we choose to respond far more often than we choose to react, and that when we react it is under control and is to the *action* the person took and not to the employee personally.

My friend Fred Smith, one of the truly outstanding consultants and management experts in America, gives us some helpful advice on this matter in his excellent book *You and Your Network*. Fred says that when others deal with us in a dogmatic or even in a mean and vicious way, it doesn't necessarily mean they want to hurt us. It could mean, and generally does, that they are acting that way because *they* are hurting.

21

If you will remember that

every obnoxious act is a cry for help,

you are way ahead of the game. Recognizing and accepting this fact makes it much easier for us to take a calmer, more levelheaded approach to our functions as managers and as people.

IT'S UP TO YOU

All of life is a series of choices, and what you choose to give life today will determine what life will give you tomorrow. You can choose to get drunk tonight, but when you do, you have *chosen* to feel miserable tomorrow. You can choose to light up a cigarette today, but when you do, you have *chosen* to die fourteen minutes early. You can choose to eat properly today and when you do, you have *chosen* to be healthier tomorrow. You can choose to be overweight, or you can choose to be the right weight. You can choose to be happy or you can choose to be sad. You can even choose, according to some authorities, to be insane—and *some* people make that choice to escape the responsibilities of dealing with life on a daily basis.

For twenty-four years of my adult life, by choice I weighed over two hundred pounds. I say this because in my lifetime (at least since infancy) I have never *accidentally* eaten anything! Every bite is carefully planned and deliberately taken. I even set aside at least three times *every* day when I concentrate almost exclusively on taking those bites of food. When I choose to eat too much today, I have chosen to weigh too much tomorrow. In 1972, I *chose* not to be overweight and took the appropriate steps to reach and maintain the correct weight. It was one of my better choices.

Never will I forget the night my wife (to whom I affectionately refer as "the Redhead") and I were in our favorite ice cream parlor when a young man and his girlfriend walked in. He appeared to be about twenty-three or twenty-four years old. I gently nudged the Redhead and pointed out the couple and the following dialogue took place.

Zig: "Do you see that couple?" The Redhead: "Yes, I do." Zig: "Wonder what happened to him." The Redhead: "What do you mean?" Zig: "Well, just look at him! He's been in some kind of accident. He's hurt!" The Redhead: "Aw, honey, he's not hurt! He's been to the barbershop." Zig: "You mean he paid money to look like *that?*" (In my lifetime, I've never seen a human being that badly mutilated from the ears up. It was awesome!) The Redhead: "Sure, honey! He's trying to be different and original, so he's chosen to imitate some rock star."

Don't misunderstand, one of the things I love best about my country is the fact that we are free and can *choose* to look any way we please. The major point I wish to make is that when that young fellow chose to look that way, he also chose to eliminate 98 percent of all employment opportunities. For example, we could not consider hiring him at our company. He would be a total distraction and we'd have to spend half our time just explaining him!

When a young person chooses to sit up late at night watching television or socializing, he has chosen to be sleepy in class the next day and, consequently, absorb less of the information he needs to know in order to be successful in the competitive world in which he lives. When we choose to be mean, nasty, and ornery to other people, we have chosen to be treated in a mean, nasty, and ornery fashion by others. By the same token, when we choose to be thoughtful and considerate of others, we've chosen to be treated in a thoughtful and considerate manner. The list is endless, but the message is always the same: *You are free to choose, but the choices you make today will determine what you will have, be, and do in the tomorrows of your life.*

You can choose to take the necessary steps to help you succeed as a manager, or you can choose to ignore the experience of successful managers and take the consequences for you and your employees. We must teach our employees that they are responsible for their attitudes and their conduct and that in life,

every choice we make, whether it is good or bad, has consequences!

Once those consequences are thoroughly understood, it's easier to make the right choices. As Mary Crowley, an outstanding Christian businesswoman and author, says, "We are free up to the point of choice, then the choice controls the chooser."

BACK TO THE AIRPORT

At the airline counter I had another choice. I could have ranted and raved and whooped and shouted and snorted and screamed and hollered. I could have made an absolute idiot of myself and embarrassed everybody around me as well as myself by screaming, "That's crazy! That's idiotic! I'm tired! I've been gone all week! My family wants to see me and I want to

see them! Who made this decision, anyway? Who runs this outfit?" Yes, I could have chosen that as the second reaction. *And the next flight still leaves at 6:05!*

THE CHOICE IS YOURS

I chose to respond as I did for one simple reason. I don't have, need, or want ulcers, high blood pressure, a heart problem, or any of the negative consequences that go with reacting. I have chosen to *respond* to negative situations in life instead of *reacting* to those situations. Even if this does not benefit anyone else, I'm persuaded that it is the best thing I can do for me. When it's the best thing for me, then obviously that puts me in a far better position to do my work, which basically is designed to help other people. That, my friend, is exactly the same position you are in. When you *respond*, you are making real progress toward living a healthier, happier life and developing effective, efficient, and happy employees.

As a practical matter, I do not know anyone who works for that monstrous airline. From the chairman of the board to the people who handle the baggage, I cannot give you the name of a single one. However, it is their airline and *if they choose to do so, they can cancel my flight. But they can't cancel my day!* It's mine. God Himself gave it to me with written instructions on how I am to use it. He told me to "rejoice—and be glad in it."

The problem with letting others "cancel your day" is that they just might want to cancel a second or even a third day (you know how folks are!). Then they might want to cancel the whole week or even a month. Some people have even permitted others to cancel a lifetime. As we go through *Top Performance*, we are going to look at specific steps and usable formulas that will help you make the right decisions while helping those for whom you are responsible to also make the proper choices!

INNOCENT—OR GUILTY?

Question: Have you ever been heading for work, driving along, minding your own business, your mind "in neutral," when suddenly somebody cuts sharply in front of you at an exit? You manage to avoid him by hitting your brakes full force while at the same time sounding your horn, shaking your fist at the offender, and even yelling, "You dummy! Why don't you watch what you're doing? I could've been killed and so could you!" Have you ever gotten upset about an incident like that and taken your anger to work, where you proceeded to tell everybody in earshot about this idiot who pulled in front of you and almost killed you? Did you wonder out loud why they allow people like that to get licenses? How could anybody have made such an idiotic mistake? And you go on and on and on as you describe in angry terms the idiot who almost killed you. "They ought to keep people like him off the streets!" you declare with righteous indignation.

In the meantime, the man who committed the dastardly deed rides merrily on, completely oblivious of the fact that you even exist or that anything unusual has happened. And yet, he is in complete control of your life. He is in charge of your mind and your emotions. He is affecting your productivity, your relationships with others, even your very future, and (once more) *he doesn't even know you exist!* One of our greatest gifts is the ability to choose the way we think, act, or feel, and the ultimate personal put-down is when we permit someone like the above-mentioned driver to take charge of our lives and our attitudes.

Think with me for a moment. If you are the way you are because "when your mother was pregnant with you she was scared by a runaway horse, and consequently you have been scared of big, brown animals ever since. . . ." If you are the way you are because they "snatched you off the potty too soon. . . ." If you are the way you are because of someone else, then here's what you do: You take the person who's responsible for the way you are to the psychologist, the psychologist will treat him or her, and *you* will get better! See how crazy that is? If you fall and break your arm, you don't send a friend to the doctor to have his arm set. You don't even send the one who pushed you! You go yourself—you take personal responsibility! It's the same for your mental and emotional health. You must accept personal responsibility.

Yes, I know that *your past is important*, but as important as it is, according to Dr. Tony Campolo, *it is not nearly as important to your present as the way you see your future.* Ralph Waldo Emerson was right when he said that what lies behind you and what lies before you pale in significance when compared to what lies within you. This is especially true when you learn to respond and not react to life's daily challenges.

It's been said before and it will be said again: You cannot change the past, but your future is spotless. You can write on it what you will. In order to do so, however, you need to learn to *respond* to the positive *and* the negative. Fortunately, you have far more control than you realize. For example, all of us have on occasion been guilty of saying, "He/She makes me so mad!" That simply is not so. As a wise man said, you can't stir the soup unless there's some soup in the pot to stir. Nobody can make you *act* mad unless there is already some mad in you. Mad rections are *learned* behaviors and consequently they can be *unlearned.*

You can watch a person go about his or her daily activities for days or weeks and learn a great deal about him. However, you can watch a person under adverse circumstances for five minutes and see whether he has learned to respond or react. Actually, you can learn more about him in a few minutes under trying conditions than you can in days of just watching him involved in daily activities.

Your response—or reaction—to the negative reveals what's inside of you. It exposes your heart and shows the kind of person you really are. The problem is that most people have a tendency to react instead of respond. They have a tendency to blame everything and everybody for the difficulties and reversals in life.

IT STARTED IN THE BEGINNING

The reaction—tendency to blame someone else for your difficulties—procedure is not new. It started back in the Garden of Eden. You undoubtedly remember the story. God placed Adam and Eve in the Garden of Eden; He gave them everything a human being could possibly desire or even imagine. It was the whole world, including the mineral rights (talk about a real estate deal—WOW!). However, He specifically instructed them not to eat the fruit from one special tree. But you know what happened: They ate the fruit.

When God came walking in the garden that evening, He called out, "Adam, where are you?" (This won't be verbatim.) Adam responded, "Over here, Lord," and the Lord asked Adam, "Did you eat the fruit of the forbidden tree?" Simple question. All God wanted was a yes or no answer. But Adam's answer set the precedent of pointing the finger of blame at someone else for our own difficulties, which the world has followed ever since. He said, "Lord, let me tell You about that woman You gave me!" The Lord then asked Eve if she had eaten the forbidden fruit and Eve replied, "Lord, let me tell You about that serpent!" (And of course, the serpent didn't have a leg to stand on!) I might not be completely right theologically with that last observation, but I am right when I say *you* don't have a leg to stand on when you blame other people and other things for your difficulties. Point: Don't waste time placing blame. *Fix the cause!*

QUESTION: DO YOU RESPOND OR REACT?

I've been beating the bushes a long time, but I seldom hear anyone make a habit of blaming someone else for his success. He doesn't say, "It's all my manager's fault. He/She spent a lot of extra time with me and made me study, drill, and prepare. He's/She's the reason I'm successful today." Most of the time we don't even say, "It was my spouse's or parents' fault. They kept after me night and day until I did what was necessary, and that's the reason I've been successful." No, most of us have a tendency to *blame* somebody else for our difficulties, but keep appropriate credit for our success to ourselves. What about you? Do you *respond* to the negative and make it better, or do you *react* to the negative and make it worse?

To be a Top Performer, you must make the proper choices. Now, if you have never had instruction on HOW to respond positively or WHAT Top Performers do to become Top Performers, then you have a "built in" excuse. But wait a minute! I'm not going to let you hang your hat on that excuse. Together, we are going to look at HOW, WHAT, WHO, WHY, WHEN, AND WHERE to make the proper choices so that you can get the most out of yourself and others!

PERFORMANCE PRINCIPLES

1. *Regardless of your past, tomorrow is a clean slate.*
2. *Every obnoxious act is a cry for help.*
3. *Don't waste time placing blame; fix the cause!*
4. *The choices you make today will determine what you will have, be, and do in the tomorrows of your life.*
5. *Top Performers learn to make the proper choices.*

Causing Others to *Want* Your Leadership

Leadership: the art of getting someone else to do something that you want done because he wants to do it.

Dwight D. Eisenhower

 In July of 1984, I was on a media tour of the country promoting my book *Secrets of Closing the Sale.* Now it just happens that I thoroughly enjoy this phase of my life. The schedule is generally hectic, but over the years the media, with few exceptions, has been extremely kind to me. Bookstores have been delighted to sponsor autograph parties because they generally sell lots of books, which is why they are in business. On this particular occasion, I ended up in a beautiful Houston, Texas, hotel at 2:30 A.M. I was really excited, since I had experienced a truly incredible day where *everything* had gone exactly right. Wonderful interviews, friendly people, lots and lots of sales, and my first interview the next day wasn't until 11:00 A.M.

A SENSE OF HUMOR WILL HELP

As I approached the desk to register, a quick glance at the night clerk told me things had not been going well for her. Her facial expressions indicated she had not only lost her last friend but had also had some M & M's melt in her hand, and might even have received some junk mail with the postage due. Despite her melancholy countenance, I enthusiastically approached the registration desk and the following exchange took place.

Zig: "Good morning, how ya doin'?" Night Clerk: "Oh, I suppose I'll make it." Zig: "I bet you not only make it, I bet you are going to win!" Night Clerk: "Well, you certainly feel good though it's so late!" Zig: "Yes, I do. When I woke up this morning I knew I was ahead of the game, because *some* people did not wake up this morning." (She *almost* smiled at that.) Night Clerk: "Well, I suppose that's the best way to look at it." Zig: "It definitely is." Night Clerk: "I suppose so, but I need to get you to fill out our registration slip." As I handed the slip back to her she said, "Now I need a major credit card." Fortunately, I was able to comply with her request and so I handed her this version of a truly major credit card.

MAJOR CREDIT CARD

Good for One Enthusiastic Laugh from Highly Intelligent Individuals with a Keen Sense of Humor and a Real Zest for Life! (or one small frown from the real sourpusses of the world).

_____
Signature

The Zig Ziglar ▓ Corporation

3330 Earhart, Suite 204 • Carrollton, Texas 75006 • (214) 233-9191

When she saw the card she burst out laughing and even demonstrated some real enthusiasm as she said, "You know,

I'm delighted you came along. I definitely feel better—but I'm going to need some other form of identification." With that comment I turned the card over and when she saw what you are now looking at, she almost did the proverbial roll on the floor:*

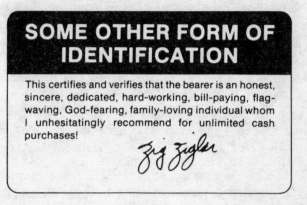

SOME OTHER FORM OF IDENTIFICATION

This certifies and verifies that the bearer is an honest, sincere, dedicated, hard-working, bill-paying, flag-waving, God-fearing, family-loving individual whom I unhesitatingly recommend for unlimited cash purchases!

Zig Ziglar

Question: Do you think she was a better employee the rest of her shift? I'll answer it for you. You betcha! Question: Why? Answer: A change of attitude.

I include this little episode because I believe that in our high-intensity world a sense of humor can play a major role in our physical and emotional health. Humor helps us relate to others and will help make them want to know us, to please us, and to want to follow our leadership and direction.

Robert DeBruyn has written an excellent book called *Causing Others to Want Your Leadership*. While this book is designed specifically for educators, I recommend it highly. There are so many practical and usable concepts in the book that it is worthwhile reading for all Top Performers. After all, one of the manager's most important functions is *teaching*.

Actually, I believe management goes beyond leadership,

*If you would like one of these "Major Credit Cards," send a stamped, self-addressed envelope to

> The Zig Ziglar Corporation
> 3330 Earhart
> Carrollton, Texas 75006

because management is that special kind of leadership where the goals of the organization must be combined with the goals of the individual for the good of both. If the individual's goals are more important than the organizational goals, or are in conflict with organizational goals, the organization will suffer. Similarly, if organizational goals overshadow individual goals or are in conflict with individual goals, the person will suffer. Excellent managers of people *cause* others to *want* them to channel energies for the maximum benefit of both.

This obviously applies whether we are talking about an office, an athletic team, a church, a home, or any situation where two or more people are gathered with a potentially common interest. Our objective must be to foster this common interest and be sure that individual and organizational goals complement each other as much as possible.

LEADERS DESERVE—AND GET—COOPERATION

No matter how brilliant or how technically capable you are, you won't be effective as a leader unless you gain the *willing cooperation of others*. For example, let's think together about the number of people you can really "force" to cooperate. Eliminate the boss because he is over you. You can't force those at your level because they are equal in authority. You can't even force a subordinate to obey without his filing a complaint, quitting, or developing so much resentment that his output will suffer, directly or indirectly. Realistically, if you have a subordinate who always agrees, watch out! It's probably because he lacks self-starting qualities, the ability to think for himself, or both. *Cooperation is not getting the other fellow to do what you want. Rather, it means getting him to want to do what you want.* And there's a great deal of difference by the addition of this one word *want*.

True cooperation generally depends on certain feelings that have been established over a period of time. It's the responsibility—and opportunity—of the leader to understand and develop these deeper feelings and then to work *with* them, rather than against them. Now let's look at some basic rules and thoughts for getting cooperation.

1. The sensitive, effective leader knows that to get real cooperation he must understand he probably doesn't have all the facts *or* feelings about anything.
2. Dynamic leaders understand that *anyone* can get along and work with those who agree with them. Real leadership involves getting along, working with, and getting maximum production from those with whom we disagree.
3. Effective leaders develop the ability to see things from the other person's perspective. They *sell* the advantages of cooperation instead of demanding it.
4. Organized leaders carefully plan their projects and choose the time and place when their ideas are most likely to be accepted, and then present those ideas in a clear, concise manner.
5. The successful leader starts with the basic premise that the other person is probably at least partially right and, consequently, doesn't let his own prejudice stand in the way of accepting valid counterproposals and ideas. He knows ideas don't care who owns or uses them, so he wins cooperation with an open mind.

WHY SHOULD ANYONE WANT TO FOLLOW YOU?

I hope that once you get past the "attention grabbing" value of the question you can turn your interest and attention to the point: Have you taken a personal inventory of your strengths as a manager? Come on, now, there must be some reason you have your position. This is not the time for false modesty. Try to recall those positive statements you have heard from others. The fact that we have trouble remembering positive reinforcement is a terrible indictment of our society and should emphasize to each of us the importance of sincerely pointing out the good we see in others. However, now is the time to honestly face some facts about yourself and your future as a manager of people. Look at areas such as Planning, Organization, Communication, Listening, Decision Making, Delegation, and Motivation. Before we go any further, right here and now list at least ten *strengths* you have as a manager of people.

Significant Reasons Others Should Want to Follow Me

1. _____

2. _____

3. _____

4. _____

5. _____

6. _____

7. _____

8. _____

9. _____

10. _____

Regardless of the length or strength of the list you made, you can become even more effective as a manager of people. John D. Rockefeller stated, "I will pay more for the ability to deal with people than any other ability under the sun." To cause others to *want* our leadership and management we must become experts in the kind of people skills to which Mr. Rockefeller was referring. According to Emerson, *our chief want is someone who will inspire us to be what we know we could be.* Dan Rather, "CBS News" commentator, took Emerson's idea a step further when he said, "The dream begins with a teacher who believes in you, who tugs and pushes and leads you to the next plateau, sometimes poking you with a sharp stick called 'truth.' " As a manager, you must embody all that these men are speaking of and more. If this sounds like an overwhelming task, it is not. Actually, becoming an expert in the people business can be very simple. I did not say "easy" . . . nothing in life is easy, but managing people should not—*must* not—be made complex.

Question: As a manager, if someone with the following qualities applied to you for a job, would you find a spot in your company or department for him or her? This individual has the evidence and can *prove* that he/she is honest, enthusiastic, intelligent, disciplined, dependable, caring, knowledgeable, humble, hardworking, persistent, loyal, organized, motivated, dedicated, patient, ambitious, energetic, friendly, goal-directed, personable, responsible, loving, and thoughtful. Not only that, but this individual has a positive mental attitude, is wise, has faith, is a good listener, has a marvelous sense of humor, a fine character, and shows integrity.

Question: Do you think this person would have a fair shot at success with your company? Two things: First, we both know this person could succeed with your company or with proper training in just about any job or profession he/she chose to enter. Second, odds are long that you think such a person doesn't exist—but I urge you, if you have that thought, *think again.*

Actually, the person with all these winning characteristics is *you.* Now before you protest too loudly, I challenge you to go over the list characteristic by characteristic. Think about it. You have *some* honesty, *some* enthusiasm, *some* intelligence, and so forth. You truly have *some* of every one of those qualities. You truly are a remarkable person—and so are the people in your company or department. Your challenge and responsibility is to further develop and use what you have and motivate your people to use what they have because they, too, have these characteristics. This short story makes a point about what you need to do to further develop these characteristics in your people.

Years ago in a remote Eskimo village, dogfights were the only diversion and "sport." One old Eskimo owned two particularly strong and vicious dogs who fought each other every Saturday. One dog won one week, but invariably the other dog won the following week. Interestingly enough, the owner of the dogs *always* bet on the winning dog. After the dogs got old and unable to fight, they were retired. At that point some-one asked the Eskimo how he had always picked the winning dog. With a twinkle in his eye, the old Eskimo replied that each week he fed only one dog and that week he bet on the one he had fed. Makes sense, doesn't it? As a manager I can tell you something which makes even more sense. To develop your abilities and further your career you need to "feed" your mind on a regular basis with good, clean, pure, powerful in-formation.

Doesn't it make even more sense to take these extremely good, winning qualities you *and* your people have (admittedly, in some of them your inventory might be fairly limited, but re-member that the mighty oak from the acorn grows), and *daily* feed your mind via good books, seminars, and cassette record-ings the information and inspiration needed to make these "acorns" of good qualities and characteristics grow into the "mighty oaks" which will carry you to your objectives?

Powerful, powerful suggestion: Write the list of qualities and characteristics identified on page 37 on a three-by-five-inch card and read them in the first person, present tense every day. This will be especially effective if you do it in front of a mirror while looking yourself directly in the eye. Be en-thusiastic and convincing. Do this just before you go to sleep so your subconscious mind can work with it all night.

I am honest
I am enthusiastic
I am intelligent
I am disciplined

DO YOU "RUSH" TO JUDGMENT?

A family counselor once said that what most wives want is a man they can look up to but one who will not look down on them. A manager's or leader's team members want *exactly* the same thing. Someone they can truly look up to—but someone who does not look down on them. This is the goal every manager should strive for in dealing with his people. This next page out of my own book of life makes the point quite well.

Several years ago, while on my way to a small town in Ohio for a speaking engagement, I had to stop in Pittsburgh to make a connection. I had a little over an hour on my hands and so, as I walked toward the connecting gate, I was in no particular hurry. Two young men had a booth and were shining shoes.

One of the guys was "Mr. Personality"—outgoing, jovial, pleasant—the kind of guy who could brighten up any party. The other was the exact opposite—somber, quiet, absolutely nonexpressive. He was "just there." I wanted the "Personality Kid" to shine my shoes, but he was still working on his customer when I arrived and the quiet young man was available, so I had no option.

As I stepped up into the chair, I cheerfully greeted the young man with, "How ya doin'?" He simply looked at me as if I did not exist and said absolutely nothing. I could not help but think that his behavior was certainly strange for somebody who was working with the public and who, to a very large degree, depended on his income from tips. However, since I am the "incurable optimist," I started rationalizing that in all probability I had gotten the one who was the best at what I wanted done—namely, shining shoes.

As the young man applied the saddle soap to clean the shoes, I immediately noticed he was very meticulous—extremely careful not to get any of the soap on my socks or my pant leg—and I was pleased with that. As he dried the shoes I again noticed how extraordinarily careful he was and how efficiently he worked. By the time he finished applying the polish, I was convinced I had come out ahead by getting him. He was very thorough and careful. As a matter of fact, he's the only guy I've ever seen who looked around at the back of my shoes to make certain he was applying polish everywhere.

When he started brushing the shoes it was obvious that he was using the artist's touch. He was very good and I was getting more enthusiastic all the time. When he applied the cloth to the leather, he had to use a little pressure to get the high gloss he wanted. It was at this point that, for the first time, I really *looked* at the young man. Since the enthusiastic kid in the next stand had finished, there was no one in the other chair, so things were extremely quiet and for the first time I heard an almost inaudible "uh-uh-uh." At this point I realized the young man was seriously handicapped.

As you can well imagine, I felt like about two cents. Here I, in my high-and-mighty judgmental way, had decided I was going to "honor" this young man by "letting" him shine my shoes! In my own mind, I was even going to be bighearted and give him a nice tip—*if* he was pleasant, courteous, gracious, outgoing, and also gave me a magnificent shine!

Needless to say, it was a very humbling experience and also needless to say, this young man got the biggest tip I've ever given anybody for shining my shoes.

I've often thought about the young man's parents and what a magnificent job they had done of raising him. He was neat and clean and he was using an extremely high percentage of his abilities. In short, his parents, or whoever raised him, were exceptional people and outstanding managers.

As managers, our job is to further the abilities our people have and then lead them to productively use those abilities. As my friend Fred Smith says, a manager "is not a person who can do the work better than his men; he is a person who can get his men to do the work better than he can." In many cases our employees have much more talent than we realize they have. It's also true that some people are a little slower than others at developing and manifesting their abilities. I think of people like Grandma Moses, who got such a late start in life; Albert Einstein, who was four years old before he could walk or talk; Thomas Edison, who was considered slow and dumb; George Westinghouse, who was labeled "impractical" and "dull," and was asked to leave college because his teachers didn't think he could make it—and yet he was awarded a patent for the rotary steam engine before he was twenty!

The point I'm making with this is—or should be—obvious. Most people have considerable ability, often undeveloped, which is not always immediately noticeable. Many others, like the young shoeshine boy, are more than willing to use what they've got to do a marvelous job. As managers, we need to be ever alert to find and develop whatever talent is available in our company or department.

A FORMULA FOR SUCCESS

I think you will agree that the responsibility of your unit—whether it is you and one other person or you and one hundred other people—is to function together for a common cause or purpose. Unquestionably, the 1984 Olympics held in Los Angeles were a great triumph. One of the primary reasons was Peter Ueberroth, the man in charge, the MANAGER. Mr. Ueberroth was successful, according to many of those who worked closely with him, because he made everyone believe they were involved in a *cause* that was bigger than the individual. The way he involved everyone in his (and their) cause was by using excellent PEOPLE SKILLS. He developed a team spirit and had everyone working together for the same end result. You can do the same thing with smaller or larger units by understanding a simple formula for success.

Much has been written and said about team effort. It's important for the family, for the athletic team, and for the work place. Recently a friend of mine was discussing a basketball team for which his son plays. The team was functioning quite well early in the season. There were no "superstars" on board, but they had learned considerable discipline and a series of plays which were enabling them to beat teams which actually had greater individual talent. They had a good record. Then two guys who had been ineligible regained their eligibility and joined the team at the change of semesters. As individuals, these two guys were bigger, stronger, faster, and better shooters, but unfortunately they did not have the discipline, nor did they know the plays. The net result was, though they had the talent, they actually were liabilities instead of assets to the team. Important point: They were liabilities because the coach did not have the courage to keep them on the bench *until* they learned the plays and developed the discipline to function as team members instead of individual talents. That coach (manager) let himself, his team, his supporters *and* the two individuals down.

As managers we frequently have similar situations arise in which an individual might have great talent and ability, but because of certain personality traits, annoying habits, or refusal to function as part of the team, they became liabilities instead of assets. The most important function a manager has is to bring the individuals together as a team—in other words, to make them "GEL."

In athletics we often hear coaches talk about team spirit. They sell their units on the importance of playing together for a common cause: WINNING! One of the catchwords that coaches use to describe unity is *gel*. They will say that the offense is just beginning to gel; or to be successful the defense must gel. Of course, they are talking about playing *together* and not as individuals; putting the objectives of the unit ahead of personal gain so that when the unit wins there will be great gain for each member of the team.

Some reporters have spelled *gel* with a *J* because of the television commercials about Jell-O, but actually *gel* means "to congeal or come together." For our purposes, let's take these three letters and use them as an acrostic to remind us how to be experts in the business of managing people.

The next three chapters will take each of these letters individually and give specific instructions on how we can use this formula to become Top Performers.

PERFORMANCE PRINCIPLES

1. *A sense of humor is vital to good leadership.*
2. *Common goals plus a common cause equals greater success.*
3. *Cooperation must be earned, not demanded.*
4. *Face up to your strengths as well as your weaknesses.*
5. *You have some of every quality necessary for success.*
6. *All resources are not obvious; great managers find and develop available talent.*

Look for
the Good

How far you go in life depends on your being
tender with the young, compassionate with the
aged, sympathetic with the striving, and tolerant
of the weak and the strong. Because someday in
life you will have been all of these.

George Washington Carver

Goodfinders

Expect the Best

Loyalty

3 The G in our GEL formula stands for *Goodfinders*—
those who are experts in Top Performance learn to
look for the good in each person they manage.

Andrew Carnegie said, "No man can become rich
without himself enriching others." He went on to
live this philosophy, as evidenced by the 43 millionaires he
had working for him. A reporter interviewing Mr. Carnegie
asked how he was able to hire that many millionaries. Mr.
Carnegie patiently explained that the men were not million-

aires when they came to work for him, but had become millionaires *by* working for him. When the reporter pursued the line of questioning as to how he was able to develop these men to the point they were worth that much money, Mr. Carnegie said, "When you work with people it is a lot like mining for gold . . . when you mine for gold, you must literally move tons of dirt to find a single ounce of gold. However, you do not look for the dirt—you look for the gold!"

It works the same way when you want to develop people to their full potential. You must look for the gold (the good), and when you find it you nurture it and bring it to fruition. Another wise man expressed it this way: The greatest good we can do for others is not to share our riches with them, but to reveal theirs to them.

Bill Hewlett, one of the founders of Hewlett-Packard, said, "Our policy flows from the belief that men and women want to do a good job, a creative job, and that if they are provided with the proper environment they will do so." Since people want to do a good job, why shouldn't we point out their success as it occurs?

The next illustration, which comes from my childhood, tells about an effective method of dealing with your people when they don't do their jobs as effectively or professionally as they can and should. As you read this, I encourage you to remember some wise words from Dr. Norman Vincent Peale: "The trouble with most of us is that we would rather be ruined by praise than saved by criticism."

CRITICIZE THE PERFORMANCE—NOT THE PERFORMER

Some of you will recognize the following story from my book *Raising Positive Kids in a Negative World*, but it so vividly makes the point, I wanted to repeat it here. When I was a small boy down in Yazoo City, Mississippi, things were pretty tight during those depression years and everybody had to work smarter and harder. As a leader, and as a manager, I honestly believe my mother, despite her fifth-grade education, would rate close to the top.

Dad died when I was five years old and there were six of us too young to work. Remember, now, that this was in the heart of the depression and things were tough for everyone. We survived because we had a very large garden and five milk cows. I was milking and working in the garden by the time I was eight years old and, for what it's worth, let me interject the fact that cows don't "give" milk—you have to fight for every drop!

Two things we always knew when Mother gave us an assignment. Number one, we knew what she *expected* (our very best). Number two, we knew she was going to *inspect* to make certain she got what she *expected*.

I'll never forget my first solo assignment in the garden. On this particular day, because my mother was also a good teacher, she showed me exactly what I needed to do to properly hoe those beans. When she finished her lesson, she pointed to three long rows of beans—which were about three and a half miles long (well, would you believe three?). But to an eight-year-old boy they looked more like ten! Anyhow, Mother instructed me that when I finished I was to call her so she could inspect what I had done. When I finally finished I called her for the inspection. As she looked the job over, she did what she always did when she was not pleased with something. She folded her hands behind her back, ducked her head, cocked it slightly to the right, and started that little left-to-right motion which I knew all too well. As she was doing this, I asked her what was the matter. She smiled and said, "Well, son, it looks like you're going to have lick this calf over."

Now in the corporate world that might seem like a strange term, but in rural Mississippi during the days of the depression, it simply meant that what I had done was unsatisfactory. Obviously, I knew what she was saying, but—hopeful for an escape—I smiled and said, "Mama, I wasn't botherin' the calf—I was hoeing those beans!" With this my mother chuckled and said, "Well, son, what I mean is this: For most boys this would be perfectly all right. But you're not most boys. You're *my* son, and my son can do better than this."

What Mother had done was extremely wise. *She had criticized the performance* because it badly needed criticism, *but she had praised the performer* because he needed the praise.

Effective management, whether in athletics, education, family, or business is measured by your effectiveness in managing your personnel to get maximum productivity and benefits for all. To accomplish this objective there are two things which great managers always do. Number one, they always *expect* every member of the team to do their best; and number two, they always *inspect* to make certain they get what they *expect*ed. (There is almost *nothing* as demotivating to a subordinate as having a completed project ignored or taken for granted after heart and soul have been poured into that project.)

Question: Suppose your inspection reveals that the project is either unsatisfactory or not up to the standards you feel that individual is capable of attaining. Do you "brag on him" or "fuss at him"? Answer: Neither. To brag on any project which represents less than a person's capability is to encourage mediocrity and the corporate world is already oversupplied with that commodity. You *owe* that person more than that. To "fuss" at him or to be harshly critical could well destroy the subordinate's confidence and stifle his initiative for future projects. You also owe that person *and* your company more than that. So what do you do? Answer: You use a page from my mother's notebook. Criticize the performance . . . not the performer!

Effective leadership demands that kind of approach. Extend the hand of encouragement to the person while making it clear that you expect—even demand—that he or she use their ability for maximum results. In short, have that person reaching for more, but do it without challenging or questioning his worth as an individual. Assure him or her that you *really* respect and appreciate their ability—and that's why work which is not consistent with their ability is unacceptable.

THE ABC'S OF MANAGEMENT

Ken Blanchard has worked with several other outstanding authors to compile a series of "One Minute" books. These books are easy to read and have really simplified some foundational concepts. Dr. Blanchard worked with Dr. Robert Lorber on a book called *Putting the One Minute Manager to Work*. In this outstanding book, these men identify the ABC's of management and reveal some startling facts.

A = Activators . . . what a manager does *before* performance
B = Behavior . . . performance, what someone says or does
C = Consequences . . . what a manager does *after* performance

For example, according to Blanchard and Lorber, "Most people think that activators have a greater influence on performance than consequences. And yet, only 15–25% of what influences performance comes from activators like goal-setting, while 75–85% of it (behavior) comes from consequences like praising and reprimands." What happens *after* a person does something has more impact than what happens *before!* To use another "one minute" phrase, "Catch them doing something right!" If you can catch people doing something well, no matter how small it may seem, and positively reinforce them for doing it, they will continue to grow in a positive direction.

Does this mean that we are to ignore the mistakes of those for whom we are responsible? Of course not, but there is a correct way to handle these errors or deal with the person whose overall job performance is unsatisfactory or begins to slip. I will address these issues later in this chapter. For the moment, however, let me simply state that the *best managers make finding the good in others a priority*. Too many managers do exactly the opposite.

ACTION OFTEN PRECEDES THE FEELING

Most of us, in our daily managerial duties, don't feel like Goodfinders. As a matter of fact, we often become the exact opposite and function in a role similar to school disciplinarians or police detectives. Den Roossien, executive vice-president of the Zig Ziglar Corporation, uses a slightly different technique I would like to recommend to you. Den is responsible for the daily operations of our company and is our chief financial officer. He comes from an accounting background. Den would be the first to tell you that people skills are not emphasized in accounting courses, and that he really has had to study and work on this area of his professional expertise. I can proudly report to you that Den Roossien has (by his own hard work, study, and dedication) become an outstanding "people" manager and communicator.

One technique Den uses, which I believe you will find extremely helpful, is to keep a running list of the minute and sometimes seemingly insignificant successes of the people who fall under his responsibility. This may include things such as staying late to see that a "rush" package gets out in the warehouse, or coming in early to set up the chairs for our Monday-morning devotions—the little things that make the big difference. He will verbally point out the fact that he appreciates the effort—*as soon as possible after the behavior.* This follows one of the most important rules of positive reinforcement: *it should be immediate.* In addition, he notes the behavior in a notebook so that at the end of the year, or at quarterly review times, he can share with our People Building Team a series of seemingly inconsequential behaviors that have worked together to dramatically impact the bottom line of our company.

The time involved in doing this is really worthwhile when compared to the goodwill and positive reinforcement benefits. Sure, it takes discipline to remember and follow through, but Den is committed to a disciplined approach when it comes to the factors and procedures which positively impact our company. Discipline and organization are both involved and fortunately, Den has developed both these characteristics in spades (there is even a persistent rumor that he is so well organized he periodically proofreads the Xerox copies).

Does he always *feel* like doing this? Certainly not, but action often precedes the feeling. When it comes to giving positive feedback, we sometimes may not *feel* like doing so; that is why it is even more important that we do so immediately. If griping and complaining can become a habit, why can't goodfinding become a habit? One reason is that we have not been trained to look for the good. Another obvious one is that we don't fully comprehend the motivational impact a word of encouragement can have on an employee or co-worker.

FINDING FAULT AS IF
THERE WERE A REWARD FOR IT

Jim Savage, my good friend, chief research associate, and coauthor of this book, tells a fascinating story about a retired professor at Louisiana State University in Baton Rouge. He was a psychology professor and though he was Chinese, he communicated beautifully in English—unless he wanted to have a little fun with his classes. Then he would do the best "Charlie Chan" imitation you have ever heard! Early one semester, a student had an examination paper returned that looked like the one in the illustration—it had only one mark in each corner of the paper. Frustrated that his paper was not graded properly (as all the other papers had been), the student stood up to demand an explanation. "Sir, I don't understand! Everyone's paper is graded properly except mine—all this test has is one mark in each of the four corners! What does that mean?" The professor got that big smile on his face that let you know his best "Charlie Chan" was coming, paused for dramatic effect, looked out over the auditorium class of three hundred students, and said, "Zero so big, not fit on paper!"

After thinking about this story, it dawned on me that as managers we often play similar games. While the professor's joke was done in fun, it still had an impact on that embarrassed student. Part of the reason we are tempted to play these deadly games is that we have been trained or conditioned to do so. You remember how it was when you were in school. You got that paper back and even though you scored 85–90 percent, the paper had so much red on it that it looked like it was mortally wounded and was in the final stages of bleeding to death. Remember? The markings screamed, "YOU MISSED THESE TWO, YOU BIG DUMMY!" I'm confident you and I are alike in at least one way. If we get 85–90 percent of our work correct, we would like to have somebody point out some of *that* part in addition to the parts we fell short on.

When I work with teachers I often tell them I'm going to ask the principal to take away all their red marking pens and replace them with blue marking pens and instructions to mark the correct answers on all exams. Now, I understand a test is not only an evaluation tool but a reteaching tool as well. And I understand that when we correct somebody we work with it's an evaluation and is designed to teach that person. But I also understand, as you do, that recognition is one of the most important tools to teach and motivate in every job. We must point out the good as well as the things that people do wrong. Instead, we too often get involved in the terrible game of "Gotcha!" You do 99 percent correct work and you may be completely invisible, but make one little mistake and . . . "Gotcha!" The manager jumps on the employee with both feet. Like a cheap suit or an ugly rash, he's all over him! One little mistake and "Gotcha!" That is unwise and unfair and is devastating in its impact on productivity.

A TOOL TO TEACH AND MOTIVATE

One of the most effective tools you can ever use to teach and motivate is a sincere compliment—with the emphasis on *sincere.* The more sincere the compliment, the more effective it will be. Unfortunately, too many of us pass out those sincere compliments as if each one were skin off our backs, or as if we had a limited supply which we were saving. In our business, personal, and family lives, we continue to play the "Gotcha!" game. You come in at the end of the day, walking kind of proud, wearing your new coat and tie, and your loving spouse greets you at the back door. Her eyes grow large as she zeros in on your new attire and your proud bearing and she says, "Honey, I like your coat and tie . . . [pause] . . . hang on to them—I hear they're coming back in style." Gotcha!

But you get back at your loving mate. As you sit down at the dinner table you look over the meal she has slaved to prepare for you and announce to the entire family, "What a magnificent meal! Why, this food is fit for a king . . . [pause] . . . here King, here King!" Gotcha!

Don't get caught up in the humor of these illustrations because that's exactly what happens in real life. We give a compliment and humorously "pull the rug" from under our "victim," thinking that no harm is done. Evidence is solid that even one nasty "gotcha" can do serious damage and a continuous barrage of them can do irreparable harm and adversely affect an entire department.

Part of our hesitancy in sharing compliments comes from the fear of being misunderstood. If a man greets an attractive lady at a business or social occasion with, "That's a beautiful dress," she might wonder about his motive. If you compliment a male acquaintance with, "That's a great looking watch you have on," he might well think you're trying to set him up for a future favor or even a small loan. So even though both compliments would be sincere, we often don't share them because of the FEAR of being misunderstood. This results in two people losing because *you cannot receive a sincere compliment without feeling better . . . and just as important, you cannot give a sincere compliment without feeling better yourself!* Sharing the compliment results in a Double Win!

A RIGHT WAY—AND A WRONG WAY

As an optimistic Goodfinder with many years experience, I'm convinced that with commitment and persistence you can find *something* good about any person, performance, or situation. After all, even a stopped clock is *exactly* right twice *every* twenty-four hours! To illustrate the point, let's look at a wrong and a right way of handling a coaching situation. The example is from athletics, but it could just as easily have been from business, education, family, or the church.

The offensive line coach of the football team had a player who did a great job of accelerating out of his stance, but he didn't roll his hips into the block, so the coach—in a loud voice—said to him, "Dummy, roll your hips!" When he said "Dummy," the player visibly slumped and his ears shrank to the size of a pinhead. He didn't want to hear anything else this misguided coach had to say. He was on the fourth team, he knew he was on the fourth team, but his mama and daddy knew he should be on the first team. His girlfriend was telling him he should be first team, and he knew full well that if he didn't have an idiot for a coach he would already be on the first team. When this "coach" addressed him as "Dummy," he didn't want to hear anything else the man had to say.

On the other hand, suppose the coach had said to him, "Man, that's a *great* job of coming out of your stance [remember, it really *was* a great job of accelerating out of the stance], now if you will just roll your hips, we can win with that block!" When the coach said *great*, and *win*, the player brightened perceptibly, smiled broadly, and made better use of his ears than Dumbo, the Walt Disney flying elephant hero with the huge ears. He wanted to hear everything his coach—obviously a combination of Vince Lombardi, Tom Landry, and Don Shula rolled together—had to say! And the coach was able to get in his correction quickly, painlessly, and far more effectively because the player listened more attentively to the coach, who was observant enough to see the *great* way he had come out of the stance.

There are two things you must remember if you are going to use this technique. Number one: *The compliment must be sincere.* If not, the people you work with will know it faster than you do and you will lose all credibility. Number two: *You cannot follow every compliment with a correction.* When this happens, the technique is viewed as manipulative because *it is.* This results in the Double Lose in the long run.

How do you feel when you get a memo or phone call and the boss says, "I want to see you, and *right away!*" Ninety-five out of one hundred people get that "glitch" in their stomachs and that *How did he find out?* thought in their minds. We have been trained to expect the worst in that type of situation. However, imagine that your boss is the kind of people manager who looks for the good and normally compliments you. When you get the call, you actually look forward to your time together—it's a whole new mind-set. The real question is, *How do you want your workers, friends, spouse, children, and others to feel when they get the call that you want to see them?*

A TOOL FOR WRITTEN FEEDBACK

Some people really do have trouble verbalizing feedback, but have no fear because this is an acquired or learned skill. However, until you learn the skill, you need a practical tool for feedback. Here is a great one for you, whether you have excellent verbal skills or are just learning. In our Zig Ziglar Corporation seminars, we use a tool or concept called the "I LIKE ... BECAUSE" pad. Each participant is given a pad like the one shown in the illustration and asked to note things they like or appreciate about class members during the seminar. This is an original idea, given to us by the Bay City High School in Bay City, Texas. It has an enormous impact on seminar participants as well as on numerous homes and businesses across America where it is used.

The I LIKE ... BECAUSE pad teaches us to look for the good and causes us to point out the positives we see in others. The comments run from the simple, such as complimenting the way a person smiles, to the more complex ideas, showing deeper levels of appreciation.

When we first introduced the concept in our three-day BORN TO WIN seminar in Dallas, there was one participant who used his body language to express his obvious disapproval. He squirmed, turned to the side, folded his arms and legs, and in general said, "I'm not having any part of this silliness!" Well, our seminar facilitators watched this man's comments carefully as they distributed the sheets to the participants. The first comments were seldom more than a few words. On day two, his comments gradually got longer, and on day three he was filling up the front and back of the sheets. At the end of class, he stood up and said, "When these I LIKE

I like _____

because _____

_____

_____

_____

You Are A Winner!!!

... BECAUSE pads were introduced, I thought it was the silliest idea I had ever heard, but it's amazing how much you people have changed over the last three days!" Obviously, the people had changed because BORN TO WIN really is a life-changing experience, but even more obviously, this man had also changed because he was learning to look for the good in others.

We have a two-day seminar called EFFECTIVE BUSINESS COMMUNICATIONS, in which we coach people on their communication skills. Over the two days, the people are videotaped a dozen times and given private coaching and feedback on how they might improve their communication skills. In addition to American Airlines, DuPont, and others, world-famous Neiman-Marcus department store had our instructors "in house" to train some of their key personnel. They liked the I LIKE concept, adapted it, and printed YOU ARE WHAT WE'RE FAMOUS FOR! on their pads. Under this great heading they write their positive comments about their peers.

DOES ANYBODY EVER REALLY USE THOSE THINGS?

Laurie Magers is my administrative assistant, and one of the most efficient people you will ever meet. In over nine years of working together, I think she made three mistakes (and two of those were my fault!). The error she probably felt worst about was forgetting to tell me (again) about a television interview. You can imagine how badly she felt, and despite the fact that I pointed out this was no major catastrophe and that it was at least 50 percent my fault, she was feeling very down for the biggest part of that day.

The next day when Laurie arrived at work, there were over thirty-five I LIKE ... BECAUSE notes hanging from the air conditioner vent above her desk. Some of her friends at the office had noticed that she was down, found out why, and decided to do something to cheer her up. Someone had written, "I LIKE LAURIE BECAUSE SHE CAN LEAP OVER A TALL BUILDING WITH HER TYPEWRITER UNDER HER ARM!" and someone else wrote, "I LIKE LAURIE BECAUSE SHE TYPES AT THE SPEED OF LIGHT!" And there were others that said, "I LIKE LAURIE BECAUSE SHE IS ALWAYS WILLING TO LISTEN!" or, "I LIKE LAURIE BECAUSE SHE IS THE MOST CONSCIENTIOUS PERSON IN THE ZIG ZIGLAR CORPORATION!" Laurie was literally moved to tears by the thoughtfulness and encouragement of her fellow employees—and talk about motivated—man alive, you should have seen her productivity! She was back to normal in no time flat. The thoughtfulness of others, the fact that others were willing to look for the good and then point it out, helped Laurie through a difficult time.

Now if you are having a little trouble with the concept, this probably means you are zeroing in on the wrong word. The key word on the sheet is not LIKE. If that word bothers you, simply scratch it out and insert *appreciate* or *respect*. The key word is BECAUSE! This word moves the concept out of the superficial and general into the sincere and specific.

All of the effective management books on the market today encourage us to give feedback to employees. Giving feedback successfully means pointing out *specific and observable behavior.* "I LIKE JOHN *BECAUSE* HE BROUGHT IN THE PROJECT ON TIME AND UNDER BUDGET!" Not, "I LIKE JOHN BECAUSE HE IS A GOOD EMPLOYEE." "I LIKE JANE *BECAUSE* SHE WORKED OVERTIME FOR THREE STRAIGHT DAYS TO FINISH AN IMPORTANT PROJECT!" Not "I LIKE JANE BECAUSE SHE WORKS HARD." Remember: *Catch them doing something right!* When you do, you build on what's right instead of what's wrong.

Unless you have written or received an I LIKE . . . BECAUSE note, you cannot fully comprehend the impact of such a simple idea. Let me offer you a challenge right now: I want you to think of someone you need to tell that you appreciate, like (love), and/or respect. Please, think of that someone and make a commitment to yourself to stop reading and share a verbal or written I LIKE *immediately!*

Our course for schools is called the I CAN course. Developed by Mrs. Mamie McCullough, it is based on the principles in *See You at the Top*. One of the assignments we give the students is to go home and tell their parents they love them. You would be shocked, but your heart would also be warmed, if you could read some of the letters or listen in on some of the phone calls we get from parents in tears because, for the first time in their lives, a twelve- or fourteen-year-old child has said he or she loves them. There's somebody in your life you need to let know you appreciate. You really need to make a commitment to *you* to do that today! Go ahead. The first time is by far the most difficult or awkward. In short order, because of the wonderful feedback, it will be fun and extremely rewarding.

UNUSUAL COMMODITIES

Love and respect are possibly the two most unusual commodities in our society today. Unfortunately, they are also among the rarest. The reason they are unusual is that the *only* way we can *get* them is by *giving* them away. If you are not as loved or respected as you would like to be, you should give yourself a "gut" check and see if you are giving either of these items away. An important fact to remember is this:

> You cannot give away something
> you do not possess!

In other words, the love and respect you should give to others is something you must have within yourself!

"There are high spots in all of our lives," wrote George Matthew Adams, "and most of them have come about through encouragement from someone else. I don't care how great, how famous or successful a man or woman may be, each hungers for applause." If you will just recapture how good *you* feel after you have encouraged someone else, no other suggestion is necessary to persuade you to seize every opportunity to give encouragement. "Encouragement is oxygen to the soul. Truly great work seldom comes from a worker without encouragement. No one ever *lived* long, happily or productively without it."

Along these lines, an article in Dr. Mortimer Feinberg's superb *Management* newsletter reinforces the point.

> William James, the noted psychologist and philosopher, said without qualification: *"The deepest principle in human nature is the craving to be appreciated."* By helping to preserve the rival's self-respect, the effective leader brings him closer to alliance by demonstrating a shared *concern in a major area of personal values.*

> This approach is *desirable* in dealing with opponents; it is *vital* in dealing with subordinates. The constant objective of higher-level executives must be to strengthen the competence and commitment of those who, in the last analysis, are responsible for implementing organizational objectives.

> As Dr. Alan C. Filley writes in his important book *Interpersonal Conflict Resolution,* the portrait we draw of ourselves is a major determinant of how we behave:

>> Various studies indicate that those low in self-esteem (1) are more likely to feel threatened in a situation, (2) are more vulnerable and dependent upon a power laden situation, (3) have greater need for structure, (4) inhibit aggression, (5) are easily persuaded, and (6) yield more to group pressure than those high in self-esteem.

> Not to be ignored is the importance of encouraging members of the group to respect each other. Acknowledging individual achievement should be done in ways that not only strengthen relationships between superior and subordinate but between the latter and his peers. Praise given to one person should never be stated in terms that criticize other members of the group. And wherever the achieve-

ment was in fact accompanied by help from others, their contribution should also be acknowledged. Any other approach is likely to lead to group tensions rather than increased cooperation.

Essentially, the key principle is the importance of *sharing the credit*, both with and among subordinates. In a rare moment of self-revelation, Casey Stengel once said in perfectly literate phrases: "Ability is the art of getting credit for all the home runs somebody else hits." But the surest way to keep the team from hitting home runs is to take the credit for yourself and never administer the athlete's salute—the pat on the base-runner's behind.

BUT ISN'T THERE A TIME WHEN WE MUST "COME DOWN" ON OTHERS?

Yes. Of course all feedback is not going to be positive. Some of you are thinking that I have overemphasized the concept of "goodfinding"—and you are partially correct. You really cannot say too much or find too much good in others, as long as each comment is sincere. The reason I have spent such an extended time talking about pointing out the good is that we (as a society in general) are so negligent in doing so. Now that the point has been emphasized, exactly how do we go about letting others know we are *not* pleased with their performance?

Answer: We start by really understanding what Jean Paul Richter meant when he said, "A man takes contradiction and advice much more easily than people think, only he will not bear it when violently given, even if it is well-founded. Hearts are flowers; they remain open to the softly falling dew, but shut up in the violent downpour of rain."

Bryan Flanagan, an outstanding speaker and sales manager of our Corporate Training Division, holds the honor of being recognized by our staff as one of the most outstanding I LIKE . . . BECAUSE writers in our office. Everyone looks forward to getting feedback from Bryan because he is so kind and so specific. He carefully validates every compliment he gives. Many times he will give verbal feedback to support the written I

LIKE and will do this in front of the supervisors of those he is complimenting—always sincerely.

Bryan also uses all the proper tools and techniques when it is time to give instructive feedback to those for whom he is responsible. On one occasion, Jim Savage, Bryan's longtime friend and immediate supervisor, observed a "less than highly motivated" employee exiting Bryan's office. Naturally, he was interested in what happened. Here is what Bryan told Jim:

> You know, Jim, that young lady is one of the best workers we have in our division. She is at work on time every day and is more than willing to stay late when necessary. She is pleased to do just about anything that will benefit our organization. Why, just last month I asked her to take on a project that is somewhat outside her area of expertise and interest and she not only took on the project but she also performed extremely well. Actually, however, this project was what demotivated her. The project I assigned took her off track from her normal duties, and since returning to these duties she has been less effective than before the project began. I simply pointed out that her productivity was not up to her usual standards and asked why . . . and *listened*. She shared her concerns and during the conversation we were able to determine the specific behaviors and factors which were decreasing her productivity. With this information we were able to come up with a plan of action, which she agreed with and felt good about, to increase her productivity. I reminded her that she is not only a valuable employee but a valuable person as well. We also set a date when we would get together again to review the program on our plan of action. She actually was relieved to discuss the concerns we both had and while she was a little nervous about the meeting, she realized she needed direction and was glad I cared enough to give her the time and direction.

Bryan Flanagan is a role model for excellence in this particular scenario. I know you were picking out the key points as we went along, but let's go back together and be sure we have analyzed carefully.

1. *The feedback was given in private.* Nothing can be more devastating than public censure. Some managers are prone to tease or "dig" at an employee in front of others about a real concern as a way of hinting that they are displeased. All this does is destroy the seeds of trust between the people involved. *All* instructive or critical feedback must be given in private.

2. *The feedback was about specific, observable behavior.* The individual involved was never under personal attack. If there is to be criticism, it must pertain to the performance, *never* the performer.

3. *The feedback was immediate.* As soon as he recognized the problem, Bryan confronted the situation.

4. *Bryan asked questions and listened to the answers.* Rather than rushing to judgment, he asked questions for which, for the most part, he already had answers. He wasn't looking for the answers as much as he was looking for the employee's perspective on the answers. As a bonus, try closing your next instructive feedback session with this question: "How do you think I feel about this meeting?" After you get the answer, follow with, "How do *you* feel about this meeting?" The answers will often surprise you and will generally give great insight about what has just transpired at your meeting.

5. *A cooperative plan of action was developed.* Bryan did not mandate what action was to be taken to correct the situation; rather, the two people involved discussed a mutually agreeable plan. The employee contributed and "shared ownership" of the plan.

6. *A date for a follow-up session to inspect to make sure Bryan got what he expected was assigned.* Too many excellent Plans of Action fall victim to the "tyranny of the urgent." With all good intentions, we try to get back to the employee, but "things" pop up and we forget. Establishing a specific date and setting an appointment creates a sense of urgency for the plan and helps prevent failure as well as hurt feelings from neglect.

7. *Praise was used throughout the session.* There is much debate about "sandwiching" criticism between praise. Some managers think they must start or end every session with praise. I

will leave the decision on when to use praise up to you. However, to measure success, you must be able to answer this question affirmatively: "Did the person leave my presence feeling good about himself?" No one should ever leave an encounter with a manager doubting his or her personal value or self-worth!

To be a Goodfinder we must often *teach* those for whom we are responsible to do something good. That is the objective of the instructive feedback session. The great managers give others instructions on how to be more successful—always giving direction *within* the ability level of the employee. The great manager does not ignore mistakes. Permissiveness is neglect of duty. For as Dr. Michael Mescon, dean of the College of Business Administration, Georgia State University, says, "When a store clerk is rude, don't blame the clerk, blame the manager. The manager is ultimately responsible and accountable for actions of subordinates." If you will look for the good, point it out verbally and in writing, give instructive feedback in the manner outlined, and accept responsibility for those who answer to you, you are well on your way to becoming an excellent manager of people!

Marshall Field, American business leader and philanthropist, said, "Those who enter to buy support me. Those who come to flatter please me. Those who complain teach me how I may please others so that more will come. Only those hurt me who are displeased but do not complain. They refuse me permission to correct my errors and thus improve my service."

As leaders, we need to hitchhike on what Marshall Field said as a method for improving performance and assisting in the personal growth of our people. Remember, if we only flatter the people, we are pleasing them. If pleasing them is all we do, we are participating in a conspiracy to prevent their further growth and opportunities for themselves, as well as service to the company.

A POSITIVE REMINDER

One of the most important aspects of motivating a force has to do with praise and recognition. That's the reason the I LIKE . . . BECAUSE approach is so effective. Before we close this chapter on "goodfinding," let me share one last story which has a different twist.

A company sent four couples to one of our recent BORN TO WIN seminars. At the end of the first day they were tremendously motivated and excited about the I LIKE ... BECAUSE idea. That evening they went to a late dinner at one of Dallas' most exclusive restaurants. They hit the jackpot. The food was exceptional and the service was superb. Their waiter was a professional with twenty-five years of experience, and over twenty of those years had been at that one restaurant. He was there when he needed to be, but he did not join the party. He served effectively and efficiently but did not smother them with attention. He was intimately acquainted with the menu and was able to answer their questions and give them concise information about the specials of the day. It seemed he miraculously appeared at their instant of need and then made his exit so that he did not intrude upon the party. Friendly yet not familiar. In short, to repeat myself, he was a pro.

The four couples were all personable and friendly and soon on a first-name basis with the waiter. The meal was particularly delicious and was greatly enhanced because of the waiter's gracious and effective service. The diners left him a 25 percent tip which, in an expensive restaurant, is substantial. Each of the guests also left him an I LIKE ... BECAUSE slip, detailing why they liked him. After they had made their exit and were about a hundred feet from the front door, they heard him calling for them to wait a minute.

The waiter briskly walked up to them and, with the eight slips of paper in his hand, started to speak but broke down with emotion and for a moment or so literally could say nothing. When he finally regained his composure, he told the four couples that in his twenty-five years of being a waiter, this was far and away the most meaningful thing that had ever happened to him. Imagine!

That waiter was living proof of something my friend and fellow speaker Cavett Robert says: Three billion people on the face of the earth go to bed hungry every night, but four billion people go to bed every night hungry for a simple word of encouragement and recognition.

Do you think that with this kind of input this already effective waiter is going to be even more conscientious in his efforts? Do you think he benefited from the experience? Wouldn't you have loved to have been seated at the next table he served? Most important, who do you think were the biggest winners? Was it the waiter, who received the I LIKE . . . BECAUSE slips, or was it the eight individuals who wrote those notes? It doesn't take much imagination to answer that one, does it? I'm confident you agree that those who wrote the slips were the biggest winners.

That's what this concept is really all about. I would like to stress that we are talking about a *principle* and not a tactic. The Bible itself says, "Give and it shall be given unto you." However, if we give or do for others with the expectation of having them do something for us, then our action is a tactic and is certain to either backfire or become entirely ineffective. However, if you buy into the concept that you can have everything in life you want if you will just help other people get what they want, and then set about helping your people become more effective and more productive by giving them honest, sincere praise, not only will they benefit but you and your organization will also benefit tremendously. The magic thought is this:

> If it's a principle, it's a winner—
> if it's a tactic, it's a loser.

Don't forget that William James of Harvard said a deep need in human nature is the craving to be *appreciated*. When you, the manager, fill that need, you have taken a mammoth step toward becoming a more effective manager.

> Remember: the G in our formula
> stands for *Goodfinder*.

PERFORMANCE PRINCIPLES

1. *Look for the good in others.*
2. *Catch them doing something right.*
3. *Remember that action often precedes the feeling.*
4. *Seize the opportunity to share a sincere compliment.*
5. *Praise in public, censure in private.*

Expect the Best

If you want to get the best out of a man, you must look for the best that is in him.

Bernard Haldane

Goodfinders
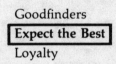
Loyalty

4 The *E* in our GEL formula is for *Expect the Best.* I was sharing some of the ideas I've been explaining to you in a seminar awhile back and a man in the audience came up to me during the break and said, "This information is fantastic. I wish some of those *morons* back at my office could be here!"

My question to you is this: Do you think there is a chance he missed a very important point?

Now let's bring it home to you. What kind of co-workers do you have? What kind of employees? What kind of children? What kind of spouse? So many times we get from others EXACTLY WHAT WE EXPECT! In short—the way we see them affects the way we treat them and the way we treat them affects the way they perform.

Several years ago, Rom J. Markin and Charles M. Lillis published an article in *Business Horizons* called "Sales Managers Get What They Expect." This article probably does as precise and concise a job of summarizing the Pygmalion Effect (sometimes called the "echo effect" or the "mirror effect") as I have read. Let me hit some of the main points of this excellent article.

> Expectations can influence behavior: therefore, a manager may get better staff performance if he expects better performance. This behavioral phenomenon is called the Pygmalion Effect.... According to Greek Mythology, Pygmalion was a sculptor and the King of Cyprus who fell in love with one of his creations. The ivory statue was created out of the desire of his own expectations. After Pygmalion's repeated prayers to the gods, Venus gave life to the statue ... the concept rests on the premise that what we see reflected in many objects, situations, or persons is what we put there with our own expectations. We create images of how things should be, and if these images are believed, they become self-fulfilling prophecies....

> ### The Evidence
>
> The feelings and tones which surround us can be changed if we work to change them by sending out the kind of signal we want reflected or echoed. Comedians as well as dramatic performers succeed in creating the kind of mood or atmosphere they want to prevail by sending out the kinds of signals they want mirrored or echoed. ... *"Once you begin laughing," a drama coach explains, "it is easy to continue, for the action and the emotion mutually stimulate each other."* ... We all have an audience of individuals and colleagues whose day, including their moods, feelings, and dispositions, will be influenced by the way we

start it. Hence, sales managers are perhaps the most important "signal generators" for field salesmen, and the expectations of the manager will profoundly affect the performance of the salespeople he leads and supervises.

Science vs. Folklore

The Pygmalion Effect has met the test of scientific analysis and hence the value of the theory is borne out both in terms of usefulness and truthfulness ... a cross section of carefully validated scientific studies reflects their significance:

• A study showed that experimenters could raise the IQ scores of children, especially on verbal and information subtests, merely by expecting them to do well. ...

• A study showed that experimenters could improve their subjects' performance on a task requiring them to drop as many marbles as possible through one of several holes in a tabletop by expecting them to do well. ...

• A study showed that worker performance increased markedly when the supervisor of these workers was told that his group showed a special potential for their particular job.

How Does It Work?

The paramount question is, how can managers implement the technique and improve their own performance while at the same time improving the performance of others?

William James, the father of American psychology, concluded that we become how we act ... so if we wish to conquer undesirable emotional tendencies in ourselves, we must go through the outward movements of the kind of tendencies we wish to cultivate. Alfred Adler, another well-known psychologist, later reaffirmed this notion by proving that *if we make ourselves smile, we actually feel like smiling* . . . in short, our moods match our posture and more important, people around us tend to feel as we feel. Mood is contagious.

B. F. Skinner, the foremost disciple of the psychological school of behaviorism, contends that our behavior operates on the environment and behavior is shaped by consequences. When a sales manager, for example, sends signals to his sales personnel that he regards them as highly competent, effective, capable, and mature, and that his work and theirs is meaningful, significant, and worthwhile, the sales personnel who receive his signals will respond in many instances by performing more competently and effectively.

And they respond further by perceiving their work as more rewarding, gratifying, and self-fulfilling. The *self-image* is the key to human behavior. Change the self-image and we change the behavior. Even more than this, the self-image sets the boundaries of individual accomplishment. It defines what one can or cannot do. Expand the self-image, and we expand the area of the possible.

Through the power of expectation, a sales manager (or any manager) can develop an adequate, realistic self-image in personnel that will imbue them with new capabilities and new talents, and literally turn failure into success.

WHEW! I'M NOT SURE I WANTED TO KNOW THAT MUCH ABOUT IT!

I give this much detail on the self-fulfilling prophecy because many people give the concept lip service but really don't buy into the proven facts. If man has suspected that the Pygmalion Effect does in fact work, and science has *proven* that it works, then why are we so unwilling to take advantage of the obvious benefits of application?

Successful Performers *do* buy in and they *apply* the principles!

If the Pygmalion Effect is going to work for you, you are going to have to help others by:

A. Encouraging achievement by providing a constant flow of positive feedback (which also creates a positive "climate").
B. Allowing for regular learning and growth opportunities for the people you expect to be Top Performers.
C. Providing activities and information that help people to understand their efforts are meaningful and productive.
D. Generating desirable and rewarding consequences for others (remember that 75–85 percent of behavior is determined by consequences).

A. Positive Feedback

We have already spent a great deal of time and energy on the importance of positive feedback and I am confident that you are sold on the importance of this vital area. Remember: Be a Goodfinder!

B. Regular Learning and Growth Opportunities

The importance of training cannot be overemphasized. According to Tom Peters, coauthor of *In Search of Excellence,* one of the companies he researched spends four full days training a teenage employee whose life expectancy on the job is only five weeks! The company: Disneyland. The job: parking lot attendant. The reason: the parking lot attendant is often the first person park guests meet, therefore these teenagers set the tone for the guests' visit.

IBM requires forty days of training per year for management personnel—eight weeks of the work year are spent in training!

The Arthur Andersen Company in Dallas, Texas, spends 10 percent of their *gross* revenues on training.

Too often in times of tight finances, training programs are

the first area cut. This is the exact opposite of what should happen. In times of financial difficulty, training budgets should be sharply increased.

To quote Tom Peters, "The excellent companies view extensive, pragmatic training as a necessity, not as a boom-time nicety . . . you gotta trust 'em, and train the livin' daylights out of them." When asked how he justified large amounts of training dollars, Peters replied, "Management from Excellent Companies would not ask a question like that!"

C. Activities and Information That Prove Our Efforts Are Meaningful, Productive, and Appreciated

I usually make every effort to stay away from absolutes such as "never" or "always," but in this case I am going to make an exception. *Never* under *any* circumstances at *any* time downplay the role of a Recognition Program in your organization, home, church, or *any* area of interest. In Part II, "The Science of Top Performance," we will get into the specifics of developing a Recognition Program. However, let me emphasize right here and now that you must never overlook the importance of this vital area.

When we look at activities and information that prove our efforts are meaningful and productive, we look at a very important area for Top Performers. This is the area in which the manager must make one of the most important "sales" ever made. Others must have a concept or a vision—an idea of what the "big picture" is all about—and how they personally fit in and contribute. The great managers regularly paint vivid word pictures showing their people exactly how this is happening now and what is in store in the months ahead.

This is important because one of the greatest problems faced in society today is the problem of "unrealistic expectations." In business, we set unrealistic goals or expect our progress within the organization to happen much too quickly. In relationships, we expect others to do certain things for us or act in a certain manner and if they do not, we are devastated. Now before you say, "Wait a second, Ziglar—a minute ago you were saying that if we expected the best, we could get the best . . . and now you are saying that 'unrealistic expectations' are a problem!" Let me finish.

Actually, this apparent discrepancy is the primary reason for the problem. Under the heading "Activities and Information That Prove Our Efforts Are Meaningful and Productive" is where we will solve this dilemma.

It seems as though no self-respecting management book could be published without dealing with Douglas McGregor's "Theory X and Theory Y" concepts. This is the appropriate place for us to look at these schools of thought. In his book *The Human Side of Enterprise*, McGregor developed two opposing views of worker attitudes based upon different conceptions of human nature:

Theory X Assumptions

*Work is inherently distasteful
*People prefer close supervision
*Most people are lazy and their work must be carefully structured
*The principle worker incentive is money
*Typical workers are uncreative
*Workers need to be coerced or bribed

Theory Y Assumptions

*Work is as natural as play
*People like to work
*Self-control is oftentimes essential
*Workers at all levels are creative
*Workers respond favorably to mature, favorable treatment
*Recognition and self-fulfillment are as important as motivation and money

According to the Pygmalion Effect, if we expect the Theory Y Assumptions to be true, more often than not they will. The Pygmalion Effect also says that if we expect Theory X Assumptions to come true, more often than not they will. The dilemma comes from the point of view of *worker expectations!*

Because of expectations that have been placed on them in the past, many workers are operating under a set of consequences or within an environment (climate) that is more closely aligned with Theory X. How do we overcome this past conditioning effectively? By providing activities and information that prove worker efforts (or spouse, children, etc. efforts) are meaningful.

Unfortunately, *there are very few workers today who know when they are successful on the job*. Oh, they have quotas and some guidelines as to what their activities are supposed to be, but how will they know when they are successful?

What about the manager? If we are supposed to give regular feedback to our people, and keep them apprised of how they are doing, and paint the "big picture" for them, how can we determine what information to pass along?

THE PERFORMANCE VALUE PACKAGE

I believe the answer is in the three-step Performance Value Package. Step #1 is *Foundational Performance*. This is the level of performance the person must achieve to continue to work with the organization (or in the case of children, to avoid punishment). I call it Foundational Performance rather than *Minimum Standard* because I don't want people even *thinking* minimum, much less working toward a minimum. With Foundational Performance thinking, not only do people maintain their positions but they also build a foundation upon which they can build future successes. We will discuss the specific "how to's" of each step in the Performance Value Package in "The Science of Top Performance," but for now let's simply say that the Foundational Performance is determined by mutual agreement of the manager and employee. The employee shares ownership in the ideas and does not feel "put upon," and the manager can lead the employee to better understand the "big picture" during the discussion. If you have never used this technique or a similar one, you will be surprised that rather than having to encourage employees to "reach" for objectives and standards, more often you will have to work to get them to be realistic and conservative about their Foundational Performance.

Step #2 in the Performance Value Package is *Successful Performance*. The Successful Performance is the level of performance that might reasonably and realistically be expected by both manager and employee. Again, the manager and employee determine this level of performance by working together and looking at past history and all data available about the position. By working together, and through discussion, both employee and manager get a reasonable understanding of what each is looking for as far as a Successful Performance is concerned. Again, let me remind you that the specific "how to's" are in chapter 8 in "The Science of Top Performance."

Step #3 in the Performance Value Package is *Value Performance*. The Value Performance is the level of performance that might be expected if everything goes according to plan and the employee excels in all areas. This level provides Top Performers with a target. Again, Value Performance is determined through sharing and discussion. The manager must be sure Value Performance objectives cause the individual to really "stretch." After having established Foundational Performance and Successful Performance levels, the manager will be able to direct the employee toward Value Performance quite successfully.

The advantages of this three-level system are numerous:

1. The manager spends directed time in specific discussion about job performance.
2. The manager and employee get to know each other and identify expectation levels through the discussions.
3. The manager can identify the performance level the employee *wants* to reach. Too often we make the mistake of classifying employees; this system allows employees to classify themselves and the manager to help them move through all levels to the extent of their comfort and desire.
4. Achievement ceilings are removed. As the self-image grows, employees have room to grow, too.
5. A basement or foundation level is established so that neither the employee nor the company is placed in danger.
6. By using this system properly, the manager will almost never have to fire an employee—some make the decision to

terminate themselves, but the manager is seldom placed in this painful and awkward position.

Chances are excellent you raised your eyebrows somewhat on #6. One of the most difficult things any manager ever has to do is terminate an employee, and to think this will seldom if ever happen again is a real boon! If you will combine the Value Performance Package with what I call *Due Process*, firings will largely be a thing of the past. Due Process leads us to:

D. Generate Desirable and Rewarding Consequences for Others (Remember That 75–85 Percent of Behavior Is Determined by Consequences)

My understanding of Due Process is going to seem somewhat simplistic to some of you, but a system does not have to have 16 graphs and 189 pages of "legaleze" to be workable. To me, Due Process means "three strikes and you are out." When an employee makes a mistake, we should be really *pleased!* Why? Simply because we learn much more from mistakes than we do from victories. We should do everything we can to congratulate people when they make an error . . . we should be delighted (well, almost) with ourselves when we make an error. Once we get over this initial euphoria, we need to analyze *why* the mistake was made, and *what* we can do to see that it rarely occurs again.

When we make the *same* mistake a second time, we must confront this mistake with a slightly different attitude. The process of analysis is the same in that we ask *why* and *what* can be done. If, after analysis, we decide that the determined performance level is fair to *all* parties involved, and it is within our control to prevent a recurrence, we design an action plan to do so. However, everyone must understand that *the same error* a third time will result in termination.

The person *repeating* errors is making a value statement about his feelings and his ability level. The statement he is making is one of two things: (1) "What happens on the job is really not a high priority in my life. My enthusiasm and commitment levels are just not very high." (2) "I do not have the ability necessary to handle this position." Our responsibility in helping ourselves and others to become Top Performers is to discover which of these statements is being made and take the appropriate action. In the case of statement #1, the proper action for employee and organization is to help the individual relocate. If this can be done within your company, so much the better. If it must be done by moving to another organization, then this is best for all concerned. To ask a person to continue performing tasks he does not enjoy, is not committed to, and fails to perform satisfactorily, dooms the individual to unhappiness and decreased productivity. Often the most helpful thing we can do for a person is to help him discover that his strengths may lie in another job or another industry. It may be a tough decision, as management consultant Fred Smith says, but the earlier the decision is made, the less actual waste.

If statement #2 is the case, then our responsibility is to help him get the training needed to handle the position. If the skill level needed is beyond the capacity of the employee, you don't have an employee problem, you have a *hiring procedures* problem. You can best help the employee by helping him find a position in which he can use the skills and abilities he already possesses—or be trained to more fully develop these skills so he may be successful.

TO GENERATE DESIRABLE CONSEQUENCES, ADD PVP

When we establish that Due Process as I have outlined it is standard operating procedure, then we need only add the Performance Value Package concept to have a fail-safe system that allows you to manage efficiently, effectively, empathetically, and with results that please both employee and organization. The Foundational Performance level is the primary key. Remember: You and the employee have agreed that the Foundational Performance level is the *minimally* acceptable level to continue employment . . . *and* if it is established properly (with employee participation), you and the employee have a foundation upon which to build. With Due Process, if the original Foundational Performance standards are not met, the manager and the employee go back and analyze by asking *why* and determining *what* can be done to assure that those Foundational Performance levels will be met in the future. When these levels are not met for the second time, and the manager is certain the burden of the responsibility lies with the employee, then a probationary period must be established. The length of this probationary period could be from two weeks to six months, depending upon the plan of action to correct the mistakes, and the position of the employee. Some assembly-line employees can show their improvement (or lack of) in a matter of weeks, while some executives may have "start-up products" that need to be on probation for as long as two years.

When Foundational Performance level is not met within a reasonable period of time (that manager and employee arrive at together), the employee has signaled that the current position he holds is not the position he should be in. If the process is handled properly by you, the improperly positioned employee will terminate himself or at least agree with you that another job would be in the best interests of both parties.

DOES THAT STUFF REALLY WORK?

Let's look at a specific incident where this concept was applied. Recently my colleague Jim Savage spoke to a group of dentists, their spouses, and entire office staffs, and they taught him this system really does work. According to Jim, they were a delightful group with which to work—very professional, very receptive, and anxious to find ideas that would help them become even more successful in their chosen profession. After the program, they were having lunch together and Jim sat with the doctors at a large round table and had one of the most interesting luncheon conversations ever.

One dentist said, "I cannot get my receptionist to make 'tension' calls." He went on to explain that "tension" calls were the daily calls to confirm appointments and/or remind people it was time to have their teeth cleaned. Jim "innocently" asked, "Then why is she still working for you?" Obviously, Jim had touched a sore spot because the dentist responded with a touch of heat, "Well, good employees are not that easy to come by!"

Then Jim asked, "How good an employee is she?" After spending several minutes rationalizing and justifying, the dentist stopped in midsentence and said, "I am being silly . . . she really is a good employee but I haven't given her the proper direction." Jim said it was exciting to see him come to the conclusion on his own. If Jim had said, "It seems to me you are not giving her enough direction," the doctor really (and rightfully so) might have become defensive. By answering questions, this man was able to discover that:

1. He must *establish* and *sell* the concept of the importance of making these calls.
2. He must *train* the people to meet his expectations.
3. He must *inspect* to make sure he gets what he *expects*.

The good doctor went back to his office and called a conference with his office manager and receptionist. He started the meeting by saying, "It is my goal to pay each of you more money! Would you be interested in discussing how this might happen?" He definitely had their attention! After their enthusiastic nods of approval, he continued, "As both of you know, our office handles sixty to seventy-five percent of our capacity (based on hours of the day and potential clients) each month. To give you both a substantial raise, we need more clients. One very good way to get additional clients is through appointment confirmation, which will cut down on our cancellations and no-shows. Another way is to make 'business building' (that's a much better name) calls. In the past, these have been called 'tension' calls because the emphasis has been on the one making the call. From now on they are 'business building' or 'helping' calls because the emphasis will be on the one we are calling. We have services these people desperately need, and it is our *responsibility* to help them by letting them know when they should be in our office." He went on to say, "Now I know these are demanding calls and I don't want you to make them all day, so let's start by figuring out how many helping calls it takes to encourage a client to visit our office."

The conversation continued and by drawing out the ideas of both the office manager and the receptionist (by asking questions), the following resulted:

1. The receptionist would make sure that 100 percent of all appointments were confirmed by starting seven days ahead on calls. She would make calls in the morning, afternoon, and even one call from home each evening, if necessary. She developed a follow-up system that allowed her to organize her time so these calls could be made during slower times of the day. In this case 100 percent of appointments *contacted* was her Foundational Performance level, Successful Performance level, and Value Performance level.

2. The office manager and the receptionist divided the "helping" or "business building" calls into two equal segments. Five calls each day was Foundational Performance; eight calls each day was Successful Performance; ten calls each day was Value Performance level. (Remember that all three levels were the same because 100% of the appointments must be contacted during the seven days before the appointment.)

3. A single sheet record report was developed by the office manager that enabled everyone involved to gather and compute the information they needed to see how the program was working. The report was submitted to the dentist weekly.

4. In only sixty days, appointment no-shows were almost entirely eliminated (a side benefit was the excellent public relations created); the office was operating at 85–90 percent capacity, and the office manager and receptionist had received their substantial raises. Note: The dentist got what he wanted (more clients) because he helped his assistants get what they wanted (a raise). The assistants got what they wanted (the raise) because they helped the clients get what they wanted (more beautiful, healthier teeth and gums).

The primary tool used in this example is what I like to call "tracking down." When a hunter is in pursuit of game, he tracks down his prey . . . meaning he divides the activities that will lead him to success into small, bite-size pieces. The hunter determines: game, geographic area, date, weapons, time of day, mode of transportation, and so on. When we hunt for Top Performance, we must do the same thing. We must "track down" success activities that take us to our goal—SUCCESS! When we break our goals into bite-size pieces and set Foundational Performance levels, Successful Performance levels, and Value Performance levels, we know *when* we are successful and *how* to get to our Top Performance level. One excellent manager stated: *"If you can't measure it, you can't manage it."*

Obviously, not all Performance Value Package programs will have the positive results this one had. In our own organization, we had a telemarketing representative who was not performing well. He and his supervisor agreed that on a daily basis he needed to average 80 attempts (numbers dialed), 20 completed calls, and $600 volume in sales as a Foundational Performance level; 90 attempts, 25 completed calls, and $800 sales volume were determined to be a Successful Performance level; and 100 attempts, 30 completed calls, and $1200 sales volume would be Value Performance level. After thirty days, the representative averaged 60 attempted calls, 12 completed calls, and $200 in sales volume. When confronted by his supervisor, the salesman had no really good reasons as to his lack of performance. In an hour-long planning session, they came to the agreement that the Foundational Performance level could be changed to 60 attempted calls, 15 completed calls, and $500 sales volume for the following week. At the end of the agreed-upon time period, the results were 58 attempted calls, 10 completions, with $180 sales volume.

These were the questions asked by the supervisor in their next meeting:

1. Do you feel that our Foundational Performance level agreed upon in our last meeting is fair? ("Yes.")
2. Is there anything I can do to help you be sure you reach this level? ("No.")
3. Do you understand that if you don't build a solid founda-

tion level on this job you might be better off somewhere
else? ("Yes.")

4. Do you understand that if you don't meet these minimum
   standards we will have no option other than to find something better for you to do with your time than work here?
   ("Yes.")

5. Is seven days a reasonable period of time to allow you to
   meet this standard? ("Yes.")

6. How do you think I feel about this meeting? ("You seem
   concerned about my success.")

7. How do you feel about this meeting? ("Good . . . and informed.")

Two days later the salesman came in and asked for a transfer to another part of our company.

The time periods and numbers may change, but the process
does not!

Let me tie down the point with one final example:

"I HATE MY JOB"

One day, just before I was scheduled to speak in Birmingham, Alabama, a lady came backstage for a brief visit. She was
attractively dressed, but she had completely forgotten to put
on a smile before she left home. She walked in and started her
little talk—which was apparently well rehearsed. "Oh, Mr.
Ziglar, I'm so glad to see you! If somebody doesn't help me, I
don't know what I'm going to do! I just hate my job! My boss
never says anything encouraging. Nobody in the company
likes me and I don't like any of them. It's a bad, bad scene and
I want out!" She was the kind of lady who could brighten up a
whole room—by leaving it, if you know what I mean!

As Cavett Robert would say, "She looked like the Cruise
Director for the *Titanic!*"

I quickly got the strong feeling that it was a little speech she
had given about eleven thousand times for all of her friends,
relatives, neighbors, and complete strangers. She seemed to
have a lot of experience in dumping a full load of garbage on
anyone who would sit still. I got the impression that she expected me to sit there and let her dump all that garbage on me.
I even felt she figured when it was all over I was going to say,

"Oh, that's terrible! Boy, that's just awful! But, my dear, you must be brave. There are those who are destined to carry the burdens of the world for others. It's just a cross you're going to have to bear and you must bear it bravely and willingly and in the by-and-by everything is going to work out for the best."

I even have an idea that in her mind she expected to leave our interview wiping the corners of her eyes with a little handkerchief, saying, "Oh, you've just helped me so much! I'm so glad you had time to share this with me!" But if I had taken that approach I would have betrayed everything in which I believe. The *last* thing she needed was sympathy. She had spent a lifetime wallowing in self-pity and as Mrs. Mamie McCullough, the I CAN Lady, would say, "holding her own private 'pity party.'" She needed empathy, not sympathy. She needed someone who was not part of the problem but who could help her find a solution.

UNFORTUNATELY, IT WILL GET WORSE

When she finally took a breath of air so I could slip in a quick word edgewise, I looked at her and said (firmly, but not unkindly), "Yes, your situation doesn't sound very good and the unfortunate thing is that it's probably going to get worse!" If I'd hit her in the face with a bucket of ice water she could not have been more surprised.

She obviously expected that "nice Mr. Ziglar" to be entirely different. I know she did because she reacted by jumping back and asking, "What do you mean?" Zig: "It's very simple: Your situation's going to get worse because there is a good chance you might lose this job, and jobs, even bad ones, aren't that easy to find." Lady: "What are you talking about?" Zig: "Ma'am, there's not a company anywhere that can have that much negativism in one concentrated spot and survive."

A few tears started to form and she asked, "Well, what can I do?" Zig: "I've got an idea, if you're really interested in solving the problem." Lady: "Please tell me what it is because I'm definitely interested."

In my mind, it's critically important to determine whether or not a person really is interested in solving the problem. Many people appear to be seeking help when in reality all they want is a listening audience and someone who will agree with what they're saying and doing. My time frame was such that I did not have the time to be just a listener. I had to feel my time was going to be utilized in solving the problem rather than just beating the problem to death.

The woman assured me she was definitely interested in solving the problem, so I agreed to share a couple of ideas which I thought would help.

START LOOKING FOR THE GOOD

Zig: "The first thing I want you to do tonight when you go home is to take a sheet of paper and list everything you like about your job and your company." Lady: "That will be easy because I don't like anything about it!" Zig: "Now hold the phone and let me ask you a question." Lady: "All right." Zig: "Do they by any chance pay you for the work you do or do you work there for benevolent reasons?" Lady: "Certainly they pay me for the work I do!" Zig: "Don't you like that?" Lady: "Of course I like it!" Zig: "Well, the number-one thing you like about your job, then, is they pay you for doing it, so go ahead and write it down. We'll start our list right now.

"Number two, do they pay you below average, average, or above average for what you do?" Lady: "I've got to confess they pay me above average." Zig: "Don't you like that?" Lady: "Of course I like it!" Zig: "Okay, the second thing you like about your job is that they pay you above average, so write it down.

"Number three, do you ever get a vacation?" Lady: "Why, of course I get a vacation!" Zig: "Don't you like that?" Lady: "Of course I like it!" Zig: "Okay, you get a vacation, you like it, so write it down.

"Number four, do you have a retirement program?" Lady: "Everybody's got a retirement program, including us!" Zig:

"Don't you like that?" Lady: "Of course I like it!" Zig: "Okay, you've got a retirement program and you like it, so write it down."

As we continued the process we discovered a host of things the lady "liked" about her job (hospital and life insurance, five days annual sick leave, all the national holidays, a profit-sharing plan which vested upon retirement, only a ten-minute drive from her home to the office, a full hour for lunch, participation in employee/employer relations, a beautiful building to work in with protected private parking spaces, and so on).

By actual count, there were twenty-two things she liked about the job which she had hated and liked *nothing* about just a few minutes earlier.

REMEMBER: YOU FIND WHAT YOU LOOK FOR IN LIFE

I could go into Mobile, Alabama, Albany, New York, or Fresno, California, and *find* drugs, crime, prostitutes, and in general the most negative, objectionable people in the world. Or I could go into Mobile, Alabama, Albany, New York, or Fresno, California, as I actually have done in times past, and *find* some of the most beautiful, loving, caring, dedicated, God-fearing, flag-waving, family-loving people in the world. You will *find* what you are looking for.

You can take the most outstanding man or woman, husband or wife, boy or girl imaginable, nitpick them to death, and manage to find some fault with them. Or you can take the average man or woman and start looking for the good qualities, and you will find them in abundance. It depends on what you're looking for.

Husband, if you treat your wife like a thoroughbred, you will never end up with a nag. Wife, if you treat your husband like a champ, you won't end up with a chump.

You can take your job or your company and find many good things you like or a number of things you don't like. It depends on what you want out of life, because *you are going to find what you're looking for.* Significantly, the more good *or* bad you find in yourself, your mate, your job, your kids, your country, or your future, the more good *or* bad there will be to find.

Message:
Look for what you want—
not for what you don't want.

ACCENTUATE THE POSITIVE

I encouraged the lady to take her list of twenty-two positive things about her job and, just before she went to bed, get in front of the mirror and slowly, firmly read the list out loud. This would plant positive thoughts in her subconscious mind before she went to sleep. The next morning she was to read the list again before she left for work.

She was also to take the list with her because in just twenty-four hours she would be adding to it, having started conditioning herself to look for the positives about her job. During that day and in the days ahead, she was to add the positives to that list. I encouraged her to follow this process for a minimum of twenty-one days, because it takes that long to substitute a *bad* habit (finding fault) with a *good* habit (finding something positive).

After about thirty-five minutes this lady left in an entirely different frame of mind. When she walked out, she was actually *striding!* She didn't walk out a beaten and defeated person. Don't misunderstand. I'm not implying that in thirty-five minutes we were able to overcome a lifetime of her making an overdraft on the bank of right mental attitude. However, we did give her some hope and a plan and those are two powerful ingredients. As a matter of fact, winning managers never make promises to their people unless they give them a plan to make the promise possible. And when managers make demands on anyone, they extract a plan *from* that person as to how they can realistically meet that demand.

Six weeks later I was back in Birmingham doing a follow-up

sales training session. The woman was seated right in the front row, grinning like she had walked through a swinging door on somebody else's push. I chatted with her briefly and asked her how she was doing. She responded, "Well, to tell you the truth, I'm still not completely out of the woods, but you would be amazed at how much the company and the people who work there have changed!" Her world changed because her attitude changed. *Yours* will do the same.

Expect the best from yourself and others!

PERFORMANCE PRINCIPLES

---

1. *We generally get from others what we expect.*
2. *The difference between good and excellent companies is* training.
3. *You find what you look for in life . . . and career.*
4. *Never a promise without a plan.*

"Wait for Me, I'm Your Leader!"

An ounce of loyalty is worth a pound of cleverness.

Elbert Hubbard

Goodfinders

Expect the Best

| Loyalty |

5 The *L* in our GEL formula stands for *Loyalty*. Loyalty, very simply, is the desire to help other people become successful.

Grant Teaff is the football coach at Baylor University in Waco, Texas. He is an outstanding man and a winner as a football coach. I once heard him share a story which says quite a bit about loyalty.

Baylor won their first conference championship in fifty years during Coach Teaff's third year. The first two years they struggled to establish a solid foundation and were not as successful as they would like to have been in the "win column." Just prior to the beginning of the third season, Baylor's offensive coordinator came to Coach Teaff and asked him to go hunting with him. It seems that a farmer out in west Texas had offered to let them hunt on his property. Seizing the opportunity for one last break before the beginning of the long (fourteen- to sixteen-hour workdays are typical) football season, they placed their guns in the truck and departed.

Upon arrival, Coach Teaff asked his assistant to wait in the truck while he let the farmer know they were there and would be hunting on his property. As Coach Teaff knocked on the door he had no idea of the enthusiastic greeting awaiting him! "Coach Teaff! Man alive, it's great to see you! You fellas are doing a great job with our Baylor Bears! I know you've not won as many games as you'd like these first two seasons, but I believe we are prepared for a championship season!"

The coach was both pleased and humbled by what the farmer said. "Thank you so much," he replied, "and if we can ever do anything for you, just let me know."

"As a matter of fact," said the farmer, "I do need your help! If you notice, about fifty yards in front of where you parked your truck is an old mule. That old mule has been in our family for nearly twenty years and, frankly, Coach Teaff, she has become just like a member of the family. Recently she contracted a disease which is most painful and she needs to be put out of her misery. I just can't bring myself to do it and my wife has never fired a weapon and wouldn't step on an ant. Since you have your hunting rifles, would you be willing to put our mule out of her misery?"

"Well, it seems like the least I can do, considering you're being nice enough to let us hunt on your property," said the coach.

"Thanks," said the farmer, "the county will remove her later and when you and your assistant finish hunting, you come back here and we'll have a big supper together."

As Coach Teaff started back to the truck, he got an idea which, as he says, "can be a dangerous thing for a football coach." His face turned to a scowl and he bit his tongue until a trace of a tear appeared in the corner of his eye. The assistant coach saw this and asked, "Coach, what's wrong?"

"Oh, that old farmer infuriated me!" Coach Teaff replied.

"Can you believe he said Baylor would never win another game while you and I coached there?"

"What?" was the incredulous reply.

"Not only that, but he said we were probably the worst coaching staff in the history of football!"

"But we were supposed to hunt on his property."

"Not only did he say to get off his property immediately, but if we don't he is going to call the law on us!"

"I cannot believe it," said the dumbfounded assistant.

"Yep, makes me so mad," responded Coach Teaff, "I think I'll shoot his mule!"

"Oh, Coach, no! You talk about trouble with the law! We'll really be in trouble if you shoot his mule!"

"Trouble or not, I'm tired of people bad-mouthing Baylor . . . this is it!"

Trying hard to hide his ever-widening grin, Coach Teaff pulled his gun off the gunrack, lined up on the poor old mule to do her a great favor, and squeezed the trigger. *Bang!* the shot rang out As he turned to see the reaction of the assistant coach, *Bang—Bang!* two more shots rang out from the other side of the truck and the assistant coach shouted, "I got two of his cows, now let's get out of here!"

Now obviously, had this happened it would be taking loyalty too far, but if you are going to be a Top Performer, there can be no question about your loyalty in three areas. You must be loyal to yourself, to those with whom you live and work, and to your organization.

BE LOYAL TO YOURSELF

To be loyal to yourself, you must *work* to maintain a healthy self-image. This is not an overinflated ego or the kind of self-confidence that the wit says, "generally occurs just before we really understand the situation." Loyalty to yourself means looking for the evidence that supports *why* you should believe in you.

In *See You at the Top,* I wrote, "You cannot consistently perform in a manner which is inconsistent with the way you see yourself." I cannot stress too much the importance of "seeing" yourself successfully completing your daily tasks. Do you think the heavyweight boxing champion of the world goes into the ring questioning his ability? Absolutely not! The champion steps into the ring *believing* in himself and his ability to win! The quarterback of the world championship Super Bowl team does not step into the huddle and timidly ask for advice from his teammates! Chris Evert Lloyd expects to win the majority of her tennis matches, Nancy Lopez expects to be among the top money winners in the Ladies Professional Golfers Association. Johnny Carson has been in front of more people, more often, than anybody in the entertainment industry, yet in an interview he reported that he still gets nervous before he performs. Believing in yourself and being loyal to yourself will help you move toward becoming a Top Performer.

A Gallup Poll revealed that the self-esteem of workers and managers plays a substantial role in economic productivity. Dr. Robert Schuller, pastor of the ten-thousand-plus member Crystal Cathedral of Garden Grove, California, commissioned the study which was paid for by an anonymous donor. Initially Dr. Schuller was not primarily concerned with productivity, but simply with the general importance of self-esteem in Americans. However, the answers in the fifteen hundred personal interviews convinced him that the relationship between self-esteem and productivity is of profound importance to business and government.

The study showed:

- Persons with a high level of self-esteem feel productive.
- Those with a low self-esteem do not feel themselves productive and seem to lack productive incentives.

Dr. Schuller concluded that "nurturing human capital, the people who make decisions and operate the tools of our increasingly industrialized society," has been allowed "to take a backseat to machinery" and this adversely affects productivity. The study showed that 37 percent of Americans have high self-esteem and 30 percent have very low self-esteem. In this low self-esteem group only 17 percent considered themselves very productive and 20 percent said they were not productive at all. Dr. Schuller concluded from the survey results that the 30 percent low-esteem group are a "drag on themselves, their employers, and American society in general."

Noting that economists and the federal government generally prescribe capital investments and new plants as the solution to the problem of static or falling productivity, Dr. Schuller said it seems that raising people's self-esteem may be nearly as important. The study showed that the elements usually conducive to high self-esteem are good family relationships, good moral standards, religion, close friends, financial well-being, hobbies, and status. Married persons tend to have more self-esteem than divorced, widowed, or single adults. Education also contributes to high self-esteem. Persons with high self-esteem are inclined to view success in personal terms; those with low self-esteem tend to look on success as a strictly material matter. One of the most important findings was that *persons with low self-esteem tend to suffer from a lot of physical and emotional stress and to have high absentee rates on the job, which definitely diminishes productivity.*

Obviously, your self-image will play a major role in how high you go in your company, because it plays a major role in your ability to develop leaders who will follow you up the ladder of success or, in many cases, pass you on the ladder of success.

The following article by James L. Hayes, former president of the American Management Association, says a great deal. The title of the article is "The Art of Self-Promotion," which might turn off someone with low self-esteem or one who does not understand what self-esteem is all about. But the article will definitely turn you on and help you develop your own potential. The last sentence in the article really gets to the heart of the matter:

> Many competent managers fail to rise within their organizations because they overlook a vital career consideration—the need to "promote themselves."

According to a recent survey conducted by Henchy & Co., a New York placement firm, it was found that 83 percent of fired executives shared one common trait—not calling attention to their abilities and achievements. The end result: they were perceived as not having any.

On the other hand, a second study by a Boston research firm found that successful managers know how to intensify their images through self-promotion.

Unfortunately, many executives conceive of self-promotion as simply meaning game playing and ego-exercising. In their conscious efforts to avoid that type of image, they go too far to the other extreme.

The executive suffering from lack of self-promotion may not approve of the behavior of the high profile executive. But he will grudgingly recognize the benefits that successful self-promotion can bring.

Since there are limited opportunities in any organization, managers who promote themselves usually have the best chances of getting better career opportunities—leading to quicker advancement, more interesting work, better pay and easier access to top management.

Managers who are skilled in promoting themselves know that it is a delicate art. There is always the risk of promoting too much. Nonetheless, there are certain promotional constants that can be applied to some degree anywhere and at any time. These techniques include:

• *Compliment colleagues.* You can demonstrate confidence and security in your own abilities by drawing attention to the achievements of others. Such reinforcement can establish you as an overall "positive" individual, and this attitude will be reflected back to you.

• *Praise subordinates.* When a subordinate does good work, tell him or her. After all, a subordinate's success is yours also. Frequent positive reinforcement will make your subordinates work harder. And your reputation as a good supervisor will grow as a result.

• *Circulate memos.* If you come across information of interest to your colleagues, circulate it in a memo. Your efforts and consideration will be appreciated.

• *Implement creative innovations.* If you develop a better way of doing something, implement it. Your efforts to improve operations will be recognized and your value increased.

• *Volunteer.* Special projects or committees will probably demand more of your time. But participation in such activities will identify you as someone who cares beyond the paycheck.

• *Talk up.* Sometimes you may be privy to information that others are not aware of when making a decision. If so, talk up. You may complicate matters, but if you are right, you will be thanked later.

• *Know all.* Don't be content in knowing what you are expected to know. Find out as much about your organization as you possibly can. You can never tell when such information will pay off.

• *Observe and respond.* Be aware of whatever goes on around you. If something happens that calls for a response, act upon it immediately. The longer you wait, the less chance you have of exerting control. If you wait too long, in some cases a situation may fester and grow out of proportion.

As you can see, none of the above suggestions prescribe loud, flamboyant, attention-getting self-promotion. On the contrary, they are sensible techniques for developing an image of even-keeled competency. *For the point is not to be perceived as the most visible, but as the most capable.*

STEPS TO A HEALTHY SELF-IMAGE

If self-esteem really is important to Top Performance, what can we do to improve our self-image? In *See You at the Top*, I listed fifteen steps to a healthy self-image . . . and I would strongly recommend that you review those steps. For our purposes here, I would like to suggest three steps the manager may take to improve self-esteem in himself and others.

Step #1 Make Out Your Own Victory List

When looking for evidence that supports *why* you should believe in *you*, make out your own victory list. The items listed do not have to include things such as "Developed the cure for cancer." List the simple everyday victories, like helping a senior citizen across a busy intersection (assuming he wanted to go across that intersection!).

Unfortunately, our human nature is such that if I were to ask you to recall your most embarrassing incident in the last two weeks, you might be hard-pressed to decide *which* incident to share. However, if I asked you to share your greatest victory in the last two weeks, you might have difficulty coming up with one. This is human nature—to hang onto the failures and forget the victories. To combat this natural tendency, you need to make out a victory list.

This list is not a "brag" list. As a matter of fact, no one should see it but you. This list has nothing to do with conceit. As I often say, "Conceit is a weird disease that makes everyone sick *except* the one who has it!" This list is to help you remember you are a person of worth.

This is not a "comparison" list. You do not build yourself in comparison to others. There will always be someone more powerful, more helpful, better looking . . . less powerful, more selfish, or less attractive than you. When you make positive or negative comparisons, you are on dangerous ground. To build a healthy self-image, you can make only one comparison: *Compare your actions to your ability.* If you will make this comparison only, and realize that even this is somewhat unfair because your abilities can be enhanced by training and growth, you will have taken a giant stride toward a healthy self-image and Top Performance.

Remember, success is not measured by how you perform compared with how others perform. You might have twice their ability—or half their ability. Success—*real* success—is measured by how you do compared with what you could be doing with the ability God gave you.

You should also have a victory list for those people you are managing or supervising. Why not keep a running record of occasions when you "catch them doing something right"? If you do, both you *and* your employees will win.

STEP #2 Determine to Live Until You Are Dead

Will Rogers made this comment in the very last speech he ever gave: "Lord, let me live until I'm dead!" Of course, he was referring to those "walking zombies" who make their way through life never wanting to be confused by the facts. You will recognize them as having been born in the 1940s or 1950s, died in the 1970s, and they will be buried in the 1990s! They are stuck in a rut, which is, you know, nothing more than a grave with the ends kicked out. The way we get out (and stay out) of the rut is by understanding that happy, successful people don't go through life, they *grow* through life!

When I think of growth, I think of the story Robert Schuller told on his "Hour of Power" television program about Sir Edmund Hillary. You will remember that Sir Edmund was the first man to climb Mount Everest, the tallest mountain in the world. He failed in several of his early attempts and on one occasion left five associates dead on the side of that great mountain. Parliament wanted to recognize these valiant efforts, so they invited Hillary into their chambers. They even placed a picture of Mount Everest at the front of the room. When Sir Edmund Hillary entered the room, Parliament rose as one to give him a standing ovation, and when he saw these great legislators standing and applauding his good effort, tears filled his eyes. Many members of Parliament noticed the tears and must have thought, *Ah, look, the tears of happiness that we are recognizing this good effort he has made.* But they were not tears of happiness and joy—they were tears of anger and frustration! For Edmund Hillary had not set out to make a "good effort" at climbing that mountain, and he certainly had not set out to leave five associates dead on the side of that mountain.

As Hillary walked to the front of that room, he recognized something that many of you have recognized and that is, yes, he had made a "good" effort to climb that mountain, but

the greatest enemy of excellence is good!

Sir Edmund Hillary walked to the front of the room and literally pounded on that picture and actually screamed at the mountain: "You defeated me! But you won't defeat me again! Because *you have grown all that you can grow . . . but I am still growing!*"

You see, my reading friend, if you are in a growth posture—regardless of what you have already accomplished or have not accomplished—there are still great things left in front of you! With that last statement, as positive and optimistic as it is, I need to remind you of what Emerson said: "What lies behind you and what lies in front of you pales in comparison to what lies inside of you." He was right, of course.

When employees move into the management role, they often feel they must know *everything* about their new position. This is an overwhelming burden to be forced to carry. You were not hired to be an encyclopedia or a computer . . . you were hired to manage. Managers must know where to find information, not have total recall. Those who can think are much more important than those who can regurgitate facts. Remember: *It's very difficult to be overtrained!* So, get involved in continuing education, seminars, books, and tapes. Your thirst for knowledge and understanding must never cease—but you don't need to memorize the manuals for every seminar you attend. Determine that you will continue to grow and learn as a manager, and you will greatly improve your self-image.

We must never overlook the fact that our company can spend millions and millions of dollars on buildings, computers, electronic gear, fixtures, communication systems, and so forth, but the full utilization of these monumental expenditures is entirely dependent on the growth, training, attitude, and capability of the people in the company. The responsibility for that growth, training, attitude, and capability rests squarely on the shoulders of management.

Step #3 Focus Your Attention on Those You Are Responsible to and For

One of the fastest ways to improve our own self-esteem is to focus our attention on others. Often, the more we think of ourselves, the less self-confidence we have. Forgetting about *us* and becoming sincerely interested in *them* will lead us directly to a healthy self-respect. When you give your full and undivided attention to others, and concentrate on making them feel comfortable, you become less self-conscious.

Dr. Alfred Adler said that we can be cured of depression in only fourteen days if every day we will try to think of how we can be helpful to others. David Dunn wrote a wonderful little book entitled *Try Giving Yourself Away*, which gives some marvelous insights as well as some simple, practical steps on *how* we can be an encouragement and help to others. When we are sincerely interested in others, we don't have time to direct negativity toward ourselves.

"MR. ZIGLAR, I HEARD WHAT YOU SAID"

One Saturday afternoon several years ago, my wife and I were scheduled to play golf at a beautiful course in the Dallas area. On this particular day we had a one o'clock tee time. However, on Saturdays the course attracts many local residents as well as people from other cities, so we were delayed a few minutes. The foursome in front of us consisted of two couples, and one of the young men was on the tee box getting ready to tee off. As my wife and I sat in our cart, I could not help but notice the young man.

He was about thirty years old, something like six feet, three inches tall, and weighed about 220 pounds. However, as the young man stood there addressing the ball, it was obvious to me that he was not a golfer. He looked a little uncomfortable and was addressing the ball in an unorthodox manner. He picked his club up, wiggled it a few times, then put it down and repeated the process for what seemed like an eternity.

Finally, I muttered under my breath that he obviously was not a golfer. My wife quietly asked how I knew. I responded I'd been playing the game a long time, had watched a lot of golfers, and just *knew* he was not a golfer. In the meantime, the young man kept wiggling the club and picking it up and putting it down. Finally, he pulled his club back and proceeded to bust that ball about 240 yards, right down the middle. So much for my expertise in evaluating golfers!

After the young man hit the ball, he walked over to his cart, put his club in his bag, and walked straight back to me. He was neither smiling nor frowning, but as he walked up to me he said, "Mr. Ziglar, I heard what you said . . ."

(Now, my reading friend, I want you to think with me just for a moment. Had you been in my position, what would you have thought—and done? I felt some apprehension and wanted to pull a disappearing act, but fortunately the young man continued.) ". . . when you spoke in my hometown three years ago, and it completely changed my life. I just want you to know, Mr. Ziglar, that it is an honor for me to even be on the same golf course with you."

Needless to say, I breathed a deep sigh of relief, thanked the young man profusely, and was grateful at the sudden unexpected and delightful turn of events. I also made a resolution that day to be far more careful in my judgmental attitude when I am observing or dealing with other people.

I've often thought of how tragic it would have been, had the young man actually heard the cutting, unkind, and, as it developed, untrue remarks I made about him. It undoubtedly would have adversely affected him and certainly would have lowered his opinion of me. Not only that, but it would have been virtually impossible for me to have positively affected him in the future from an inspirational and instructional point of view.

As managers and leaders, one of the things we cannot escape is the fact that when people look to us we have a responsibility to let them see we deserve to be in that position of leadership. They evaluate and respond to us to a large degree based on the way we see them, feel about them, *and* treat them. That's why it's so important for us to look for the good, expect the best, and always remember that as managers we are role models for many of the people in our group or company. It is at least reasonably important that they like us. It is critically important that they respect us. It is difficult, if not impossible, for them to either like us *or* respect us if we make snide, judgmental, unkind, and/or untrue observations about them as I did the young golfer.

Don't misunderstand. Each one of us—including that young man—is responsible for his own actions and conduct. By no stretch of imagination am I responsible for what he does. However, I am responsible *to* him to be fair, honest, objective, and exactly what I appear to be. As managers in your organization, you are not responsible *for* your people, but you are responsible *to* your people.

HONESTY + COURTESY = LOYALTY

Top Performers are loyal to those with whom they live and work. Mamie McCullough, the I CAN Lady, says her idea of Judgment Day is that the Lord is going to line up everybody we have ever said anything ugly about and make us repeat it to their faces. That's a sobering thought, and I'll bet it will make all of us think twice before we say anything unkind about others, won't it?

There is a statement you have heard since you were a child that is no less true today than it was when you first were told: "If you don't have something nice to say, don't say anything at all." I know the admonition has become a cliché and may seem oversimplified, trite, and worn out, but wouldn't we all be better off if we took this bit of sage advice?

The Forum Corporation of Boston, Massachusetts, did an

in-depth study of 341 salespeople from eleven different companies in five different industries. Of this group, 173 were top salespeople and 168 were average salespeople. The primary difference between the two groups was not skill, knowledge, or ability. The 173 super salespeople were more productive because their customers *trusted* them, and customers are far more likely to *believe* the honest salesperson. They discovered that people do not buy based on what you tell them *or* what you show them. They *do buy* based on what you tell them *and* show them, which they believe. The same principle applies in directing the activities of those under your leadership. They will "buy" and act enthusiastically on your leadership based *only* on what you show and tell them, which they believe. Anything less than that trust and confidence simply means they will give it less than their 100 percent support.

In managing people, trust and honesty are commodities we can take to the marketplace and cash in at any time. Top Performers in management learn to create trust in others by *complete* honesty in all dealings. The second characteristic these supersuccessful salespeople possessed in spades, according to the *Forum Report*, was plain, old-fashioned courtesy. These salespeople are just as nice and courteous to the switchboard operator and file clerks as they are to the office manager and accountant. They are as pleasant with the shipping clerk and service personnel as they are with the president of the company. The reason is simple: They clearly understand that the sales process is not complete—and future sales are in jeopardy—until the current sales order has been delivered, installed, serviced, *and* paid for. For this reason they *know* they need the cooperation, effort, and goodwill of the entire team back at the home office.

In any business or family where two or more people are involved, there is always going to be a certain amount of discussion and conflict about who does what. One of the best opportunities for teaching trust and honesty is in the area of responsibility or doing what needs to be done. Unfortunately, in most businesses and homes the battle cry is, "That's not my job!" Top Performers, however, are loyal to those with whom they work and live and show this loyalty by doing what they are supposed to do, when they are supposed to do it. They give strong verbal support, and never say negative or unkind things about their associates. They clearly understand that when you're slinging mud, you're not doing anything but losing ground. Top Performers also are willing to go the extra mile and do the extras because they instinctively know that the more successful their company or department is the more likely they are to move ahead in their own careers.

Burke Marketing Research, Inc., asked executives in one hundred of the nation's one thousand largest companies, "What employee behavior disturbs you the most?" The result was a "hit parade of things that stick in the boss's craw, the kind of behavior that hits a nerve," said Marc Silbert, whose temporary personnel agency commissioned the survey. "They can blind employers to employees' good qualities. They become beyond redemption," he said. Liars, goof-offs, egomaniacs, laggards, rebels, whiners, airheads, and sloths—these are eight banes of a boss's existence, according to the survey, with *dishonesty* and *lying* topping the list. *"If a company believes that an employee lacks integrity, all positive qualities—ranging from skill and experience to productivity and intelligence—become meaningless,"* said Silbert, vice-president of Accountemps. Loyalty to those with whom we live and work is a prerequisite to Top Performance.

BE LOYAL TO YOUR ORGANIZATION

When I say that loyalty to your organization is important, I do not mean you should accept every thought that comes from upper management as if it had come down from the mountain on tablets. No one expects you to leap with joy when the commission structure has been changed so that there is more for the company and less for you. You are not expected to thank ownership when the working hours are changed and you are allowed to work more hours for the same or less pay. Loyalty to your organization means handling these aggravations in the proper manner.

Let's take a "negative break" and talk about how *not* to handle these situations. You do not complain about your areas of concern over coffee with a co-worker who has no authority to change the situation. You do not identify internal problems externally—meaning to someone outside your organization. The person who takes either of these avenues becomes a cancer to the organization. As you know, a cancer is a cell that lives within the body independently of the other cells of the body, and unless it is removed it will eventually lead to the death of the body. There are few diseases that will affect your organization in a more deadly manner or will creep up on the company with less notice than lack of loyalty. I have already mentioned that I feel very strongly about the importance of Due Process, but if there were ever a reason for dismissal without Due Process, it would be a lack of loyalty.

How, then, should the loyal employee manage the situation? The proper method of handling any situation that concerns you is to take the "problem identified" to someone who has the authority to handle the situation. Present it and several "potential solutions" for consideration. If after a realistic amount of time the company takes action on your recommendations or another satisfactory solution, you should congratulate yourself for working from within the organization to make it stronger.

However, if after a realistic amount of time the company fails to take action to change the situation, you now have two options: (1) shut up; (2) move on. There are no other options! If you continue to identify a problem over which no action is going to be taken, then the cancer grows. Continuing to identify a problem on which no action is going to be taken is beating your head against the proverbial brick wall. I believe that ulcers, serious headaches, burnout, stress, and even heart problems often begin in this very manner. Dr. David Schwartz, in his book *The Magic of Thinking Big*, says that over 80 percent of our hospital beds are filled with people with "EII," or Emotionally Induced Illness. This does not mean that the people are not sick, just that their illnesses *began* in their minds.

You owe it to *yourself*—as well as to your organization—to either support what is happening or find another company to work for. Now some of you are saying that jobs are not that easy to come by, and I agree. Neither is the human body that easy to come by—at least, spare parts are in great demand! The answer is simple but not easy: Get with the program or find another program to get with!

THIS COIN HAS TWO SIDES

Loyalty to the company is important, but the other side of the coin is that management and the corporation owe that same loyalty to their people. A classic example is Ross Perot and EDS. First a little background. His story is one of those rags-to-riches American stories with which many are so familiar.

In 1958 a young man drove into Dallas, Texas in a 1950 Plymouth automobile. He had virtually all of his possessions in the backseat and his wife and baby in the front seat. He was a top producer with IBM in 1958, but later he came up with a better idea in the use of computers. The idea was so good that he decided to start his own company. I don't believe there are many people in the United States today who don't recognize the name of Ross Perot and EDS (Electronic Data Systems).

Now remember, Ross Perot is one man. With a limited amount of money of his own plus some from his family and friends, he started his own company. EDS has made a major contribution to the computerized age of which we are a part. And in 1985 EDS was purchased by General Motors for more than three *billion* dollars.

One interesting and encouraging side to this story is the fact that although EDS deals in computer services, it is a very "human" company. Its management feels that qualities such as loyalty to country and family, high business ethics, and a sense of fair play to one's fellow man are all more important than job skills in a "total man, total company" growth concept.

The purchase of EDS by General Motors made Ross Perot one of the wealthiest men in the world. However, the key for Top Performers is to understand *why* he was able to become so successful. The following incident will give you some real insight into the character of this very successful man.

JUST HOW FAR CAN YOU GO WITH LOYALTY?

When the American Embassy in Iran was overrun in 1979, two of Ross Perot's key executives were captured by the Iranians and put in prison. Ross Perot is known as a man of decisiveness and a man of action. He is even better known among his employees as a man of intense loyalty. He stands by his people and supports them and they, in return, are intensely loyal to him. The problem in this situation was what to do about these two men who were in an Iranian prison. The answer—as far as Ross Perot was concerned—was fairly simple. He had little confidence (because of the political ramifications) that his men would see the light of day for a long, long time. He even feared their lives were in jeopardy. He quickly called a conference of his key executives in the United States. They mapped out a daring plan for the rescue of their co-employees.

The details are so exciting and so involved that space does not permit their being told here. However, I encourage you to read *On Wings of Eagles*, by Ken Follett, and get his full and exciting account of the story. In a nutshell, Ross Perot was able to organize a campaign to get those men out. He created a false riot situation, hired his own loyal people, and they freed those two men from that Iranian prison. Is there any wonder his people are so loyal to him?

Obviously, most of us will never be called on to get involved in such a situation, but

every day we have an opportunity to be loyal and to stand by our people.

A FINAL WORD ON LOYALTY

We began this chapter with a quote from Elbert Hubbard, and now let's close with some wise words from the same man.

> If you work for a man, in heaven's name, *work* for him. If he pays you wages which supply you bread and butter, work for him; speak well of him; stand by him and stand by the institution he represents. If

put to a pinch, an ounce of loyalty is worth a pound of cleverness. If you must vilify, condemn, and eternally disparage—resign your position, and when you are outside, damn to your heart's content, but as long as you are part of the institution do not condemn it. If you do that, you are loosening the tendrils that are holding you to the institution, and at the first high wind that comes along, you will be uprooted and blown away, and probably will never know the reason why.

PERFORMANCE PRINCIPLES

1. *Loyalty begins with loyalty to self.*
2. *You cannot consistently perform in a manner which is inconsistent with the way you see yourself.*
3. *Make every effort to be perceived as the most capable, not the most visible.*
4. *The greatest enemy of excellence . . . is good.*
5. *If you don't have something nice to say, don't say anything at all.*
6. *Support your organization or go to work for an organization you can support.*

"People
Just Don't Care..."

One learns peoples through the heart, not the eyes or the intellect.

Mark Twain

---

6 Unfortunately, as managers of people, we often feel like the speaker who was met with less than a resounding welcome and said, "In the words of William Shakespeare, it's nice to be among friends ... even if they are somebody else's." So many times managers and their employees almost seem to work at developing an adversary relationship. Instead, we have to be like the small boy who was confronted by the three big bullies, any one of whom could have obliterated him. (They even gave some indication they were going to do exactly that.) Like a lot of us, the little guy wasn't too well qualified to fight, but like *all* successful managers, he was qualified to think. (In this case, his physical well-being depended on it!) With this in mind, the little guy backed up dramatically, drew a line in the dirt with the toe of his shoe, looked the leader of the group in the eye, and said, "Now you just step across that line." Well, as you

might imagine, the big bully confidently—even arrogantly—stepped across the line. The small boy then smiled broadly and exclaimed, "Now we are both on the same side!" If we are going to be successful in managing people, we have got to remember that the manager and the people he manages *are* "on the same side."

You probably recall that Sir Edmund Hillary and his native guide, Tenzing, were the first people to make the historic climb of Mount Everest in 1953. Coming down from the mountain peak, Sir Edmund suddenly lost his footing. Tenzing held the line taut and kept them both from falling by digging his ax into the ice. Later Tenzing refused any special credit for saving Sir Edmund Hillary's life; he considered it a routine part of the job. As he put it, "Mountain climbers always help each other." Can we, as managers, afford to be any different? Aren't we obligated to work with our people to direct their energies and help them to develop their skills and talents to the fullest?

YOUR BILLION-DOLLAR ASSET

It is my firm conviction that if you could take only one thought or one idea out of *Top Performance*, it would be the thought I will share with you now. If you would really be an expert in the "people business" (that determines 85 percent of your success), then you should look into this statement:

People don't care
how much you know, until they know
how much you care ... about them!

Chances are great you have heard that phrase before and as an achiever, you really don't need to be told ... but it doesn't hurt to be reminded. You see, whether we are talking about parents, brothers and sisters, children, spouse, friends, associates, co-workers, employees, or employers—people don't care whether you are a Phi Beta Kappa from MIT, or if you got your Ph.D. from Harvard. They don't care if you have twenty years of experience (or one year of experience repeated twenty times!), sold more units for more dollar volume than anyone else ever has, or set every record the company keeps . . . *until* they know how much you care about them.

Anyone can do a job; anyone can do a *good* job. But it's not until there is love in a person's heart for a job that the results are something which others will call GREAT! Love is caring— caring enough to invest your life, caring enough to give it your all, to stick it out, to do the best you possibly can.

Love comes forth to contribute, to invest, to help, to be a loyal part of an effort or enterprise. Love will draw out from a person the very best he can do, which is often more than he himself or anyone else thought he could do. Love motivates one's entire potential for that individual's total success. But love also serves to inspire others to motivate the ones who follow them.

Several years ago I heard this story, which comes from Dr. George Crane's daily newspaper column "The Worry Clinic," but its real impact hit me much later and I think it applies to what we are discussing here.

> Jimmy, age ten, was devoted to his little sister, age six. One of the older staff doctors at Wesley Hospital told me of this case. It occurred about 1910 when blood transfusions and other medical miracles were not yet common.
>
> Jimmy's sister had fallen off her bicycle and cut a large artery in her leg. Bleeding was profuse, so by the time the doctor arrived at their house, she was failing fast.
>
> Quickly, the doctor managed to clamp the cut ends of the artery with his hemostats, but her heart was failing. In desperation, the doctor turned to Jimmy and said, "Jimmy will you give your blood to help save your little sister's life?"
>
> Jimmy swallowed hard, then nodded his head, so the doctor lay him on the kitchen table and began

withdrawing blood from one of his veins. Then he injected the blood directly into the little girl's vein.

For the next thirty minutes the doctor and family watched the little girl anxiously and prayerfully. The doctor kept his stethoscope over her heart to note its beating. Finally it showed she was over the crisis, so he wiped the perspiration off his forehead and turned around. Only then did he notice that Jimmy was still stretched out on the kitchen table, tense and trembling.

"What's the matter, Jimmy?" asked the doctor. "W-w-when do I die?" Jimmy replied through his clenched teeth.

That's when the doctor realized that Jimmy had misunderstood what the request for his blood really meant. For Jimmy had imagined his sister was going to need *all* his blood! Which meant that Jimmy, though hesitating a moment and swallowing hard at the doctor's original request, had silently agreed to die for his little sister!

The doctor had tears in his own eyes when he reassured Jimmy that he had extracted only a little of his blood and that Jimmy was not going to die. The doctor's tears demonstrated Descartes' comment about those divine sparks that God places in the brains of all of us. Jimmy's willingness to die that his sister might live is the type of thing which you empathetic readers will find makes your own divine sparks glow just from reading about Jimmy's sacrifice.

Now sacrifice and giving part of ourselves is not a popular concept in our society today, but think with me for just a second. When you come in at the end of the day and your spouse greets you at the door, chattering like a magpie about something in which you are totally disinterested, and you stop and give him or her your undivided attention, aren't you giving your loved one a part of your life? Aren't you giving up a little bit of yourself?

When you have been dealing with people—not always successfully—all day, what you really want is a few minutes of peace and quiet in front of the evening news or with the newspaper. Just as you settle down, your children, whom you dearly love but want to do so from a distance for the next few minutes, come climbing on you as if you were a jungle gym. At this point, when you either turn the TV off or put the newspaper down so that you can give them your love and undivided attention, you are investing a part of your life in theirs and giving up a little bit of yourself. When you are dead tired because it's been "one of those days," and an employee needs an empathetic ear and counseling and you take the time to listen, aren't you giving up a part of yourself?

If you would be an expert in the people business, read the Performance Principle at the end of this chapter, brand the words on your heart, and live them every day of your life.

PERFORMANCE PRINCIPLES

1. People don't care how much you know, until they know how much you care ... about them.

PART II

THE SCIENCE OF TOP PERFORMANCE

Science is organized knowledge.
Herbert Spencer

"But I Thought You Said..."

Precision of communication is important, more important than ever, in our era of hair-trigger balances, when a false or misunderstood word may create as much disaster as a sudden thoughtless act.

James Thurber

7 Every manager has heard about the importance of *communication.* Yet, we all need to be reminded occasionally just how important it is, and we need some specific suggestions on *what* we can do to be more effective. *We also need to remember that miscommunication, poor communication, or no communication can create incredible problems.* For example, take a look at this legislative summary of a bill introduced by California Assemblyman Alister McAlister (D-San Jose):

"The existing probate code does not expressly provide that its provisions are severable, in the event any of them are held invalid; that the singular number includes the plural, and the plural, the singular; that the present tense includes the past

117

and present, and the future, the present; or that designations of distinct portions within the code, without specific reference to the code, means such portion of the probate code. This bill would make specific each such provision."

Yes I know this is an extreme example, but isn't all communication, when it's *mis*communication, extreme?

In this chapter we will examine some of the problem areas that inhibit communication, review some of the rules for better communication, and take a closer look at specific situations, such as public speaking and meetings, in order to maximize effective communication. Finally, we'll see how communication plays a part in creating a work environment that is conducive to productivity.

According to the *Harvard Business Review*, the most promotable quality an executive, manager, salesperson, or anyone can possess is the ability to communicate. Alan Loy McGinnis, in his excellent book *Bringing Out the Best in People*, tells why:

> Motivators always use words lavishly and intensely as they outline their dreams to prospective supporters. Such diverse leaders as Lyndon Johnson, Winston Churchill, and Lee Iacocca have all possessed something in common: a mesmerizing ability to talk. Some may have had their shy sides, but when the occasion presented itself, each could pour out a profusion of words. "The inspiring talker produces zeal," said Aldous Huxley, "whose intensity depends not on the rationality of what is said or the goodness of the cause that is being advocated, but solely on the propagandist's skill in using words in an exciting way." Words are a remarkably powerful vehicle. Much of Franklin D. Roosevelt's success was due to his ability to coin a phrase and use slogans to summarize his dreams, and those slogans became a part of the fabric of our national life. Gandhi and Martin Luther King, Jr., both knew that if one speaks long enough, there is an uplifting and elevating, almost intoxicating power in words. Most

of us have experienced it hundreds of times—listening to another speak, either before an audience or in one-on-one conversation, until the sound of their words and the sheer weight of their flow eventually persuades us.

You can gain a considerable following if you are willing to relate your message to enough people and not be deterred by the large numbers who will not buy it. Instead, you pick up your idea and present it to the next prospect. Eventually, with enough presentations to enough people, a few people become enthusiastic, they join the parade, one by one, and soon a movement is on its way. Talk may be cheap, but the right use of words can generate in your followers a commodity impossible to buy . . . hearts on fire!

Yet, every day in our business and home life we encounter examples of miscommunication that bring grief and despair. This little bittersweet story could be true, and says much about life's communication problems.

An elderly couple were celebrating their fiftieth wedding anniversary. Their children, grandchildren, and great-grandchildren, as well as the townspeople, really rose to the occasion and recognized them in every conceivable way. The mayor gave them the key to the small town; there was a brunch at the country club; an afternoon tea; a banquet that evening, and all the townfolk as well as kinfolk came by to extend their congratulations. Finally, at about ten o'clock that evening the public celebration was all over. As was his custom, the husband headed for the kitchen to prepare the buttered toast with jam and the small glass of milk which he and his wife always enjoyed just before retiring.

Perhaps it was exhaustion from the long day, but when the husband called the wife into the kitchen for their little snack, as she sat down she broke into tears. Naturally concerned, the husband rose, walked around the table, embraced his wife, and asked her what the problem was. Through teary eyes she proclaimed that she thought on this most special of all occasions he would not have given her the end piece of bread. In some shock and surprise, the husband replied, "Why, sweetheart, I thought you knew that was my favorite piece!"

Isn't it ironic—and tragic—that for such a long period of time the husband had been giving what he thought was the best, but his wife had been receiving it as what she perceived to be the worst. Unfortunately, many of us have had similar miscommunication in our lives.

WHAT INHIBITS COMMUNICATION?

As this story illustrates, one of the greatest inhibitors to effective communication is the simple word *assume*. The husband *assumed* his wife knew he was giving her what he considered the best piece of bread. The wife *assumed* the husband was deliberately giving her the least desirable piece of bread. In the family setting, that leads to family dissension with dire consequences. In the corporate world, the consequences can have a disastrous effect on productivity. Any time you think, *They probably know*, let that be a red flag to remind yourself that they probably *don't* know—and seize the opportunity to *remind* them of what they should know.

According to AT&T, the lion's share of time spent in any office is spent communicating: listening, talking, chasing down stray facts, dealing with mail, etc. Were you to keep a log you'd be appalled at how little time you have for actually producing work (par for senior executives is about 15 percent of the workday).

In addition, communication can be very difficult, and it takes a constant concise effort to make sure you are understood. For instance, the five hundred most commonly used words in the English language have about fourteen thousand different meanings. And then there is the tendency to compound the problem by using words that don't fit together at all and force them into the same phrase. Take these examples:

"It's the **same** *difference!*"
"I would like the **jumbo** *shrimp.*"
"He worked with **military** *intelligence.*"

Word meanings and usage can complicate your life. Take the story of the woman who went to her pastor for counseling concerning her marriage. After a few preliminaries, the pastor said he had a few questions that would help identify the problems if she would just answer his questions as openly as possible. When the lady agreed, he began by saying, "Do you have any *grounds?*" To which the lady responded, "Why, yes we do, we have about ten acres just north of town." "No, ma'am," the pastor replied, "that's not what I mean. What I mean is do you have . . . well, do you have a *grudge?*" "Oh, no," she replied, "but we do have a nice little carport!" "No, ma'am," said the pastor, "that's not what I meant. One more question: Does your husband beat you up?" "Beat me up? Oh, no, I get up before he does just about every morning!" In complete exasperation the pastor said, "Lady, you're not listening to me. Why are you having trouble with your husband?" "Well," she said, "the man just doesn't know how to communicate!"

Communication should be as crisp and to the point as the sign I saw when I was in Chicago recently. It read WARNING! GUARD DOG ON DUTY—SURVIVORS WILL BE PROSECUTED! Now that communicates! I didn't want any part of that fence, that dog, that yard, or anything to do with that house. To be effective communicators, we should always be just that clear, though not necessarily that threatening.

AS EASY AS EBC

The problems in communication in the management area, and in society, for that matter, are so great that we at the Zig Ziglar Corporation have developed a seminar for companies and individuals called EFFECTIVE BUSINESS COMMUNICATIONS, which we are tremendously excited about. Our corporate staff instructors will spend two days helping your middle- and upper-management people become more effective in all-important communication skills.

Seeing yourself as others see (and hear) you is important, so participants are videotaped a dozen times, given private coaching sessions, and instructed in twelve Vital Skill Areas.

EFFECTIVE BUSINESS COMMUNICATIONS is an extremely strong skill builder because approximately 30 percent of the time is spent in instruction while 70 percent of the time is spent in practicing skills each individual needs and can use *immediately* upon returning to the job. Now this is beginning to sound a little bit like a commercial because it is . . . a commercial for gaining communication skills! Let me give you a sample of some communication skills and ideas from our seminar that you can use immediately.

DID YOU KNOW THAT . . . ?

You have about four minutes to be either received or rejected when you first meet someone. You gather 87 percent of your total lifetime information by sight; 7 percent by hearing; 3.5 percent by smell; 1.5 percent by touch; 1 percent by taste. So when you encounter a prospect or an employee, what they *see* is vitally important. Listeners need visual stimulation—a point of activity to focus on. Gestures, body language, and facial animation, in addition to other visual stimuli, are crucial. The average person *speaks* at about 150 words per minute but *thinks* at about 600 words per minute—or about four times faster. You may think your mind wanders, but in fact it often is *galloping* ahead of you like a runaway racehorse. As a communicator you must do everything possible to hold the listener's attention, including keeping your thoughts in order and paced with your speaking.

People respond 55 percent to your body language and expression, 38 percent to your vocal inflection, and only 7 percent to what you say. And, because of TV, the average person's attention span is now said to be from about seven to eleven minutes. Then it's time for the commercial. As communicators we must work to overcome these habit patterns which have become ingrained in our listeners' minds.

THE DAZZLING DOZEN

You can become a more effective communicator by becoming aware of what we call the twelve Vital Skill Areas of communication. These areas are: Appearance, Posture, Gestures, Eye Contact, Facial Expressions, Voice, Padding, Involvement, Handling Questions, Humor, Introducing Others, and Visual Aids.

Appearance means your clothes, plus the way you groom, the way you carry yourself and your accessories. Your appearance makes a statement about you; it tells others what you think of yourself. Does it add to or detract from the message you wish to communicate? What does *your* appearance say?

Posture means body language. Does your body language say that you are confident and in control, that you really care about the person you are communicating with, and that you are comfortable—or does it communicate just the opposite?

Gestures are the specifics of body language as it relates to arm and hand movement. You have heard people say they couldn't communicate if they were tied up and couldn't use their hands, and that is at least partially true. Natural arm and hand movement allows the communicator to express himself or herself much more clearly.

Eye Contact is to the eyes what the handshake is to the hands. When we "clasp" eyes with someone, we either send positive signals of confidence, courage, interest, and concern or negative signals of boredom, irritation, disgust, antagonism, or even anger.

Facial Expressions include the smile and frown. Your face is one of your greatest assets to effective communication. With controlled facial expressions, you set the tone for conversations and let people know what's coming. You also show what you mean, and make your thoughts easier to follow.

Voice includes not only the pitch of your voice but also volume, inflection, and pace. When you vary the volume level, place emphasis on certain words and phrases, and speak at a varying pace, you become more effective and are far more likely to be understood.

Padding is the nonworking words that we so uh, often um, insert ah, into you know, our—well, like our, uh, um, ah, spoken conversation. Just for fun, record a telephone conversation (your side of the call only) and count the number of nonworking words. You may be surprised.

Involvement means active listening both on your part and the part of those who *might* listen to you. Using a person's name, asking questions, and listening to the answer, and speaking in terms of others' interests are examples of how we involve others in communication.

Handling questions is especially important in business conversations. All too often we do not listen to the question or do not answer the same question that is asked. If integrity and trust are important in business (and they are), then the way you handle questions can increase your "trust level" with those with whom you work.

Humor can be used to relax your audience (of one or ten thousand) and make friends with them. It can also be used as a bridge when you are shifting into other perhaps more serious subject matter, and to give your audience a mental stand-up. It can be especially effective in lengthy presentations to bring a tired or drifting audience back to the session. Careful—don't overdo it. Too many would-be communicators sacrifice message for humor. Incidentally, the rule in sharing questionable humor of an off-color nature is this: If you have to ask the question "Should I share this?" you already have the answer: *No!* (I've never known a speaker to get a speaking engagement, an employee to get a promotion, a salesperson to make a sale, or a politician to win votes *because* he or she used profane language or told off-color stories. However, I do know of countless instances when extremely negative reactions were the result of profane language or tasteless stories.)

Introducing others may not seem very important to you, but someone very wise said, "You never get a second chance to make a first impression." In introductions, you have the opportunity not only to make an excellent first impression but also to make others feel important through sincere recognition of their strengths.

Visual aids are not only used in board meetings but may also be used in one-on-one conversations as well. Anytime you can impact more than one of your listener's senses, you are ahead in the communication game.

By just being aware of these Vital Skill Areas, you will move ahead in communication skills . . . and if you spend time working and studying these areas, you can substantially increase your communication skills.

DIFFERENCES BETWEEN ORAL AND WRITTEN LANGUAGE

Even though you may be an excellent writer, you will not be an excellent oral communicator if you use the same approach in speaking you do for the written word.

- Spoken language must be easily and instantly understandable to the listener. If the listener misunderstands, he cannot go back and reread.
- Spoken language should be more repetitive. It is important to rephrase several times key ideas you want the listeners to take away with them.
- Spoken language should be more idiomatic. Otherwise, it sounds somewhat stilted and stuffy.
- Spoken language should be simpler in structure than written language.
- Figurative language adds life and color to spoken words. Colorful, descriptive words can turn an otherwise colorless phrase into a memorable one. Lincoln described a nation "conceived in liberty . . ." Kennedy spoke of freedom as a "torch passed to a new generation . . ." J. F. Bere, chairman of the Borg-Warner Corporation, described untapped human assets as "waiting like a coiled spring to release enormous potentials . . ." Problems were called "smoldering fires . . ." and new programs being developed as "a brick here and a brick there."

COMMUNICATION: MANAGER TO EMPLOYEE

Let's take an overview of how a Top Performer creates an environment for communication by looking at several points which I think are excellent guidelines for Top Performers.

Openness sets the basis for knowing your employees personally. Communicate the desire to know your employees, and then make the effort to know them personally as well as professionally. The personal goals, interests, hobbies, family relationships, thoughts, and beliefs should be known as openly as possible so that the employee becomes more than an object. Managers should recognize employees as dynamic, unique individuals. Openness communicates dignity. No longer an object, the employee can enjoy the benefits of involvement and commitment, a platform for an exchange of trust. Mutual honesty and confidence create a model of behavior that becomes a positive emotional and mental support system.

Listen and communicate. To know employees openly, listen to what others say and encourage them to communicate their motivation, concerns, personalities, and unique mental sets. Listen to their ideas. Doing so makes possible the sharing of responsibility not only for work but also for the quality of personal relations.

People carry out their own ideas best. Your responsiveness generates employee responsiveness: mutual responsiveness sets the stage for growth and training. Commitment to such evolution is a grand design to help people recognize their own capabilities.

Communicate compassion and recognition. By listening carefully, you come to know your employees intimately. The human condition is vulnerable to both joy and pain. The manager who communicates compassion for the strength and potential of others can generate a friendship that brings about maturity and mutual acceptance of responsibility. The opposite is probably true as well. Being a friend is preferable to the adversary relationship of "us and them."

Communicating compassion is a kind of recognition, a key ingredient of people development. Good performance is an evolution of people development.

Communicate co-management. The trappings of authority inhibit human growth and stunt organizational development. Co-management is the key to each individual's opportunity to become interwoven with a dynamic organization's progress. Together, in an informal and intricate away, commitment becomes a working definition of the quality of life possible for everyone.

Communicate fallibility and involvement. No one is perfect. When you make a mistake, admit it and ask for help. If you've taken the preceding steps, employees will not mistake your humanity for weakness. Communicating fallibility communicates involvement. When the manager admits a mistake, everyone can err. With that freedom, shared decision making, authority, and responsibility are possible. People become committed because they can afford to do so. The axiom "Management is getting things done through people" becomes reality.

Communicate initiative through "parenting." We "parent" everyone, including ourselves, when we are striving to become viable human beings. Like a good parent, a good manager implements organizational mechanisms so that decisions are forced down the chain as far as possible, thus fostering initiative. Authoritarianism for its own sake destroys initiative; people will want to be told what to do. The manager as parent can foster the evolution of autonomous, responsible workers who are involved and can expend initiative for furthering the organization.

Communicate trust, missions, and expectations. The manager as parent shares the responsibility and decisions of work, and in turn, the meaning in work. Sharing meaning in work inspires commitment. When trust and meaning generate commitment, communicating missions and expectations is possible. Attainable, clearly understood objectives shared synergistically in organizational missions are the results.

Communicate confidence. The freedom to bring missions to fruition should be sustained by confidence in employees and the courage to stand back and let them make mistakes that can lead to modified objectives. Proper parenting includes giving credit where it is due, suggesting and requesting, not ordering and driving. People will know the reasons for your suggestions and requests. Praise in public. Reprove in private. Do both constructively.

Communicate fun and happiness. Be positive. Self-esteem, confidence, and happiness beat their alternatives for generating both productivity and quality of work life. A child's enjoyment of life comes from the hope and joy of tomorrow and the potential of numerous opportunities. Maturity is becoming the parent of the child within yourself. That simply means that you nurture the child's natural abilities, the greatest of which is the ability to "have fun."

Communicate expectations. Treat people as what they can become. New missions are natural outgrowths of expectations when dignity and responsibility are shared. People perform according to what is expected of them. Building in employees a sense of the importance of their work will give them goals, a sense of direction, something to strive for and achieve. They can become what they choose to become. [These points were made in the August 1985 issue of the *Training and Development Journal* by Gerald D. Baxter and John K. Bowers.]

To the thoughts expressed by these authors, I might simply reinforce the fact that the Baby Boomers of today, who constitute 48 percent of the work force, are vastly different from the work force of forty years ago and, to a large degree, even of twenty years ago. The Baby Boomers were raised in permissiveness and have rejected authority figures, to a large degree. Not only that but they are more outspoken and have a real desire to participate in the decision-making process. Most of them have attitudes which would have appalled their fathers, and that's not all bad. They do not respond to dictatorial managers or leaders but are far more responsive to those leaders whom they perceive as having an interest in their personal growth and development.

According to Glen Raschick in a January 1986 article in Air Canada's magazine, these new members of the work force are more "people oriented" and respond more to the gentle approach than they do to harsh discipline. Results indicate that this nonpunitive approach has positive effects on these Baby Boomers, such as less absenteeism, dismissals, disciplinary action, an increase in morale, and a reduction in wrongful termination.

Now let's take another look at the new work environment.

A recent survey showed that the number-one job of top executives is to communicate successfully. Aside from communicating—including speaking, writing, listening, reading, and thinking—company presidents and chairmen of the board do virtually nothing.

"Which courses best prepare one for business leadership?"

This was the question posed by the University of Michigan graduate school to 1,158 newly promoted top executives. Business communication was the most common response, with 71.4 percent rating it as very important. Finance was the second highest, with 64.7 percent.

Bruce Barton, congressman, author, and ad agency founder, said, "In my library are about a thousand volumes of biography. A rough calculation indicates that more of these deal with men who have talked themselves upward than with all the scientists, writers, saints, and doers combined. Talkers have always ruled. They will continue to rule. The smart thing is to join them."

COMMUNICATING TO TWO OR TWO HUNDRED

From time to time, most of us are forced to stand up and address some kind of meeting somewhere at some time on some subject. Inevitably, that experience will happen in every leader's work environment. Since all of us—especially leaders and managers—are judged by our peers, underlings, and supervisors by the way we present ourselves, our ability to communicate on our feet is extremely important. Since you might not have the time or inclination to join the National Speakers Association, take the Dale Carnegie Course, join Toastmasters, Toastmistresses, or come to Dallas for our specialized training, I'd like to give you a few additional tips and reminders that will offer some immediate benefits for you.

Chances are good you know that former Vice President of the United States Alben W. Barkley died in the process of giving an address. I mention that simply because to the best of my knowledge, he is the only person who ever passed on while making a speech. Since the beginning of time there have been ten or twelve billion people to walk this earth. Mathematically speaking, therefore, I can tell you with considerable confidence that public speaking is easily the safest occupation on the face of this earth. Although your knees might knock, your heart race, your palms get sweaty, your mouth feel like cotton, and your blood pressure go up considerably, the odds are dramatically in your favor that you are going to survive. That should give you added confidence.

As Bruce Barton said:

> I never want to speak if I'm not scared; when I'm not scared I tend not to care enough about what the listener thinks. I don't care whether I get the subject across or not; all I want to do is get done and go home. But if I'm scared, I know I'll have the proper tension to do the right kind of job. I know of nothing that will give the energy and creativity that healthy tension and stress will give.

Let me remind you that if you should lead an old mule—or, for that matter, even a young one—in front of the group to whom you're going to speak, he would look as if he were bored to tears and might even stand there and go to sleep right in front of the group. However, if you were to lead a beautiful thoroughbred horse in front of the group, he would be extremely nervous and fidgety. So, if you are "scared to death" or nervous and fidgety when you stand in front of a group, just be grateful you're a thoroughbred and not a mule! As Toastmasters International is fond of saying, "Effective speaking is not the result of eliminating those butterflies in your stomach, but simply getting them to fly in formation."

REAL VS. IMAGINED FEAR

But the fear of speaking is anything but a laughing matter. In fact, in the *Book of Lists*, speaking before a group was listed as the number-one fear among Americans. It ranked ahead of the fear of death by fire or death by drowning. So the fear of speaking is a legitimate one. The way to overcome fear is by taking action on that fear, and that's how training can benefit you. Let me give you some specific hints on successful speaking.

First, remember that speaking is a safe thing to do. More people die getting out of the bathtub daily than have died in the history of the world speaking. (I don't say this to discourage bathing, rather, to encourage speaking.)

Second, if you don't like public speaking, don't do it. Stick to private speaking because chances are excellent that since you're this far into *Top Performance* you are doing a lot of private speaking in small meetings for the people under your supervision. Yes, I know you're thinking, *But I often have to address a significant number of people.* I still insist that you stick to private speaking. On occasion I have addressed as many as twenty-three thousand people—and that's a bunch! However, I can honestly tell you that it was a private speech. What I do is select certain individuals in the audience and key on them most of the time. I pick friendly, responsive, supportive people whose body language tells me they agree with what

I'm saying and they even like me for saying it. If there's a sourpuss in the crowd who looks like his ancestors descended directly from Attila the Hun, I do not play hero and try to win him over. I ignore him and concentrate on the supportive, friendly people. In most cases, if I'm effectively doing my job, the sourpuss eventually joins the meeting, but in the meantime he has not been a drain on my own enthusiasm and energy. (I'm responsible *to* him so I give him my best effort, but I'm not responsible *for* him, his attitude, and the way he receives my message.) I encourage you to select one friendly person (in your own company there should be lots of them), look him directly in the eye, and talk to him. Then move to another friendly person and do the same. You'll find this to be helpful and a tremendous confidence builder.

Third, I can tell you that in my many years as a speaker and teacher, I do not believe I've ever come across any one thing which builds self-image and personal confidence as much as the ability to communicate on your feet. I encourage you to become skilled in this area. Once the initial fright subsides, you will probably discover that you actually enjoy speaking! And if you are ever called on to give a presentation, and feel those butterflies flying radically out of formation, just think of this little story:

Back in the days of the Roman Empire during a circus in the Colosseum, a Christian was thrown to a hungry lion. As the spectators cheered, the wild beast pounced. But the Christian quickly whispered something in the lion's ear and the beast backed away in terror. After this happened several times, the emperor sent a centurion to find out what magic spell could make a ferocious lion cower in fear. A few minutes later the guard returned and said, "The Christian whispers in the lion's ear, 'After dinner you'll be required to say a few words.'"

PERFORMANCE PRINCIPLES

1. Miscommunication, poor communication, or no communication will create problems.
2. Get involved in communication training that teaches both sides of the communication process—speaking and listening.
3. Remember these key phrases for important communication:
   a. openness sets the tone
   b. listen, listen, listen
   c. send signals of compassion and positive recognition
   d. communicate co-management
   e. communicate personal fallibility
   f. communicate initiative through parenting
   g. communicate trust
   h. communicate confidence
   i. communicate fun and happiness
   j. communicate a vision

SPECIAL BONUS SEGMENT ON COMMUNICATION

Since so much information is communicated in meetings, we decided to include a bonus section dealing with all facets of a meeting. As our company has grown so much in the last ten years, I have personally seen the importance of effective meetings.

Meetings, like certain forms of wildlife, are protected under the law. The First Amendment to the Constitution of the United States says in part that "Congress shall make no law . . . abridging . . . the right of the people peaceably to assemble." Under this guarantee, meetings seem to have multiplied like rabbits . . . until today it seems that everyone is on his way to or from a meeting. But remember this simple definition of a *meeting:* "A meeting is a group of people who have come together for a common purpose." The challenge for a Top Performer is to see that that purpose is accomplished. Because meetings are so vital to business communication and hence productivity, I want to give you a few tips, hints, and secrets for maximizing their effectiveness.

Ten Commandments to End Meeting Madness

Prior to the Meeting

1. *Meet only if necessary.* If a decision can prevent a meeting, make it. If a substitute will do (like a conference call), do it. If it's not of maximum importance for you, delegate participation to a subordinate.
2. *Limit attendance and attendees.* If you're needed for a minute, stay for only a minute. Invite only those people who must be involved . . . and then involve them.

3. *Pick the best time and the right place.* If you don't base your schedule on every attendee's schedule, you'll end up holding another meeting. Make sure everything you need is in the room before starting.
4. *Make your agenda their agenda.* Be sure everyone knows the purpose of the meeting, the items for discussion and decision, and the time requirements involved. Number the items on your agenda in order of priority so the most important gets done first, and the least important may be sacrificed.

During the Meeting

5. *Assign a time watcher.* No one keeps time . . . so watch it! (Often your best time watcher is your keeper of the minutes.) This person is a key and objective observer of the agenda and of meeting dynamics. Your time watcher starts on time, calls out time segments, drives you toward completion.
6. *Steer the meeting along the agenda track.* Control digressions, delays, and denouements while you drive toward your destination: the action that accomplishes your stated purpose.
7. *Conclude, assign, depart.* Sum up what you did or how you're going to do what you decided to do. Remind whoever is going to do it to do it (and tell him when it should be done). Then leave.

After the Meeting

8. *Make sure that attendees get minutes in hours, not weeks— twenty-four or forty-eight maximum.* Nothing is more frustrating than receiving minutes for a meeting you can barely remember. They won't be read. Use minutes to reinforce assignments, and as a checkup at follow-up meetings.
9. *Assign someone to report to the person in charge.* Establish a reporting method to assure that decisions are executed and progress is being made.
10. *Evaluate meetings and abolish standing committees that are sleeping.* Did your meeting *work*? Did it actually do the *work*? Did it make subsequent *work* easier? If not, fire it! Evaluate

meetings, all committees, and any important get-together regularly. Was the meeting well prepared for, well run, a creative, communicating session that accomplished its purpose and involved people in a meaningful way? If the answer to any of these questions is no, go back to the First Commandment and start all over again.

To help you prepare for meetings that really work, I'm including a checklist for planning meetings, one for controlling participation in a meeting for maximum effectiveness, and another for evaluating meetings. By using these instruments you can help your team, company, or group be a Top Performer.

Checklist for Planning Meetings

Prior to the Meeting

Publicity
___ Notices
___ Letter of invitation
___ Bulletin boards
___ Personal contacts
___ News release
      (if apropos)

Agenda
___ Plan agenda
___ Plan for involvement
___ Contact people on agenda
___ Previous minutes
___ Committee reports

Space and Equipment
___ Place reserved
___ Equipment reserved
___ Materials needed

Just Before the Meeting

Space
___ Room arrangement
___ Seating arrangement
___ Extra chairs
___ Climate control

Equipment and Supplies
___ A-V equipment set up, checked
___ Extension cords
___ Microphones
___ Gavel, felt pens, pencils, pads
___ Newsprint
___ Visual aids
___ Agenda, other handouts
___ Name tags

At the Meeting

___ Meeting, greeting, seating participants and guests
___ Greeting and seating latecomers
___ Handing out materials
___ Operation of equipment
___ Recording equipment

End of Meeting . . . and After

___ Collect unused materials
___ Return equipment
___ Clean up

___ Thank helpers
___ Read and analyze evaluation, feedback
___ Remind people of follow-up commitments
___ Make plans for next meeting—date, etc.

Dealing With Individuals in Meetings

In every meeting you will find basically two kinds of people—those who talk and those who don't. But within those broad classifications, there are several types you as a presider or presenter need to know how to handle.

BEHAVIOR	SOLUTION
Talks too much	Cut across their talk with a summarizing statement and direct a question to someone else. If they continue to talk, say, "Let's hear what Jerry thinks." If they're difficult, get other participants on your side by asking what they think about what the talker is saying.
Quick, helpful	Even though this type often has the right answer, it keeps others from participating. Thank them and direct a question to someone else. Be sure they understand that you appreciate their help. Suggest, "Let's get several opinions." Use them to summarize.
Rambler	When they stop for breath, thank them, rephrase one of their statements, and then move on.
Arguer	If they are naturally troublesome or trying to make trouble, get them placed in your blind spot right next to you. Pretend not to hear. But recognize legitimate objections and side with them when you can. Sometimes the group will take care of them if they persist. If all else fails, talk to them privately and ask for their help.
Obstinate	This may be someone who really doesn't understand what you're driving at. Reflect or ask them to say more. Get others to try to help them see the point by stating it a

BEHAVIOR	SOLUTION
	different way. If that doesn't work, tell them you'd like to discuss the question further after the meeting.
Wrong subject	Focus on the topic. Say something like, "That is interesting. I'm sorry, though; it's beyond the scope of our meeting."
His own problem	Tackle the problem if it is pertinent to the subject under discussion. Otherwise, acknowledge the value of the problem and ask to discuss it privately.
Racial or political question	Frankly state what you can or cannot discuss. Say something like, "Problems do exist, but our meeting can't deal with them."
Side conversations	Pause and let others listen to the conversation. Draw them into your discussion by asking for their opinion.
Poor choice of words	Their ideas may be good, but they just don't know how to express them. Help them out by putting their idea in your words. Say, "In other words, you mean . . ." Protect them from ridicule.
Definitely wrong	Comment, "Well, that's an interesting way to look at it," or "Of course, you're entitled to your opinion." And go on.
Clashing personalities	In the midst of dispute, cut across with a direct question on the topic. Bring another participant into the discussion. If it still continues, frankly ask that personalities be left out.
Question you can't answer	Redirect the question to the group. If you don't know the answer, say so. Offer to find out.
Bored	Try to find an area of interest. Call on them for their experience.
Never participates	Use direct, provocative questions.

BEHAVIOR	SOLUTION
Shy, unsure of self	Ask direct questions you are sure they can answer. Ask if they agree. Build them up in the eyes of the group.

HOW DID IT GO?

To avoid having meetings that "self-destruct," evaluate them afterward. Here are some of the more obvious problems and a few tips to prevent falling into common meeting traps.

Lack of involvement in the planning by those who will be at the meeting. Members need to feel "ownership" and will support what they have a part in planning and developing.

Same plan, same place, same time. While sameness gives security to some people, it bores others. Participants can add spice and zip to meetings by using different methods and techniques.

Equipment that doesn't work. Check equipment beforehand. Have extra bulbs and cords. Have an alternate plan.

Illegible visual aids. Prior to meeting, check visuals to make sure they can be easily seen and deciphered.

No planned agenda. Make sure that the purpose and plan of activities are defined and participants know what is to happen.

Inappropriate seating plan. Formal classroom-style seating is all right for an audience. Semicircles, seating around tables, and other less-formal arrangements, however, invite and facilitate communication.

Long, drawn-out speakers. Give the speaker a specific topic and a time block, and keep the meeting moving.

No record. Keep a history of the meeting, the plans, discussions, and commitments made.

Neglect to carry the group "into the future." Plan for who will do what and when.

"Show" run by only a few. Get the total group involved.

These tips are adapted from Eva Schindler-Rainman and Ronald Lippitt, *Taking Your Meetings Out of the Doldrums.*

"The Firings Will Continue Until Morale Improves"

Every man takes the limits of his own field of vision for the limits of the world.

Schopenhauer

8 The paramount responsibility of every manager is to obtain successful results, which can be done by getting the proper performance from the people we manage. As we just learned, communication is an essential element. So is establishing standards for evaluating performance. Question: How can we supervise or plan performance if the parties involved don't understand *and* agree on what is to be done? The answer to this question lies in mutual goals and mutual understanding. The process of developing these mutual objectives and this common understanding is called the Performance Value Package. We discussed this in chapter 4 in "The Art of Top Performance," and in this chapter we need to get into the specific how and why of the Performance Value Package (PVP).

As a reminder, let me repeat:

The Foundational Performance level is the level of performance a person must achieve to continue to work with the organization. It is called Foundational because when this level is achieved the person not only maintains his or her position but he also lays a foundation upon which he can build future successes.

The Successful Performance level is the level of performance that might reasonably and realistically be expected by both manager and employee.

The Value Performance level is the level of performance that might be expected if everything goes according to plan and the employee excels in all areas. This provides overachievers with a target.

When introducing the employee to the Performance Value Package, you are really introducing him or her to a three-level goal-setting or management-by-objective concept. The idea that makes PVP so valuable is that the employee participates in the decision-making process rather than being dictated to. This "shared ownership" principle is a powerful motivator. The one possible exception is the Foundational Performance level. Since this is the basic level at which an employee can function and maintain his position, it is often dictated by the company and by historical data about the position.

For example, here at the Zig Ziglar Corporation, our telemarketers must average six hundred dollars in volume per day to cover their overhead (including phone time, salary, commission, product cost, building maintenance, employee benefits, and so forth). We have learned that to average six hundred dollars per day over a thirty-day period, the telemarketer must make a minimum of eighty attempted phone calls per day. This number of attempted phone calls will yield twenty completions (opportunities to make a sales presentation), which will result in the correct volume. This is our break-even point. These numbers are carefully studied and constantly monitored to see if they are changing.

However, we know that if a telemarketer cannot achieve these quotas, we cannot afford to have him on staff. This leaves little room for negotiation on Foundational Performance level, so the supervisor introduces the new employee to concepts during the initial interview.

The Successful Performance level is a different story. To determine the Successful Performance level, the supervisor will start with the salesperson's goals. We set goals in primarily two ways at ZZC: (l) number of people helped (sold); (2) dollars earned, keeping in mind that dollars earned is a yardstick for success and not our only objective. However, we do know that the only way we can stay in business is to operate at a profit, so we do not apologize for being fairly rewarded for delivering an excellent product. When the employee has determined the number of people he wants to help (sell) and the amount of money he wants to earn, it is fairly simple to "track down" his Successful Performance level goals. The Value Performance level is figured last and serves as a real "stretch" goal.

What happens when I don't meet my Foundational Performance level?

One of the concerns about PVP is what happens when minimum standards are not achieved. This is the really exciting thing about the program. By following a three-step outline, everyone wins.

I. Consultation. The manager must have the courage to confront the employee with his or her concern. If the manager does so in a nonaccusatory, nonpersonal manner (attack the problem, not the person) by attempting to see the situation the employee's perspective, then the manager and employee can work together to solve the problem and not be on opposite sides of the situation.

II. Problem definition. The manager and employee must agree on *exactly* what the problem is. If they cannot agree, they must at least have an agreement that there is a problem and they must agree to identify the "pieces of the puzzle" so that they may define the problem.

IIA. Brainstorming alternatives. The manager and the employee work together to contribute ideas for solving the problem. There must be no "value judgements" on these alternatives since to judge them at this point would stifle creativity.

IIB. Choosing the best alternative. The manager and employee work together to evaluate each alternative and identify the one that will be most effective for solving their problem.

III. Plan of action. The manager and employee agree on a specific Plan of Action including timetable, activities, and outcome for immediate implementation.

IIIA. Inspection. The manager and employee meet regularly to assess progress. If the alternative selected is not working, it may be that the problem was not properly identified. Or, if the alternative solution is not working, the manager and employee may need to select another alternative.

THE SCIENTIFIC AND ANALYTICAL APPROACH

Let's take each step in the process and break it down into small, digestable parts and use the scientific and analytical approach to problem solving.

I. Consultation. One of the most difficult aspects of management is confronting employees who don't seem to be getting the desired results. We often confuse sympathy with empathy and end up sympathizing with them instead of managing them with empathy. Because this is such an important aspect of the process, I want to deal with it in a more detailed manner.

> Every manager comes up against the problem of someone whose progress is being blocked by some deep-seated attitude or behavior. It might be a person who can't organize his time effectively; or someone who is always fighting with others. Or, it might be one of those people who will never admit that he has made a wrong decision and bridles at the slightest criticism. . . . The precise nature of the problem is usually immaterial. The real difficulty is that the individual concerned sees nothing particularly wrong with his behavior.

Adapted and reprinted by permission of the publisher, from PERSONNEL, May–June 1963 © 1963 American Management Association, New York. All rights reserved.

Everyone has blind spots but no one can continually and profitably evade reality. In the final analysis, it is what others think of a person that determines his or her acceptance and progress in life.

For such problem people, there is only one remedy. You must guide them to reexamine their values and behavior. Admittedly, this is not easy, but it is not beyond the capability of any manager with empathy and an honest desire to help people develop their fullest potential. And it is a vital part of every manager's job, for it is in guiding and influencing the behavior of his subordinates in such a way as to make them better and more effective employees that the manager fulfills one of his key roles—the role of performance counselor.

Effective counseling is not only fundamental to the development of people, it is synonymous with it. Yet the chief reason so few managers succeed in mastering the art of counseling is that they fail to understand their true role in the counseling process. Asked to define this process, many people would say that it meant "having a heart-to-heart talk." Others might define it as "giving fatherly advice," while still others might call it "constructive criticism." However, true counseling is really none of these things. A manager's object in counseling is to change the attitude and behavior of a person by changing the thinking. . . .

In short, the aim of a manager's counseling, or coaching, is to clearly present to a person a behavior or attitude that negatively affects performance in a way that convinces that person to change.

Here are some pointers for every manager who needs to coach a person about his performance:

1. Remember that counseling is a routine management responsibility and should be treated as such. It should not be regarded as, or allowed to become, a

psychological exercise or a major emotional crisis.

2. Recognize that the essential work of counseling goes on within the counselee. It is there that changes must be brought about and it is there that the drive to change must be developed. In this process you can rely on a person's desire to succeed.

3. Acquaint yourself with your employee's background, work history, and relations with others in the organization. Much of this information is available in personnel files and previous evaluations. Sometimes it is helpful to record observations about the person's behavior over a given period, such as the year between formal evaluations. You must have a clear understanding of the problem you are trying to resolve.

4. Pick a comfortable place to talk, preferably, a routine business setting, either your office or your subordinate's, if there is sufficient privacy. Managers supervising a field sales force might find suitable opportunities in the course of driving with their salespeople. Wherever the discussion takes place, make every effort to give the employee the feeling that he or she is in a relaxed and confidential setting, thus enhancing the feeling of security.

5. Remember that people differ in their ability to see their personal biases. Those who are mature and used to viewing themselves critically can be brought to such realizations fairly quickly; others, particularly if they are immature and burdened with deep emotional needs to avoid the truth, often take considerable time. You need to make a decision about the pace he should employ in a particular case.

6. Focus on the barriers to the person's "progress." Try to show him that he is working against the very thing he really wants to achieve. It often helps to proceed from a person's remarks, since this reduces the possibility of friction, and keeps the emphasis

on his values. As we saw earlier, if the man has some attitude or behavior problem that he has failed to recognize for what it is, he is overlooking facts that have a direct bearing on his business success. The uncovering and cautious evaluation of these facts is in itself a most potent therapy.

Finally, there is the question of follow-up. You should do this as unobtrusively as possible. If no change takes place, or the change is temporary, you should try again. If after a few attempts the problem is still unresolved, it is time to consider other action, including termination.

MAKE CERTAIN YOU ARE—OR WANT TO BE—A MANAGER

Some managers will balk at the thought of having to "counsel" employees. To those of you who feel this way, I want to challenge you to consider whether management is really for you. If you are so caught up in activities that you cannot spend time with your people, then I submit that you are *not* a manager. If you will go back to the first pages of this book you will see we agreed that *management is getting things done through people.* To impact people's performance, we must be willing to confront, counsel, lead, and direct. The next steps in the PVP process are *problem definition* and the action which follows.

II. Problem definition. Very few problems are singular in nature. They probably consist of several aspects. What you usually see are a variety of symptoms of a problem. Long hair was not a problem in the 1960s, it was a symptom of the problem: unwillingness to conform to established standards.

To effectively identify the problem of a person you manage, you must list on paper the "parts" or primary "factors" of the problem as you see them and ask the employee to do the same. On paper, some of the factors will not be as pertinent as you originally perceived them to be. Stick with the specific observable facts when listing the facets of the situation. You can support facts with evidence. If there is little or no evidence, you may not have many facts.

Together, you and the employee must determine the answers to the following questions in identifying the problem:

1. In what areas do you feel you are performing proficiently?
2. Why are you doing so well in these areas?
3. Could you give me some specific examples?
4. Where do you feel (think) you did an acceptable but not necessarily commendable job?
5. Why was this work only average?
6. Could you give me some specific examples?
7. In what areas did you perform below Foundational Performance level?
8. Why?
9. Could you give me some specific examples?
10. Are you interested in developing a Performance Improvement Program?
11. How do you think the performance might be improved?
12. How can I help implement *your* plan?

While these questions may seem somewhat obvious, this list should result in over one hour's worth of counseling and conversation. There will be important points along the way where you will need to interject your own point of view and shape or guide the direction of the session. The manager must help the employee to *see* the situation. Then the manager must help the employee develop the *desire* to make the improvement and a *plan* to overcome any obstacles. You are not sitting in judgment, in your long black robes, waiting to render your verdict; instead, you become a partner in helping another Very Important Human Being become a Top Performer!

IS IT ALWAYS AS EASY AS IT SOUNDS?

Absolutely not! Most management books make the coaching and problem identification sessions between manager and employee sound like the easiest part of the job, when in fact it is often just the opposite. Just asking the list of questions I shared with you takes a great deal of courage and considerable skill to come across as a concerned manager instead of a prosecuting attorney. Combine this with the fact that many times employees see no problem, and the result is they often don't cooperate and give the answers you hoped for. So what do you do? Well, I'm glad you asked, because that's the next agenda. As I've said before, we need to break each situation into its smallest components. The same is true for problems. Here are some guidelines and questions for exposing and defining a problem.

A. Beware the potential for problems and don't ignore danger signals.
 1. What changes have occurred in your areas of responsibility?
 2. What facts led you to notice the change?
 3. Exactly what has changed? What has not changed?
B. Identify the crucial elements of the problem.
 1. What first led you to notice a change?
 2. What are the problem indicators in concise terms?
 3. When did you first notice these indicators?
 4. Who is involved?
 5. Where do these indicators occur?
 6. Are the problem indicators causing members of the team to fall short of their objectives?
 7. Are there any similarities or patterns to the indicators?
C. Identify the obvious causes of the problem indicators.
 1. Which indicators have you seen before?
 2. What are the causes of the indicators?
 3. What action must be taken to eliminate the indicators?
 4. What would happen if you did not take any action?
D. Expose and define the problem.
 1. Write out the problem in one clear and concise sentence.
 2. List the evidence that indicates this is a real and not imagined problem.
 3. Who, What, How, When, Where, and Why?

POOR PERFORMANCE INDICATORS

It seems almost too simplistic to list some of the indicators that managers should be on the lookout for in dealing with poor performance. However, if we will recognize the earliest indicators, we can avoid big problems down the road. The attitude of poor performers is one of defensiveness, and they often become disinterested and fail to communicate with you or their peers. They have a tendency to take very little initiative and when forced to take action that doesn't work, they will blame failure on others instead of accepting personal responsibility. They often keep to themselves and seem to have no real enthusiasm for their work. This will result in poor performance as indicated by making careless errors and appearing disorganized. They may turn in work incomplete or not at all. If you have established some time limits for work, they rarely meet a deadline. These poor performers avoid the difficult tasks and spend enormous amounts of time on the easier aspects of their jobs.

When you suspect any of these indicators, do the right thing for both you and your employee: confrontation. Remember:

Permissiveness is only neglect of duty.

The rationalizations you have been using for procrastinating on facing the poor performer—"It's tough to get replacements; if my predecessor didn't help them how can I; I simply don't have the time [the worst excuse of all]; I don't want to hurt her feelings"—will eventually come back to haunt you in the worst ways. Take courage and action! Know that if you have answered the questions in "tracking down" the problem, then you have sufficiently prepared to work positively to eliminate the problems and not the employee.

IIA. Brainstorming alternatives. Before your session with the employee, look over these key points:

1. Make no value judgments on ideas. To criticize *any* alternative will diminish creativity and render the session ineffective.

2. Wait to discuss the alternatives. The purpose of this portion of the meeting is to generate a large number of possible solutions, not to discuss implementation.
3. List all alternatives on paper or flip chart.

I can't emphasize too much how important it is to consider *all* alternatives. If you and your employee feel comfortable in letting the ideas flow, the "creative juices" are released. No matter how ridiculous the idea may seem, encourage sharing. As a matter of fact, I sometimes start these sessions with a humorous or ludicrous example just to make the point.

IIB. Choosing the best alternative. This is the all-important step where you determine the best of the alternatives. Evidence and specific reasons must be given for making the choice. This is a good time to use the Ben Franklin "Plus and Minus" method. When considering each alternative separately, use the form shown in the illustration. This helps keep your ideas on the specific and not the speculative. Write out:

Possible Alternative Solutions

Positive Reasons (+)	*Negative Reasons (−)*

III. Plan of action. When developing this plan of action, we must be sure to not only "track down" our activity, but we must also be sure that these activities are measurable and inspectable. Daily, even hourly, activities may need to be planned. If you start with the desired outcome and track the result down to its smallest component, *only then* do you have a realistic plan of action.

In *See You at the Top,* I explained how I lost 37 pounds in a ten-month period. Thirty-seven pounds was the desired outcome. That tracks down to 3.7 pounds per month and 1.9 ounces per day. While thinking of losing 37 pounds is overwhelming, 1.9 ounces per day is conceivable. The next question I must answer is: "What must I do now—today—to lose 1.9 ounces?" Some ideas (specific, measurable, inspectable) include: eat only the correct foods (chicken, fish, salads, fruit); leave off the extra bread and butter and desserts; drink only unsweetened tea rather than soft drinks. I think you see what I mean, but let me give you an example from the business community.

A successful real estate agency manager noticed that one of the women who worked for him was not as enthusiastic about her work as she had been when she was hired eighteen months before. During the last thirty days Mary had been late in attending meetings, seemed to be somewhere else mentally during the meetings, and in general had kept to herself. This was quite unusual since she had previously been a real people-oriented person. While she had never been his top performer, her results had always been consistent and had improved steadily. Her performance in the last thirty days had been miserable. The one sale she had the opportunity to close had to be postponed due to careless errors on her part in the paperwork.

Realizing that he had to take some action or lose a very solid performer, the manager called Mary into his office. As soon as he closed the door, she started to cry. "I know you're going to fire me," she sobbed, "and I don't blame you one bit!" (Right then and there the manager knew he had waited too long to call the meeting and vowed to himself that he would never wait that long to confront a problem again). "No," he said, "I have no intentions of firing you. I just want to see what can be done to help you regain the level of productivity you have enjoyed for so many months. Has something happened to upset you?"

After regaining her composure, Mary went on to explain that she was embarassed by the fact that her automobile was the oldest one driven by any of the agents and that she had set her goal several months earlier to buy a new car by the beginning of the current month. She was devastated that her earnings had not allowed her to do so. "So, you see, " she said, "my problem is that I have a car I am embarassed to drive and it is limiting my productivity." Her manager thought for a minute and replied, "Is that really your problem, or could it be a symptom of your problem?" He went on to take her through the series of questions we have already shared on page 147.

1. In what areas do you feel you are performing well? ("None.")
2. Why? ("I'm not meeting any of my Foundational Performance level goals.") The manager worked with each agent to establish all three levels of activity for each agent based on their personal goals. This lady knew what her Foundational Performance level was to be as well as her Successful Performance level and Value Performance level. The manager had "tracked down" the success activities needed for each level.
3. Give me a specific example. ("My Foundational Performance level calls for me to knock on five doors per week in looking for possible listings; I have knocked on none.")

This response allowed the manager to skip questions 4 through 9 and get right down to business. He asked Mary, "Are you interested in developing a Performance Improvement Program?" She said, "What I am really interested in is driving a new car!" They both laughed and agreed that they needed to delve more deeply into the problem. The manager took the agent through the series of questions for exposing and defining a problem which we outlined on page 148. Under part A. *Beware the potential for problems and don't ignore danger signals,* they were able to agree that the problems had begun when her activity levels had decreased. Under part B. *Identify the crucial elements of the problem,* they were able to agree that not reaching her goal seemed to be the crucial element since her activity had been good with the same car up to that point. Under part C. *Identify the obvious causes of the problem indicators,* the manager and the agent agreed that her goal setting had been unrealistic and she had not allowed herself a realistic amount of time to reach her goal of having a new automobile.

Under part D. *Expose and define the problem*, they wrote out the problem as follows: "Mary did not understand the goal-setting process well enough to set a realistic goal to purchase a new automobile." The evidence that indicated the problem was real and not imagined was the seven-year-old car in her driveway. The positive action step that needed to be taken was to get the proper input on how she could realistically set the goal. So the manager and the agent began to work together to develop a Plan of Action.

They started with the desired result—a new automobile. Mary knew exactly what kind of car, what color, all the options, and the price, down to the last penny. By carefully studying Mary's performance records for the first seventeen months she spent with the company, they were able to determine that to purchase the automobile she wanted would take nine months instead of the four months she had originally allowed. They also discovered that she could reduce that time to six months by improving some of her activity levels.

Next, Mary and her manager got involved with the final step.

IIIA. Inspection. This step is not a subversive activity that requires you to go through subordinates' desks at night or plant listening devices on their phones. The employee must know *when* to expect the inspection and *what* to expect from the inspection.

Mary and her manager set a weekly appointment to monitor her progress. By doing this, Mary's manager not only let her know that he was interested in her career but also that he was going to hold her accountable.

Next, Mary and her manager evaluated alternatives to her not improving her performance. Mary agreed that she could not afford to keep her position if she did not improve, and her manager assured her that though termination was a possibility, it was *not* his first choice. The manager assured Mary that through their regular meetings she would be kept posted on progress so that termination would not come as a surprise to either of them and that she could be confident that Due Process would be observed.

In reality, the Performance Value Package is nothing more than goal setting on three levels. The seven steps in determining a goal, an objective, a standard, or whatever you want to call it, do not change. You may not be able to tell me what 782 × 411 is; however, you do have a formula that you can use to determine the answer. The seven steps in the goal-setting process are the steps in the formula that you can use to establish each performance level.

THE SEVEN-STEP GOAL-SETTING FORMULA

1. Identify the goal.
2. List your personal benefits for achieving the goal.
3. Identify the major obstacles you must overcome to reach this goal.
4. Determine what skills or knowledge are required to reach this goal.
5. Identify the individuals, groups, companies, and organizations you must work with to reach this goal.
6. Develop a specific plan of action to achieve the goal.
7. Decide on a realistic time limit for achievement.

MY GOAL IDENTIFIED:

MY BENEFITS FROM ACHIEVING THIS GOAL:

I, _____, COMMIT MY FULL EFFORTS TO

ACHIEVING MY GOALS NO LATER THAN _____ ! I AM BORN TO WIN!

_____   _____
(signature)   (date)

In our three-day BORN TO WIN seminar, we not only teach this formula but we also practice using it. We have developed a format which contains all seven steps and helps you to organize the steps on a single sheet of paper which we call a "Detail" sheet.

With a realistic goal in mind and her boss's support, Mary's productivity (and results) took an immediate turn for the better. Eight months later she was driving a new automobile. She hadn't improved her performance to the level that would have allowed her to get the car in six months, but she had improved it so she could have the new car in less than nine months. Both she and her manager were extremely happy.

This manager had done what all good managers do in a similar situation. Let's recap the major points.

1. He confronted the poor performance.
2. He helped the employee come up with well-defined and clearly understood goals.
3. Together they determined a time frame for goal attainment.
4. Together they determined a means to inspect to make sure they got what they expected.
5. They scheduled meetings regularly to assess progress.
6. Together they determined the specific assistance needed.
7. They examined alternatives if the improvement was not achieved.

When they were looking at the time factor, they considered: her prior history with the company; the time required to reasonably meet her goal; what contributed to her poor performance; and just how unsatisfactory her performance was. By putting all these ideas together, the manager was doing exactly what a good manager should do:

1. Provide performance standards that are realistic, understandable, and measurable.
2. Identify as soon as possible the poor performance.
3. Criticize the performance, not the performer.
4. Pay attention to specific observable behavior, not hearsay.
5. Clearly express the consequences of failing to meet the agreed-upon performance level.

Outstanding managers give their employees every opportunity to succeed. They view employee failure as personal failure and use every means possible to help their employees succeed. They are intolerant of losing behavior on the employees' part as well as their own. Great managers demand excellence . . . and use the Performance Value Package as a success tool!

PERFORMANCE PRINCIPLES

1. *The Performance Value Package consists of three levels of goal or objective setting:*
   a. *Foundational Performance level—minimum standard*
   b. *Successful Performance level—realistic goal*
   c. *Value Performance level—stretch goal*
2. *These are the steps in the PVP process:*
   a. *consultation/confrontation*
   b. *problem definition*
   c. *brainstorming alternatives*
   d. *choosing the best alternative*
   e. *plan of action*
   f. *inspection*
3. *Outstanding managers often ask questions they already know the answers to in an effort to understand employee perspective.*

Recognizing, Rewarding, and Role Modeling for Top Performance

The greatest humiliation in life is to work hard on something from which you expect great appreciation, and then fail to get it.

Edgar Watson Howe

 Bringing out the best in people means appreciating what they do, rewarding them for it, and giving them the role models they need to become Top Performers. In this chapter we'll take a look at these three important aspects of successful management.

RECOGNITION

Several years ago I was scheduled to speak at a banquet in Dallas for an insurance company. During the meal, I was seated at the head table between two company vice-presidents. We were chatting amiably as the meal was being served. When our waitress placed a salad in front of me, I said, "Thank you." A few minutes later, when the bread was placed in front of us, I again said, "Thank you." When she brought the entree I not only said, "Thank you," but added, "you know, I want to tell you how much I appreciate the good service you're giving us. It's amazing how you work so efficiently and yet don't seem to be in any kind of hurry. More important, you're so pleasant and gracious and I just want you to know I appreciate your efforts." She beamed broadly, thanked me for my comments, and said I had made her day.

While all of this was going on, the two vice-presidents on either side of me were ignoring her or acknowledging her service with a grunt. They directed all of their comments and attention to me and our conversation. Dessert time was quite an eye-opener. When the scoop of ice cream with chocolate syrup was delivered, the two vice-presidents received a scoop about the size of a golf ball with their syrup. I received one about the size of a baseball. The difference was so obvious that both of them simultaneously commented, "Well, Zig, I see you know this lady." I laughingly said, "No, I've never met her before tonight, but I do know a lot about her." They jokingly asked how I knew. I pointed out that she was a human being and, like everybody else, she wanted appreciation and sincere interest, and I had given her both of these things.

The same thing is true of every member of your organization and family. Everyone likes to be appreciated. What better way to express your appreciation than to share a simple, courteous "thank you" when something pleasant has been said or some simple service has been rendered. Obviously, I was not being nice to the waitress in the hope I'd get a bigger scoop of ice cream. To be honest, I didn't need the bigger scoop—I needed the smaller one. But by feeding her needs, she responded in the only way she could—which was to dig deeper and get a bigger scoop of that ice cream. I believe that in helping others to become Top Performers by teaching them to be thoughtful, kind, and considerate of the other person, we are teaching them to dig deeper and get a bigger scoop out of life.

Not a "Pollyanna" Philosophy

The December 6, 1982 issue of the *Wall Street Journal* carried the following article by Jack Falvey entitled, "To Raise Productivity, Try Saying Thank You." I believe you will benefit from these concepts, which have been italicized for emphasis.

People work for love and money. Few of us ever seem to get enough of either. There are no great behavioral science secrets to good management. *If you will give top priority to supporting and paying your people, you will be blessed with results beyond your dreams.*

Managers often think of themselves as systems specialists or problem solvers or functional experts. *They lose sight of the commonsense practicality of getting others committed to doing things for them willingly. The essence of good management is letting people know what you expect, inspecting what is done, and supporting those things that are done well.* The experts acknowledge that we don't know the design limitations of a human being. All we do know is that even the most committed people seldom exceed 15% or 20% of their brain capacity in a normal day's work. Average people can double or triple their output with increased confidence, more encouragement, better organization, a deeper commitment, and a surprisingly small amount of effort. Additionally, if managers would begin thinking in terms of doing things *for* their people—instead of *to* them—we would see productivity increases off the scales. . . .

Here are a few things you can do right now with no increase in budget, but with big returns.

Make a list of everyone who works for you. Before the week is out, tell each one personally what he has contributed this week and how much you appreciate his efforts. Criticism is to be avoided at all costs (there is no such thing as constructive criticism, all criticism is destructive). If you must correct someone, never do it after the fact. Bite your tongue and hold off until he is about to do the same thing again and then challenge him to make a more positive contribution. If you can do that consistently, you will be earning your pay as a professional manager.

Set up informal visits with your people. Listen and use your eyes to pick up on what is going on. Don't look for problems, look for strengths and things done well. Make something out of every positive thing you can find. As a manager, your words and actions carry impact much greater than you expect. Just a small effort with these techniques will have almost immediate effect. A concentrated, disciplined, and sustained thrust in these directions will produce incredible returns. Publish everything positive you can find. Print is cheap. Its rewards are long-lasting.

Put positive notes on solid productive efforts and send them back to the producers. . . .

How innovative can you be? Do you realize the impact you have on others? Can you reduce or eliminate the negatives in your dealings with your people? Will you do the searching and analysis necessary to uncover positive contributions? Can you name the strengths of all your people? Can you say something complimentary to everyone by the end of this week?

As simple and as straightforward as all this is, it is really a tremendously difficult professional challenge. Just how good are you as a professional manager? *If results are produced by committed people, just how much love and money can you spread around to build that commitment and those results? Go, do something nice for someone or say something nice to someone right now.*

Recognizing Top Performance

Most managers would like to have employees and co-workers who take PRIDE in their careers. Now since PRIDE means many things to many people, let's look at a workable definition for our purposes.

To me, PRIDE is *Personal Responsibility In Daily Effort.* If we are going to encourage those around us to take Personal Responsibility In Daily Effort, we must recognize the importance of RECOGNITION in this process.

Mary Crowley, the extremely successful businesswoman who founded Home Interiors and Gifts (a half-billion-dollar company), says that *everyone* carries a sign which is constantly on display: MAKE ME FEEL IMPORTANT! If we can do this (make others feel important)—*sincerely*—then we have taken a giant stride in developing Top Performers.

Everyone needs recognition. The blue-collar worker is recognized for being the family provider; the white-collar workers are recognized for having great potential; the sales-marketing person is recognized for having high-income earning power. The point is that some people's recognition needs are very basic while the needs of others may be quite complex. The Top Performers in the world are BUILDERS, DOERS, and COMPETITORS and they want to, and even need to, make a contribution to whatever they do. They must know when they are contributing, and how much they are contributing. Those who manage Top Performers develop a "scoring" system that keeps *everyone* informed on how they are doing. Please remember that negative scoring should be done in private and positive scoring should be done publicly.

Developing Enthusiastic Optimism

To develop Top Performers we must teach them how to be enthusiastic about life, how to graciously deal with other people, and how to encourage others.

When you develop a pleasing personality by being a little more friendly and outgoing, it can be enormously helpful to you socially, professionally, and for that matter spiritually. Let me share an incident with you which demonstrates some important concepts.

I never realized just how tough working on a cafeteria line could be until my youngest daughter, at age sixteen, tried to find a job—and the only one she could find was on a cafeteria line. As I watched what she had to do and contend with, from both customers and management, I promised myself I would never again go down a cafeteria line without saying something pleasant, gracious, optimistic, and enthusiastic to every person on the serving line. And I still do this today.

Recently, one particularly hot August day, after the lunch-hour crowd had departed, a friend of mine and I were going down the cafeteria line and I was "doing my thing." The gentleman in front of me was apparently from the same school of thought and he, too, was giving pleasant greetings and encouragement. This worked quite well until he got to the meat department and made the mistake of saying something about the day. The woman serving the meat put her hands on her hips, then wiped her forehead with her right hand and literally slung the perspiration to the floor as she proclaimed, "Yes, this is one of *those* days!"

Now I'd like to point out that she was not talking to me, but when you understand the business I'm in and the reputation I have as a positive thinker, combined with the fact that I had an associate with me, you must understand that my reputation was at stake. So, though it definitely was none of my business, I proceeded to stick my big nose in and say, "Yes, today is absolutely beautiful, isn't it?" With that she looked at me with disgust and said, "You have been out in the sun too long!" I replied, "No, actually I've just come back from overseas—and I've seen grown men and women without anything to eat, small children without any clothes to wear, sanitary conditions which are impossible to describe, and poverty beyond your wildest imagination. And I look at you today. You're young, pretty, employed, and an American citizen. I know for a fact that you could take this job, do it to the best of your ability, and someday you could well be the manager of this place. For that matter, if you really bought into the American Dream, with all its possibilities, you could eventually own a place of your own."

Personally, I thought it was a superb, impromptu, off-the-cuff speech, and I was reasonably confident she wanted to express her appreciation for my willingness to share with her those words of hope and encouragement. However, for fear she might miss her lead-in, I decided I'd better assist her a little, so I paused and said, "Now you feel lots better, don't you?" This time she looked at me with even more disgust and said, "You—are—sick!"

Stinkin' Thinkin' At Its Worst

As we'd say down home, you win some, you lose some, and some get rained out! This lady was hard-core negative. Her stinkin' thinkin' had gone into an advanced case of hardening of the attitudes, which gave every indication of being terminal. I meekly walked on down the serving line, getting the rest of my food and picking up my ticket. My buddy and I sat down to have our lunch and, after a few minutes, ran out of tea. A little lady who was at least sixty—and she could well have been seventy—came by, serving the extra tea. I don't recall ever seeing anyone her age with as much of a twinkle in her eye, so I smiled pleasantly and asked my famous question: "How ya doin'?" She literally took a half-step, half-jump, half-dance backward, grinned very broadly, and said, "Honey, if it was any better I'd think the deck was stacked!" I laughed and said to her, "Well, why don't you go tell the ladies on the serving line what you just told me?" In mock horror she threw up her hands and said, "Oh, no! I don't want to have anything to do with those girls! If I fool around with them very much, I'll end up being just like they are!"

I don't know where the lady learned her psychology, but she's right on the button. The way I read my Bible, it teaches, "Be not deceived—evil companions corrupt good morals." It's an established fact that your associates do have a strong bearing on your feelings, attitudes, moral values, and conduct. The classic example which I often use is this: You can take a Southern boy or girl and send him or her up North or out West and, after a period of time, he or she will end up with an accent. Or, you can take a Northern or Western boy or girl and send him or her into the South and pretty soon we'll have them talking normally! (Yes, I expect you Northerners and Westerners to turn this example around.) You need to be careful who you associate with, because we do become part of what we are around.

Chances are about 4000 to 1 that if you were given the choice of being with or around either the girl on the serving line cutting the beef or the older lady serving the tea, you would, without hesitation, choose to be around the lady serving the tea. This book is written so that you can help others to be Top Performers, and you do so by helping them become more like the senior citizen serving the tea and not like the young cynic on the serving line. You affect this important dimension of the Top Performer's life by recognizing outstanding performance.

Bees, Fleas, and Trees

In June of 1984, we determined that our company needed a formal recognition program. Since outstanding programs recognize the qualities that are pertinent to company and individual employee success and "sell" them, we began by deciding what qualities we wanted to foster. Based on our needs and beliefs, we determined it was important that our employees come to work regularly with a good attitude and demonstrate leadership qualities that show they are "part owners" in the company. Top Performers must realize that while the boss may sign their checks, the employee determines the amount.

Our basic needs—attendance, attitude, leadership, and loyalty have evolved into four recognition awards which we distribute quarterly. Here is the information we present in our employee manual:

> The Zig Ziglar Recognition Program is based on the premise that "what gets recognized and rewarded is clearly what the company values." Our philosophy challenges each team member to look for the good in others. The Zig Ziglar Corporation Recognition Program allows us to find that good and recognize exceptional performance. There are four areas considered.
>
> *Attendance* . . . The "Chinese Bamboo Tree" Award. Those who are at work, on time, for the full day throughout the quarter receive a $50 cash award and a certificate of merit. Increased productivity and less dollars spent on replacement personnel makes this award a real "bonus builder" for the Zig Ziglar

Corporation. The name comes from the Chinese Bamboo Tree, which shows no sign of growth for five years . . . then grows approximately 90 feet in a six-week period. The years of watering and fertilizing when no progress is seen are what causes the tree to grow. This quarterly award allows an employee to be recognized in a single quarter, or in all four quarters.

Attitude . . . The "Bumble Bee" Award. You have read that aerodynamically the Bumble Bee cannot fly; its body is too heavy and its wings are too light . . . but the Bumble Bee doesn't read—it flies. This I CAN attitude is what the Zig Ziglar Corporation clearly values. This award is voted on by the entire People Building Team. The winner has his or her picture prominently displayed in the foyer, receives a plaque, a $50 cash award, has his or her picture in our *At the Top* newsletter, and has lunch with the president and executive vice-president of the Zig Ziglar Corporation.

Criteria for the Bumble Bee Award:

A. This person must actively demonstrate the physical, mental, and spiritual ideals that the Zig Ziglar Corporation embraces.

B. This person responds rather than reacts in difficult situations.

C. This person helps others' attitudes and lifts spirits when others come in contact with him or her.

Leadership . . . The "Flea Trainer" Award. Flea Trainers teach others to jump out of the jar (overcome limitations) and keep others from becoming "S.N.I.O.P.s" (Susceptible to the Negative Influence of Other People). This leadership comes from all positions in the organization and does not necessarily have to be a supervisor or department head. These leaders strongly discourage gossip, criticism, and negative talk from their areas in the office. This award is nominated by the entire People Building Team (our staff), and determined by the president, executive vice-president, and divisional vice-president. The winner receives the same rewards and recognition as the Bumble Bee Winner.

Criteria for the Flea Trainer Award:

A. This person must actively demonstrate the physical, mental, and spirtual ideals that ZZC embraces.

B. This person "looks for the good" in others and shows it through written and verbal feedback.

C. This person demonstrates leadership in a way that helps others grow.

D. This person leads others in such a way that placing their picture on the wall will encourage others to emulate them.

Loyalty . . . Loyalty and Perseverance are recognized as follows:

A. 5 years of service = employee's choice of pin, ring, or watch.

B. 10 years of service = paid vacation trip.

C. 15, 20, 25, etc. years of service = will be determined by the Executive Committee.

Recognition Awards are shared on a quarterly basis. Any ties or questions will be settled by the Executive Committee.

As you can see, we have spent a great deal of time determining what we want and selling the importance of specific criteria.

How Do You Make It Happen?

If you agree that *everyone* needs recognition, and are ready to make a commitment to "making it happen" with your group or organization, here is a step-by-step procedure:

1. *Determine what you want and need to be recognized.* Involve as many people as possible in this process. You may choose an employee survey (written or verbal), an open forum discussion, or individual conferences. The key is to find what employees think is important to their success. This will give you great insight into employee values, as well as allow them to participate in "ownership" of the recognition program. According to an article in the April 1982 issue of the *New York Times*, in 1981, workers at a GM bearings plant in New Jersey purchased it to prevent the plant's closing. Now *productivity is up 80 percent* and the percentage of defective parts has dropped from 10 percent to 7 percent. Grievances have plummeted from a one-time high of two thousand pending to a recent total of only three. And the workers, now the owners, have agreed to new work rules to increase flexibility. Good things happen when employees are aware of shared ownership.

2. *"Sell" the program.* Employees *must* believe in the recognition program and see that it is administered fairly. Talk to them in terms of benefits they will enjoy by participating and "talking up" the program.

3. *Control the "competitiveness and popularity contest" aspects of the program.* Mary Kay Ash's Cosmetic Corporation recognizes *all* who qualify for recognition at varying "levels." Thus her people do not compete as much with one another as they do with themselves—in other words, internal competition. One of the real dangers of doing damage to our self-esteem is when we compare ourselves to others. We must remember to "be the best that we can be . . ." compared with our capabilities—not compared with others!

4. *Judgment must be carefully used when establishing criteria for award winners.* The policies must be as objective as possible. For example, what are the manifestations of a good attitude? Can you develop and identify "specific and observable behaviors" that demonstrate the qualities you want to recognize? Obviously, a sales volume award winner is much more objectively chosen than an attitude or leadership award winner. But are the latter awards less important? Attach as much specific criteria to the awards as possible.

5. *Recognize winners regularly and promptly.* Don't delay, postpone, or cancel recognition programs.

6. *Do not recognize inferior performance.* If there is no winner in a particular category, it is much better to say so than to award someone undeserving.

What Happens Without Recognition?

According to pollster Daniel Yankelovich, who was quoted in *Psychology Today* magazine, over the ten-year period from 1972–1982, workers keeping on-the-job diaries reported that they had been working 10 percent less. That's enough of a change to account for the *entire* drop in national productivity. But before we start blaming workers, he cautions, his own surveys have shown that the "work ethic" is stronger than ever—workers want to work hard and do a good job. He explains the paradox with the result of another survey, showing that workers don't believe that they themselves benefit from increasing productivity. Because they think greater productivity benefits only management, consumers, and shareholders, workers have no incentive to be more productive. The answer, says Yankelovich, is to *directly reward workers for their productivity gains.*

REWARDS

Usually when we think of rewarding people we think of money. *Incentive motivation* is a much-debated form of motivation and for many organizations a viable alternative, especially the sales field. One of the important things to remember about incentive motivation is, "Today's fringe benefits are tomorrow's expectations." This means that in incentive motivation, we must constantly be willing (and able) to "sweeten the pot" to come up with truly motivational incentives. *Sales and Marketing Management* magazine selected several very successful incentive programs in their September 10, 1984 issue so that we could learn from the experiences of others. The following is taken from the article entitled "Getting a Kick From Experience."

When it comes to planning, announcing, and implementing sales incentive programs, executives are letting the past be their guide. By analyzing what has worked best, as well as what has failed, they are, to paraphrase the old song, accentuating the positive and eliminating the negative to get the most kick out of incentives. . . .

• Rather than tie incentives to total sales volumes, managers try to match programs to specific products or objectives.

• More managers regard merchandise and travel incentives as the most effective motivators, although some still prefer cash incentives.

• Careful attention to the timing of incentive programs can affect such areas as production and shipping that are crucial to the total sales and marketing effort.

• Continuous reminders or teasers relating to continuing programs can help maintain enthusiasm.

• Incentive programs should be easy to understand and participate in so that they offer something to everyone. . . .

While matching incentives with production can become a lesson in logistics, choosing the type of incentive that works best is a subject for debate. To say, as one executive does, that "different things motivate different people," is just not enough. Although experience has taught some managers that certain incentives work better than others for them, the decision between merchandise, travel, or cash programs—or some combination of the three—is a subjective one. . . .

Another major lesson reportedly learned by sales and marketing executives is that incentive programs, like the products they motivate salespeople to sell, must be properly promoted and supported. . . .

Reprinted by permission of *Sales and Marketing* magazine, September 10, 1984.

If there is one overall lesson that experience teaches managers, it is that incentive programs must be carefully thought out, planned, and executed. Even if programs include administrative headaches, such as splashy announcements at sales meetings and regular follow-up promotions, they should remain simple enough for everyone to understand and want to participate in enthusiastically. . . .

Another way to get salespeople involved in incentive programs is to simply ask what motivates them. Look at how a specific incentive impacts an individual. Speak with individuals to let them know what you're trying to do and to find out what kinds of incentives they'd like to see. . . .

Positively affecting the role of the salesperson perhaps sums up management's overall intent when designing incentive programs. The ways and means of doing so, however, are as varied as the experiences of the executives involved. Actually, this may be a good sign. It shows that managers are willing to try new ideas in their attempts to motivate salespeople.

In the legal world the competent attorney asks probing questions to get at the heart of the problem. In medicine the effective, sensitive physician largely depends on his questions to the patient to uncover the problem. The minister or counselor follows the same approach, as does the professional salesperson when calling on prospective customers. With these facts in mind, let's take a look at some questions professional managers need to ask about incentive programs.

Incentive Program Questionnaire

1. What has been the most effective form of incentive motivation I have used in the past? Will it work in this instance?
2. Have I spent enough time in planning this incentive program to get the best results?
3. Have I tied the incentive to the most beneficial and measurable area (product, objective, instead of sales volume)?

4. What is the best incentive: cash, merchandise, travel, or personal choice?
5. Is the timing of this program going to benefit all areas of the company (production, shipping, sales, and so forth)?
6. How am I going to constantly remind everyone involved about the contest so I can maintain enthusiasm?
7. Is this contest explained in as simple and understandable a form as possible?
8. What impact will the contest have on the business when the contest is over?

Now, let's take a look at an unusual incentive program created and used by an imaginative middle school administrator.

It Doesn't Have to Be Real Money

In the summer of 1981, Charlie Pfluger from Indianapolis, Indiana attended one of our BORN TO WIN Seminars for Educators. He really got motivated about the positive approach to education and what could be done with the right attitude under almost any circumstances. Charlie was particularly enthused because he was the principal of an inner-city school which was just one year away from closing its doors. He went back home with a tremendous amount of enthusiasm and with the wholehearted support of his principal and the staff, they devised a game plan for the coming year.

Charlie took a silver dollar and used it for the outline of a neat little project. On one side he wrote I CAN and on the other side he put PLA MONEY. As you can see from the diagram on page 173, we've fancied it up a bit and made it out of plastic for greater durability.

Charlie's original version was cut from a sheet of paper and was fairly crude, but enormously effective. He reproduced them by the hundreds and gave each teacher a supply. When a youngster was "caught" doing something good, such as picking up paper in the school yard without instructions, cleaning the blackboard without someone ordering him to do it, welcoming new students to the school, returning "lost and found"

articles, and a host of other things, the student was given an I CAN by the teacher.

When a student received one hundred of these I CANs he or she was awarded an I CAN T-shirt. Out of a student body of 594, 587 of them won an I CAN T-shirt. It truly became a status symbol. Charlie smilingly says it got to be slightly ridiculous to see a sheet of paper blowing across the school yard with five kids out there running it down!

Some of the students helped old ladies across the street who did not want to cross the street, and when a new student showed up, he was individually greeted by about ninety-seven students. In short, the entire school got involved in the project.

There are some who might contend that 587 T-shirts was expensive and, of course, they are right. However, when you consider the results, it's got to rate as the finest investment the school ever made. First of all, there was not a single case of vandalism for the entire year. There was not a single drug bust for the year. Attendance for the year was measurably better; grades were better (in many cases, substantially so); and perhaps best of all, for the first time parents, teachers, and students felt they all were on the same team seeking the same objective.

ROLE MODELS

The primary role of leadership is to create a team headed by someone the team can follow because they respect his or her integrity and leadership abilities. Our example from the educational world achieved that objective. The principle will work just as effectively in the business world, as you can see from the following article:

> Question: What do Tom Selleck, Brooke Shields, and Farrah Fawcett have in common with Lee Iacocca, William Norris, and Malcolm Forbes?

> Answer: Not much. But they are all models.

> The fact of the matter is that the first three have been, are, and will be supermodels in the world of fashion. Each is known by millions of fashion aficionados, television watchers, and moviegoers from Kansas to Kenya. Each is easily recognized and admired by throngs eager to emulate the "look" that these supermodels have created. Each represents excellence in his or her field of work.

> On the other hand, the latter three are neither dashing, smashing, nor particularly debonaire. They, too, are known by millions. Each is easily recognized. Each represents excellence in his field of work. These men are role models.

> *A supermodel is someone we aren't and someone we will never be. A role model is someone we aren't and someone we can be. Today, unfortunately, our society seems to be brimming with an affinity and affection for supermodels rather than role models. We are actively striving for something we will never be when we should in fact be pursuing something that we ought to be.* In short, we have systematically replaced our true American heroes of yore with The Hulk, Strawberry Shortcake, and Papa Smurf!

> The simplest and most direct route to excellence is to emulate, shadow, and replicate what works. Un-

Printed by permission from Dr. Michael H. Mescon, Dean, College of Business Administration, Georgia State University, and Holder, Ramsey Chair of Private Enterprise, and Dr. Timothy S. Mescon, Assistant Dean, School of Business Administration, University of Miami, and published by Mescon Group, Inc., Atlanta, Georgia.

fortunately, the media has a somewhat morbid pre-occupation with failure or success. So we must be content to peruse advertising pages of periodicals inhabited by supermodels rather than role models.

We are inundated with form not function, with quantity not quality, with illusion not substance.

What characterizes a role model? What rings a tone of excellence that is loud and clear? What separates the role model from the rest? Let's look at one:

Nicola Iacocca immigrated to the United States from Southern Italy in 1902 and eventually settled in Allentown, Pennsylvania, where he built a small auto-rental business. His son, Lee, surrounded by cars all his life, aspired to work for Ford. With a Bachelor's degree from Lehigh and a Master's from Princeton, Lee joined Ford Motor Company in 1946. By 1970, only the grandson of Henry Ford held a higher position in the company than Iacocca. On July 13, 1978, thwarted by Ford's obsession with nepotism, Iacocca was fired. On October 30, 1978, Lee Iacocca was named president of the Chrysler Corporation; on that same day, Chrysler announced its largest-ever quarterly loss.

On Thursday, April 21, 1983, The New Chrysler Corporation triumphantly announced it earned $172.1 million in the first quarter, the highest quarterly profit in the automaker's history. Initially, many dismissed Iacocca as a hypersalesman. After all, the demise of Chrysler was imminent. Wall Street laughed, the public taunted, Congress scrutinized, and *Iacocca persevered*. After effectively cutting the size of the company in half, Iacocca went to work on the people at Chrysler.

His managerial style has been described as charming, demanding, arrogant, ruthless, and confident. The truth is that *Lee Iacocca demands no more than he gives.* He is the ideal role model. He sets quarterly goals for Chrysler, for himself, and for his management team. Iacocca exudes confidence. He is impeccably tailored and groomed . . . and literally oozes assuredness. He is a winner. . . .

Three A's for Excellence

There is, indeed, a common thread of excellence that weaves its way through men like Lee Iacocca. Not surprisingly, although these men are involved in completely unrelated businesses, there is a remarkable degree of common factors among them. These common factors, these ingredients for success, represent our three A's for excellence: *Attitude, Aggressiveness, and Appearance.*

Attitude. Excellence is a mind-set. You must believe. Each person who achieves success seems to have an unwavering commitment and belief in his own abilities. They adhere to a very basic tenet of business: rely on no one. Their beliefs, their mind-sets, their attitudes are communicable. This is a top-to-bottom phenomenon in organizations. We all want to believe. But when the CEO believes and that belief is transmitted throughout the organization, the belief is catchy. Says Chrysler St. Louis plant manager, John Burkhart: "All of us at Chrysler believe in the man. . . ."

Aggressiveness. Our society today is overcome with a national lethargy that has reached epidemic proportions. In a multinational, hypercompetitive business environment we can no longer afford this luxury. The global business community is populated by competitors who are both hungry and aggressive. Perhaps we, too, are hungry, simply not hungry enough. The search for excellence is a top-to-bottom aggressive process. It is a preemptive strike on the business community. First you win, second you lose.

Appearance. A brilliant student could not find a job. He mailed resumes to dozens of businesses. Many responded favorably, invited the student to visit and interview for a position. The student visited a number of firms but no offers were forthcoming. The student wanted to know why.

"Are you absolutely certain you want to know why?" his professor asked. "I am," replied the student. The professor then responded, "You look like you've been on a six-month camping trip." The student indignantly responded, "Are you referring to my hair and my beard?" The professor answered, "Yes, and your clothes and your shoes, and your breath." The student said, "That's not fair." And the professor patiently replied, *"You didn't ask if it was fair, you simply asked why."*

Fair or not, the business community responds to appearance. Naturally, appearance must be fortified with substance but, nevertheless, appearance is important. *You must reek of excellence.* Much of the initial high marks received by the Reagan administration were based not on substance but simply on appearance; the White House once again appeared "Presidential." Reagan and his staff looked the part. The sartorial splendor of Iacocca is not an act. The third *A* is simply a visual manifestation of attitude and aggressiveness. . . .

Special Recognition: Treat Everyone as if They Are Hurting

Role models can be found everywhere, if you just look for them. Several years ago at one of our BORN TO WIN seminars, I had a moving experience. At the end of one particular session, a beautiful black woman from the Midwest asked if she could speak with me for a moment. When everyone else had departed, she and I sat down for a visit.

Let me qualify this by saying that had anyone asked me to identify the one person in the class who "had it all together," I would have quickly identified this lady as being that person. She was a beauty queen, and she walked, talked, and acted like one. Although her voice was feminine, it was strong and clear, and she could easily be heard in a large room. She was a college graduate and a very successful businesswoman. She truly gave every indication of having it all together.

As we sat down, the young woman started to talk slowly and quietly, almost hesitantly at first, as she said, "You know, I finally found out this afternoon why I came to attend this seminar." Then she paused and had to compose herself before she could continue. She said, "You know, in my lifetime, I believe you're the first person who ever looked right at me and told me you loved me and I did not have a feeling anything was involved other than the fact that I was a human being and I, like all others, needed to be loved." She finished with tears in her eyes. That day I learned a vitally important lesson: If I treat everyone as if they are hurting, I will be treating most of them right. As my good friend Pastor Bill Weber says, "You can go up to anyone on the street and say to them, 'I heard about your problem,' and they will reply, 'Who told you?'"

I'm not implying that as managers and leaders we can go around as mother confessors or father counselors, but I am suggesting that many people are hurting, and if a person hurts in his or her personal life, he's not going to be as productive as he could be in his business life. A sensitivity to the needs of others will make us more effective in leadership roles.

If you will give *everyone* the recognition, rewards, and role models he or she deserves, both of you have taken a giant step toward becoming Top Performers!

PERFORMANCE PRINCIPLES

1. *Everyone needs recognition.*
2. *Pride = Personal Responsibility In Daily Effort.*
3. *Outstanding recognition programs recognize the qualities that are pertinent to company and individual success and reward these qualities.*
4. *The six-step Recognition Program setup:*
   a. *Determine what you want and need to recognize*
   b. *"Sell" the program*
   c. *Control the "competitiveness and popularity contest" aspects of the program*
   d. *Evaluate carefully the criteria for award winners*
   e. *Recognize winners regularly and promptly*
   f. *Do not recognize inferior performance just for the sake of giving an award*
5. *The three A's for Excellence are:*
   a. *Attitude*
   b. *Aggressiveness*
   c. *Appearance*
6. *Treat everyone as if they were hurting in some area of their lives and you will help them to function more happily and more productively.*

Getting to Know You...
and Me, Too!

The primary skill of a manager consists of knowing how to make assignments and picking the right people to carry out those assignments.

Lee Iacocca

---

10 Have you ever wondered why you hit it off so well with one person and never could seem to get along with another? Why is it that your new boss seems to be so much more difficult to deal with than the last one? What is it that really accounts for the difference in personality types and styles? The person who can unlock the key to these questions has a definite advantage in understanding himself and others.

What does this have to do with Top Performance? Quite a bit. Top Performers know themselves and know how to deal effectively with different personality types. We don't treat everyone the same. The manager who says, "I treat my people all the same," is going to be very ineffective. If you can recognize some of the basics of different personality types, you will be surprised at the difference it will make in your ability to deal with people.

There is a great deal of information on the market today that gives us insight into the personality types of ourselves and others. Psychologists administer the Briggs-Meyer Analysis; Dr. Carl Jung, the Swiss psychoanalyst, wrote in *Psychological Types* in the 1920s, "What really accounts for personality differences is that every individual develops a primacy in major behavioral functions." He went on to elaborate on the inherited and developed traits we all possess. Here at the Zig Ziglar Corporation we have used two types of analysis in our hiring procedures for several years. Walter V. Clarke and Associates has an analysis called "The Activity Vector Analysis," which has been an exceptionally good tool for us. In many of our seminars and consulting opportunities we use the Personal Profile System from Performax Systems International, Inc. The more we know about ourselves and others, the better suited we are to deal with people in our complex society. Ten years ago I would not have considered using a personality profile in hiring employees, and today I cannot imagine hiring anyone without this tool—not just for our sake, but for the sake of the employee as well. Let me give you two specific examples.

When Ron Ezinga was considering my offer to become president of the Zig Ziglar Corporation, we agreed that it would be wise for us to be tested for compatibility. Neither of us was interested in getting involved in a business relationship that was anything less than a permanent one, because joining our firm meant Ron would have to resign the presidency of a larger company and move his family over a thousand miles to Dallas. It also meant major changes in our company and a substantial change of direction for me personally. Our getting together seemed natural, because I was speaking over two hundred times a year and was substantially less than effective in running our business. Ron's job was financially rewarding but did not permit him full use of his creative skills, organizational abilities, and management expertise. We wanted to get together but we wanted it to be "right" for our families and our careers.

As prudent decision-making businessmen, Ron and I went through extensive testing and found that we really had the potential for an excellent business partnership. My style is to be quick to act and make decisions, while Ron's is to be very deliberate and gather the facts. The psychologists said, "Zig, if you can speed Ron up a little, and he can slow you down a little, you guys are gonna be really successful!" There were many areas where it seemed his strengths compensated for my weaknesses and my strengths for his weaknesses. The scientific tools validated what we both suspected and prayed would be the answer—that we could successfully work together. And I can tell you that I am so grateful God led Ron to our company. Under his effective and imaginative direction we have moved into many new areas and are currently reaching five to ten times as many people as we were before Ron joined our team.

The second example I would like to share pertains to a young lady we hired as a backup receptionist. She was very pleasant and quite good on the phone; however, she was never in her seat when it came time for her to "back up" on the phones. She had so much energy that "sitability" came hard for her. We had reached the point that we were considering asking her to find other employment when we got involved in "Activity Vector Analysis." From the analysis we saw that *she* wasn't the problem—*we* were! We had completely misplaced her. Fortunately, we had an opening at the time for an assistant office manager. The job required that about fourteen different projects be handled at one time (ordering office supplies, getting office machines repaired, hosting visitors to our offices), and she was magnificient! She was one of the best we have ever had in the position. We all shed a tear when her husband's career called for them to relocate.

The point is this: With scientific validation we can get reinforcement for making career decisions—both in hiring and in choosing a profession. Am I recommending that your organization get involved with one of these personality profile analyses? The answer is yes and we even list the addresses of some excellent companies at the end of this book. We also have a consulting team which specializes in developing personalized personnel programs for your organization.

A VOYAGE IN "SELF" *AND* "OTHER" DISCOVERY

A personality analysis is somewhat like the analysis of the notes on a musical score. This analysis will reveal the nature, even the quality, of the performance. Every musical instrument and every human being is different. Take any group of people who interact together in pursuit of some common goal and you will see that each possesses personality traits different from the others. Each of these people is motivated differently, and the differences can result in effective performance (as with Ron Ezinga and me), or in complete discord. This does not necessarily mean that one person is right and the other is wrong—just that we are different. And that's good! If we always agree, then one of us isn't necessary.

The beauty of the personality analysis (regardless of the system used), is that not only does it enable you to understand why you and those around you behave as you do but it also enables you to take advantage of this knowledge (not take advantage of the people) so that you might channel energies and focus talents in existing relationships for the better. Understanding personality differences helps people appreciate each other more and, consequently, work together more effectively.

Here's how it works: Most of the studies we have done categorize behavioral style into four broad dimensions. Obviously, no one person's personality can be defined as belonging totally to one of these four categories. We are, after all, human beings and not computerized mechanisms. Our personalities reflect many subtle differences of tone and texture, and we all have some of all degrees of each of the characteristics. However, some characteristics are dominant and will surface on a regular basis.

HOW AGGRESSIVE ARE YOUR EMPLOYEES?

Think of four beakers of liquid that you might find in a chemistry laboratory.

Each beaker represents a personality characteristic. Let's call the first beaker our *Aggression* container. If the Aggression container is filled below the midline, the person usually is willing to let others make decisions and glad to reach decisions by consensus. This individual is often quiet and unassuming and is perceived as being mild-mannered in dealing with others, and usually modest about personal achievements.

To motivate these people, place them in low-pressure situations and allow them to lead with a "let's do it together" style instead of a demanding style. Incentive motivation will do little to motivate these good-natured individuals who are turned off by pressure. They are willing and unselfish, which is one reason they are sometimes taken advantage of by more aggressive people.

People who have their Aggression containers filled above the midline are often perceived as strong-willed, task-oriented "doers." They have a tendency to drive themselves and others and enjoy change and challenge. You recognize these people by their "steely eyed" (stern and intense) expression and clenched fists that pound the table for emphasis (or pointed finger for the same effect). They "stride" rather than walk, and always seem to be going somewhere with a purpose and in a hurry.

You motivate these people by challenging them and grant-

ing authority. The less tied down they are, the more effective they become. Give them direct answers and stick to business when in the business environment. When you disagree with them, take issue with the facts and not the person. The more you refer to objectives and results and provide facts about success probability, the more you have their attention.

These people will be turned off if you continually require documentation or require them to follow policies and procedures. They are pioneers, not followers. If you question their authority or place a ceiling on their earning potential and advancement possibilities, they will go to work for someone else.

One of the key concepts to remember when looking at personality characteristics is that *our weaknesses are often extensions of our strengths.* These individuals are goal achievers who are forceful, decisive, confident, persistent, and strive to achieve. This may lead to impatience, workaholism, lack of attention to detail, abrasive interaction with co-workers, and overstepping of privileges.

WHO ARE THE "PEOPLE" PEOPLE?

The next container is our *People* container. If the container is filled below the midline, it usually indicates a person who is willing to spend time without other people. Others may perceive him or her as aloof and pessimistic. This person is usually slow to speak out and at times is suspicious of the motives of others. He is usually very conscious about the way he handles himself in the social and work environment and is careful about his appearance.

You motivate this person by providing a work environment free from social contacts. Allow this individual to think out a problem by himself. He is at his best on projects requiring logical analysis. Superficial and loud people really turn him off.

This congenial though rather reserved person can be quite a problem solver, but if placed in a position of solving "people" problems, will be quite uncomfortable.

The person who has his People container filled above the midline is normally a very spontaneous person. He is enthusiastic, friendly, and good at persuading others to join him. He is perceived as being poised, charming, emotional, and optimistic. You will recognize him by his ready smile and relaxed and friendly manner. He is very expressive with arms and hands and, if you are around him for any extended period of time, he will hug you or pat you on the back, shoulder, or hand.

To motivate these people, give them time to socialize and talk. Let them express their opinions and ideas, especially those regarding people. Help them by being supportive of them in relationships.

These people are turned off by work with long periods of intense concentration, record-keeping, and criticism of their friends. Put them in a nonparticipative environment (computer terminal, accounting tasks) and you won't be able to keep them for long. These "People" people are trusting, sociable, generous, popular promoters. But if you go too far in extending these strengths, it may result in more concern with popularity than results, overselling, problem avoidance, and heart-over-mind decisions.

A MEASURE OF PATIENCE

The next container is our *Patience* container. If the container is below the midline, the person is usually actively involved and prefers an unstructured environment. He or she is frustrated by the status quo and invites change. Impulsive, ready to move about, and good at initiation, he is excitable and anxious to get the job done.

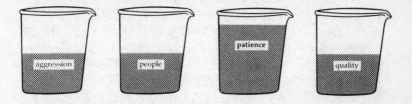

You motivate this individual by giving him a variety of activities and the freedom to move about on the job. The nervous energy he brings to the work force can be very positive when channeled; however, if left undirected, anxiety, nervousness, and tension will result. The strength of this person lies in the initiative he is willing to take. This becomes a weakness when he initiates so many projects that none are completed.

People who have their Patience containers filled above the midline are very stable and have "sitability." They are recognized for being kind, patient, quiet, disciplined, and service-oriented. You recognize these people by their willingness to listen to others and by their friendly countenances. They appear to be relaxed; body movement is smooth and effortless. To motivate these people, give them time to adjust, few changes, and *no* surprises. If you show sincere appreciation for tasks completed, these folks will be extremely loyal to you. Create a secure environment and allow them to develop work patterns for maximum productivity.

These people will be turned off by pressure placed upon them. New tasks and new people presented on a regular basis will produce diminished productivity. These people are loyal, team players, deliberate, sincere, hardworking, consistent, and dependable. Their strengths become weaknesses when they procrastinate or are asked to initiate projects. They may have trouble meeting deadlines. They always finish the project—they just like to do it on their own time schedule.

QUALITY, NOT QUANTITY

The last container is our *Quality* container. If the Quality container is below the midline, people may be perceived by others as being strong-willed (that's a nice way of saying stubborn). People who are low in this container are normally very independent and couldn't care less about details. Quantity wins out over quality with these folks.

You motivate these people by letting them do a job their own way, and granting autonomy. They are persistent and will stick to a chosen course of action. This strength becomes a weakness when they stick to a project which would be better off given up.

The people who have their Quality container filled above the midline are known for conscientiousness and concern for detail. They are intuitive and sensitive to the environment. These cautious individuals insist on competence and accuracy. You recognize them as thinkers who are seeking facts. They are not highly animated in gestures and are uncomfortable with those who easily show emotions.

To motivate this person, give him personal attention, exact job descriptions, and a controlled work environment. If you allow him to be part of a group or team and provide solid, tangible evidence for your position in discussions, you can win a friend. He is turned off by those who demand quick decisions on important matters and don't allow him enough time to check for accuracy. If you place him in an unstructured en-

vironment where no performance guidelines exist, he will find somewhere else to work.

These quality-conscious people are normally mature, accurate, logical, precise folks with high standards. If they take their strengths to the lengths that they become weaknesses, they may overanalyze and get "paralysis of analysis," become inflexible and bound by procedures and methods. They may have a tendency to get bogged down in details and hesitate to act without precedent.

HOW ARE YOU DOING?

I hope that as we've been looking at each of these containers, you've been doing a little self-evaluation. On a scale of 1 to 10, with 1 being very little and 10 ready to overflow, how would you rate your *Aggression, People, Patience,* and *Quality* containers on the chart below? How would your parents rate you? How would you be rated by your employees? And so on, down the list. Let me remind you of something I said earlier. We all have *some* of each of these qualities. There are times when our containers seem almost empty and other times they are almost full. However, I think you can see that each of us has dominant characteristics.

Aggression	*People*	*Patience*	*Quality*
I say___	I say___	I say___	I say___
Parents___	Parents___	Parents___	Parents___
Employees___	Employees___	Employees___	Employees___
Spouse___	Spouse___	Spouse___	Spouse___
Children___	Children___	Children___	Children___
Boss___	Boss___	Boss___	Boss___

ANOTHER METHOD FOR COMPARISON

If we take each of these containers and line them up next to one another, we can get a comparison of how we stand in each area. Remember that the further away from the midline, the stronger the characterisics are perceived by others.

Aggression	People	Patience	Quality
10 Direct	Enthusiastic	Predictable	Perfectionist
9 Daring	Persuasive	Relaxed	Accurate
8 Risk Taker	Emotional	Nondemonstrative	Systematic
7 Decisive	Trusting	Deliberate	Conscientious
6 Competitive	Sociable	Stable	High Standards

——————————— Midline ——————————

4 Calculated Risk taking	Reflective	Outgoing	Opinionated
3 Self-critical	Factual	Eager	Persistent
2 Weighs +/−	Controlled	Fidgety	Independent
1 Peaceful	Self-conscious	Restless	Rigid
0 Quiet	Suspicious	Active	Firm

Some of you (those in the upper half of the Quality container and lower half of the People container) have noticed the overlapping characteristics. These feed each other. In other words, the person rating himself a 3 in People and an 8 in Quality have the ability to analyze and should excel in positions allowing them to use these strengths. To place them in a public-relations role might not be advisable for long-term consideration. It is not that they could not perform in this position. The question is, for how long and at what cost could they do that job?

The beauty of these tools when they are applied in a scientific manner is that for hiring purposes you get the round pegs into the round holes and the square pegs in the square slots. When they are used after people are already in position, they allow you to help the employee take advantage of his strengths by working in a position which he can not only enjoy but can also excel in.

The information shared in this chapter is meant to be an introduction to the scientific tools and not to replace them. You have operated strictly on "guesstimates." The research that has gone into making the kind of tool I am talking about is enormous. I don't pretend to be able to understand the mathematical formulas and data-based information that make these analyses valid.

One idea must be reinforced: *There are no right or wrong characteristics, no good or bad characteristics. We are where we are and what we are because of what has gone into our minds. We change where we are and what we are by changing what goes into our minds.* Don't be satisfied with the broad generalities we are forced to work with in this book. If this area of personality characteristics interests you, find a good counselor who can give you information on yourself and those with whom you work.

Let me emphasize again: there is no wrong character for management, and no wrong type for achievement and Top Performance. Every profession seems to have its stereotypes ... hard-driving, goal-oriented stockbrokers; laid back, people-oriented social workers, etc., and you may want to take those stereotypes into consideration when making career or employment choices. Yet even though different industries or companies may tend to breed a particular type of personality, you will find variations and degrees everywhere. Remind yourself that different management styles are appropriate to different times and situations. If you are directing the fire drill, don't call for a consensus vote on exit plans. But don't grimly demand that people be creative in a brainstorming session, either. Their ideas will simply dry up.

It's worth reviewing the ways in which your character type generally works best. Are you a Theory X manager or a Theory Y manager? Each can get the job done with and through people. Which works best for you? When? Here are some of the positive and negative aspects of each style of management.

Self-Oriented

• Maintains control and makes decisions, but may not get the input of others.
• Has confidence that his views are valid, but may be intolerant of other views.
• Goal-oriented and demanding in work objectives, but may make others feel he is overbearing.
• Driving and competitive, but may use excessive pressure for

attaining objectives or excessive discipline on those who don't do the job in exactly the prescribed manner.

- Willing to work hard to gain recognition, but may not give recognition to others.
- Is decisive and able to confront poor performance, but expects no criticism from subordinates and will not allow his ideas or decisions to be questioned.

Other-Oriented

- Rarely makes major decisions without getting input and helping others feel a "shared" ownership, but works more slowly.
- Has enough confidence in himself to be willing to listen to others, but may not have the confidence to drive home his own decisions.
- Focuses on stimulating creativity and encourages team to take the initiative, but may not take initiative himself.
- Coaches his team and acts as a facilitator and producer who leads by example, but may not want to carry the ball.
- Seeks every opportunity to provide proper and positive recognition, but may not take enough credit himself.
- Values the ideas of others and considers the team more important than any individual (including himself), but may not allow Top Performers to stand out.
- Competitive with himself in constantly striving to do a better job, but may avoid competition with others.

So you see that both styles of management have strengths and weaknesses. The best manager uses both styles at the appropriate time with the appropriate people.

Self-Oriented Leadership
Can Be Properly Used When:

A. employees misuse or abuse their authority
B. organizational policies are neglected
C. new employees don't completely understand their objectives

D. an emergency situation exists, such as when people's safety is at stake
E. the manager/leader is solely responsible for project completion

Other-Oriented Leadership Can Be Best Used When:

A. people have become competent in carrying out their routine, daily objectives
B. creative problem solving is needed
C. the manager needs to motivate the highly qualified personnel
D. conducting "ongoing" planning for the organization
E. there is a need for creative work and "co-ownership" in ideas

One of the men who best exemplifies the correct combination of all the characteristics we have been sharing in this chapter is Robert W. Woodruff of Coca-Cola. He was nicknamed "Mr. Anonymous" despite being the CEO of the Coca-Cola Company. Here is the text of a leaflet he carried in his pocket that summarizes a solid business and personal philosophy.

Life is pretty much a selling job. Whether we succeed or fail is largely a matter of how well we motivate the human beings with whom we deal to buy us and what we have to offer.

Success or failure in this job is thus essentially a matter of human relationships.

It is a matter of the kind of reaction to us by our family members, customers, employers, employees, and fellow workers and associates. If this reaction is favorable we are quite likely to succeed. If the reaction is unfavorable we are doomed.

The deadly sin in our relationship with people is that we take them for granted. We do not make an active and continuous effort to do and say the things that will make them like us, and believe in us, and trust us, and that will create in them the desire to work with us in the attainment of our desires and purposes. Again and again we see both individuals and organizations perform only to a small degree of their potential success, or to fail entirely, simply because of their neglect of the human element in business and life. *They take people and their reactions for granted. Yet it is these people and their responses that make or break them.*

It is believed that these words are those of Mr. Woodruff's friend Bernard F. Gimbel, the late chairman of Gimbel Brothers, Inc. So greatly was he impressed by the message in these words that he had the pamphlet reprinted to pass out among the key men in his organization. You might say that over the years these words have almost become the spirit of Coca-Cola. These are words that all Top Performers would do well to live by.

PERFORMANCE PRINCIPLES

1. *The more I understand myself, the more effectively I can work with others.*
2. *Personality profiles are valuable tools for getting the round pegs into the round holes and the square pegs into the square slots.*
3. *Self-evaluation (with a scientific tool) is more valuable than self-condemnation.*
4. *Our weaknesses are often extensions of our strengths.*
5. *There are no good/bad, right/wrong profiles—they simply help us evaluate where we are so we can determine where we want to go.*
6. *You are what you are and where you are because of what has gone into your mind; you change what you are and where you are by changing what goes into your mind.*

Management Gems

Find the essence of each situation, like a logger clearing a log jam. The pro climbs a tall tree and locates the key log, blows it, and lets the stream do the rest. An amateur would start at the edge of the jam and move all the logs, eventually moving the key log. Both approaches work, but the "essence" concept saves time and effort. Almost all problems have a "key" log if we learn to find it.

Fred Smith

---

11 Throughout *Top Performance*, we have made every effort to give credit where credit is due. We have painstakingly tracked down every traceable bit of information to keep from claiming originality when there was none. In this final chapter in "The Science of Top Performance," we want to share with you some "management gems" that frankly are difficult to credit. These are timeless truths that have really been shared by most, if not all, effective managers. Hopefully you will find some "key logs" in these concepts and formulas that will answer your "opportunities" to solve problems more efficiently and effectively.

FORMULA FOR TOP PERFORMANCE MANAGEMENT

1. Show honest and sincere appreciation at every opportunity—make the other person feel important.
2. Don't criticize, condemn, or complain.
3. Make your cause bigger than your ego.
4. Work for progress, not perfection.
5. Be solution conscious, not problem oriented.
6. Invest time in the activity that brings the highest return on investment according to the priority list of responsibilities—effort alone doesn't count; results are the reasons for activity.
7. Fulfilling responsibility is a good reason for work; discipline is the method.
8. Recognize and accept your own weaknesses.
9. Make checklists and constantly refer to them.
10. *Always* show the people in your life the humility of gratitude.

SIX ACTION STEPS FOR PERFORMANCE-ORIENTED MANAGERS

1. Give regular, specific, and observable behavior feedback on performance.
2. Respect the lines of communication and authority.
3. Make timely decisions.
4. Be accessible.
5. Encourage creative ideas.
6. Provide personal support.

THE TEN "DOUBLE WIN" RULES THAT LEAD TO TOP TEAM PERFORMANCE

When dealing with others:
1. Remember that a *smile* is the most powerful social tool we have at our disposal.
2. Listening is the most neglected *skill* in business (or home)

today. The person who listens controls the final outcome of the discussion. Encourage others to talk, and then consciously remove any barriers to your good listening skills.

3. Talk in terms of the other person's interest. You will find a "uniqueness" and "specialness" in every individual you meet. Others are interesting when discovered; check out the other person's point of view.

4. Ask questions you already know the answer to and you will get to see the other person's perspective. Most ideas are more palatable if we "discover" them ourselves. People who truly care about others lead them down the "discovery path."

5. "What you are speaks so loudly I can't hear what you say." Remember to model the behavior and attitude you want the other person to have.

6. Give assignments that allow you to express faith and confidence that the other person can successfully perform in the task assigned.

7. Always make requests, never give orders.

8. Develop your ability to use the narrative story and the meaningful analogy—these are powerful teaching tools.

9. Always be respectful of others. Show your respect by being on time for meetings or letting others know why you must be late.

10. Return phone calls and letters immediately—there is no excuse for not doing so.

EXPLODING SOME "MANAGEMENT MYTHS"

1. *Manipulation and Motivation are often the same thing.* Absolutely not! Manipulation is getting people to act for you in ways that may not necessarily be for their own good. Motivation is helping people recognize mutual interests and getting them to join the "cause" because there is a benefit for them as well as you.

2. *Making your best effort is all that really counts.* No! Too many people substitute effort for accomplishment. The reason for working is to get *results*. The person who gets the most

results with less effort is working smarter and harder. Fatigue is not an indicator of success.

3. *Delegation is the key to management success.* Wrong again! Delegation is not telling someone what you want, when you want it, and how it is to be done. This is *direction*. Delegation means assigning the *results* you expect and designing a follow-up system that allows you to *inspect* what you *expect*. New employees get direction, experienced employees get delegation. Determining which employees need direction, giving it to them, and delegating results and the authority to get those results is an important key to management success.

4. *Managers are normally superior physically, mentally, and spiritually.* Nope! Very few managers are "normal"! And, there is nothing in the books that says a manager is a "superior." Very simply put, managers are people willing to take responsibility and work through others to achieve results. As Fred Smith says, "An executive is not a person who can do the work better than others, rather, he is one who can get others to do the work better than he can." Are you trying to be a "supervisor" or "superworker"?

5. *Managers must control all circumstances.* No way! Managers deal with problems and situations, and there is a distinct difference between the two. A situation exists because you cannot control it—people get ulcers trying to control the uncontrollable. A problem is something you can take action on. Excellent managers learn the difference between the two, take action on problems, and stop worrying about situations.

YOUR CHALLENGE

There really are no "great revelations" in this brief summary chapter. However, professionals don't need to be told, but they are glad to be reminded. If you will read these few pages every day for twenty-one days, your career will be greatly enhanced by the principles you will be putting into action.

PERFORMANCE PRINCIPLES

1. Reread the principles listed in this chapter daily for twenty-one days!

PART III

MOTIVATING THE TOP PERFORMER

It is motive alone that gives character to the actions of men.

Bruyére

A Formula
for Motivation

You can't sweep people off their feet, if you can't be swept off your own.

Clarence Day

---

12 One evening an associate and I flew back into Love Field in Dallas and got on the shuttle bus to take us to the outlying parking lot to pick up our car. As we stepped aboard, a client of mine warmly and enthusiastically greeted me. We exchanged a few pleasantries and then, to no one in particular and yet to everyone on the shuttle bus, he said, "From time to time I bring Zig in to talk to my organization. He's enthusiastic and optimistic and he gets 'em all charged up and convinces 'em that everything's going to be fine and that they need to have a good, positive mental attitude." Then he continued by saying, "Of course, I look at things a little bit differently. I tell 'em exactly how it is and from time to time I chew 'em out pretty good!"

A passenger on the bus entered the conversation at that point and said, "In other words, Ziglar is unrealistic because he's so optimistic, and you're realistic in your approach."

With this, I turned to the man and said, "Friend, let me ask you a question. What percentage of the bad things you expect to happen actually happen?" At that point another passenger entered the picture and said, "About five or ten percent of them." Then I commented, "In other words, over ninety percent of the time the expected negative events just don't happen. This is realistic *and*, according to the experts, factual. From my perspective, the conclusion is obvious. *It's completely unrealistic to be negative and totally realistic to be positive.*" However, it *is* unrealistic to deny that problems do exist, so let's take a serious look at a major problem and then look at some positive solutions.

BRIDGING THE GAP

The general trend in business in the last five years has been toward growing employee dissatisfaction, according to many of the research associations and news magazines which study business climate. Workers at all levels—hourly, clerical, professional, and even managerial personnel—are down on employers. Gripes have less to do with money and more to do with the work environment.

Now, if you are wondering what this "less than cheerful" news is doing in such a positive book, let me explain that we should look for the positive in all situations. However, that must not keep us from identifying obstacles to becoming even more positive. Just because the ostrich buries its head in the sand does not make the trouble disappear. As a matter of fact, until and unless you specifically identify the problem in a company, you cannot solve it any more than your doctor could successfully treat you for an illness until he has correctly identified the illness. Identifying obstacles or problems is the first step toward discovering solutions. *The key is to be solution-conscious and not problem-oriented.*

One study shared by *Research Institute Report* showed that four classes of workers were surveyed: managers, professionals, clerical, and hourly. For three of the four categories, over 20 percent fewer people are satisfied with their companies now, compared to twenty years ago. Seven percent fewer professionals are satisfied with their companies. The problem is not in the work; rather the problem lies in *those who create and manage the work environment*. And, though some attitudes toward employers have begun to improve, according to Opinion Research Corporation of Princeton, New Jersey, it will be a long time before most employers regain the favor the workers felt ten to twenty years ago.

What this means to us is that there is a *growing gap between managers and workers*. A major objective of *Top Performance* is to close that gap and substantially improve employee job satisfaction, which is a *must* for greater productivity. In order to reach that lofty goal, we need to examine some of the facts and *attitudes* discovered in the research:

- Age had little to do with the study—all ages showed a decline in satisfaction.
- Only professionals rated "sense of accomplishment" high ... clerical, hourly, and even *managers* don't feel a sense of accomplishment.
- Everyone was less contented with benefits and job security.
- All except professionals showed less respect for supervisors and most workers charged that their superiors don't know the job.
- All classes were down on whether they get sufficient information and advancement opportunities.
- Only two in ten employees believed performance and pay are related.
- The "grapevine" was described as the source of information for most employees. All said they preferred to get information from supervisors and management.
- *Fully 50 percent of managers felt top management had lost touch with employees. Among all others, over 75 percent voted the same way.*

WHAT ARE WE GOING TO DO?

Obviously, we need to take constructive measures to reverse this trend. The answer lies in this statement:

Management's imperative is to cultivate its human resources!

And, since you are involved in *Top Performance*, obviously you realize the importance of your greatest resource, your people. Here are some suggestions from researchers which we are reinforcing and expanding throughout *Top Performance*:

- *Show respect for a job well done.* Get rid of second-class job citizenship regardless of pay differences. Real job equality is feeling we have a stake in our company's success.
- *We must* involve *employees.* This means providing opportunities to make decisions and give useful input. This does not mean surrendering basic decision-making powers. It does mean giving employees a chance to participate, to be involved, *and* to hold them accountable.
- *As a company leader, keep skid chains on your tongue.* Talking about others may be destructive and probably is just gossip unless it's specifically designed to help.
- *Cultivate a calm, persuasive voice. How* you say it is often more important than *what* you say. In any type discussion or confrontation, your objective is to "win them over" . . . not "win over them."
- *Make certain you are short on promises to your people and long on fulfillment.* Action does speak louder than words.
- *Be interested in the goals, welfare, homes, and families of those with whom you work.* People have many facets in their lives. Don't be a one-dimensional supervisor. You may not supervise their private lives, but you can let them know you *really care*.
- *Keep an open mind on all debatable questions* (being the boss doesn't necessarily mean you are always right). Discuss but don't argue. The mark of superior minds is to be able to disagree without being disagreeable.
- *Be careful of employees' feelings.* Wit, put-down, and any form of ethnic or racial digs are no-no's. Leaders instinctively know that when someone is resentful and has a chip on his shoulder, the best way to remove the chip is to let him take a bow.
- *Since employee morale is affected by many factors in and outside the work place, those who have confidence in management's integrity are most likely to deliver their best work and to do so consistently.* The

best way management can build this confidence in itself is to *communicate its abilities honestly, confidently, and directly. A well-run company is the best employee morale-builder available.*

In summary, what the researchers and their statistics say is very important; however, what they *don't* say is even more important:

What the work force really wants is management leadership whose competence and concern they can trust.

The work force desires and feels it deserves an opportunity to grow mentally, socially, spiritually, and physically, while sharing in the financial recognition and security rewards which come as a result of their growth and effort as part of the team.

Andrew Carnegie once said, "A man can succeed at almost anything for which he has unlimited enthusiasm." Lonnie Shealey, president of Lone Star Builders, adds, "Whatever we call it—enthusiasm, motivation, ambition, drive, desire, or energy—it's a quality which plays a major role in success. *People who are unable to motivate themselves must be content with mediocrity, no matter how impressive their other talents.*" Now let's take a sobering look at why he makes that statement and why motivation is a must in our personal and corporate lives.

OUR WASTED TIME

One shocking statistic which costs America and its people a great deal of money and countless lost opportunities is the incredible amount of time which is wasted. The December 9, 1985 issue of *U.S. News & World Report* cites one estimate that in a year American workers will "steal" $160 billion from their employers by arriving late, leaving early, and misusing time on the job. That's a lot of corporate dollars, but the truly big loss is the individual's, because Emerson was "right on" when he said, "The right performance of this hour's duties will be the best preparation for the hours or ages that follow it."

Professor Tor Dahl, an internationally respected productivity expert from the University of Minnesota, and president of his own consulting firm, has done considerable study in the area of time utilization and productivity. He says that well over 40 percent of the time spent on the job is wasted. One of the biggest time wasters on the job is smoking. The average smoker, according to Dr. William L. Weis in an article published in the *Personnel Administrator* May 1981, is absent 2.2 days per year more than a nonsmoker and "steals" over 30 minutes per day, which translates into 18.2 more days per year. Prediction: Since the dollar loss averaged $4611 in 1981 dollars for the employer, by the end of this decade the young person entering the job market as a smoker will find it difficult—if not impossible—to get a really good job.

The most conservative nationwide survey I saw revealed that the average worker wastes nine full work weeks a year simply putting off or postponing work that should be done. Burke Marketing Research, Inc. conducted the survey for Accountemps, an accounting, bookkeeping, and data processing personnel organization. The survey was based on interviews with vice-presidents and personnel directors of one hundred of America's one thousand largest companies. Those responding to the survey estimated that *the average employee procrastinates 18 percent of the time, or nine full thirty-five-hour work weeks each year*. Why? Well, the last survey question was: "What do you believe are the main reasons for procrastination in business?" The answers make up the following list. Read it and see if you agree that motivation could be the most important ingredient leadership can bring to a company.

- unwillingness or inability to make a decision
- failure to understand responsibilities
- lack of communication

- boredom
- low morale
- lack of interest in the job or particular task
- absence of clear-cut goals or objectives
- fear of failure or of making a mistake
- too large work load
- lack of discipline
- poor self-esteem

To this list we must add the thought that far too many people get carried away with what Charles E. Hammel identifies as the "tyranny of the urgent," and permit the "urgent" things to crowd out the "important" things. Basically, we have a *prioritizing* problem and not a *time* problem.

The proper utilization of our time and resources, according to Thomas K. Connellan, president of the Management Group, Inc., of Ann Arbor, Michigan, involves some truths which are so simple and basic that many people miss them completely. First, we need to understand that *there is no point in doing well that which you should not be doing at all*. When you take on a task, you should ask yourself if this is something you should be doing, or is it something someone else should be doing. Focus on *effective* use of time rather than *efficient* use of time.

Efficiency is doing things right. Effectiveness is doing the right things.

According to Mr. Connellan, 10–15 percent of the tasks managers are personally handling should be delegated and 10–15 percent should be eliminated.

Question: What happens to these effective people who take their jobs seriously and use their time wisely? Answer: According to a December 10, 1985 Associated Press release, they get promoted:

CHICAGO Dull people may not be the first invited to parties, but they are usually the first in line for promotion, according to a research team at a medical college here. The team made a study of eighty-eight executives and found that those people with a "low pleasure capacity" make the most successful executives. This is because they can concentrate on their work without being distracted. . . . Executives who were categorized as "fun seeking" tended to have lower salaries. [Author's note: The key word is *seeking*. You should, even must, enjoy your work and have fun performing your job.]

There is something else about those men and women who were promoted. They were masters of the utilization of their time. My friend Dan Bellus from San Diego, California is—in my judgment—the number-one time-management authority in our country. Dan, president of Human Development Unlimited, says this:

"When the Colonists declared their independence from Great Britain, a statement was written: 'All men are created equal.' There has been a lot of discussion about the truth of that statement since the time it was written. I don't propose I can clear it all up, but this I *do* know—everyone is equal in the amount of time he or she receives.

"Everyone gets twenty-four hours a day—sixty minutes for every hour and sixty seconds for every minute. No one can get more; no one can get less. You can't play the 'army' game with time: if you know the guy who's handing out the chow you can say, 'I want more.' Not so with time. You can't build a bigger time pipeline and say, 'I want more.' No one can live more than one second at a time. In this sense, then, everyone is truly equal. Now this one fact alone makes time the most precious of all commodities. This factor forces us to an inescapable conclusion: We've got to make our time work for us—it's the most perishable and nonnegotiable possession we have. We have to get production out of every second.

"Now, if we're low on money we can go to our friendly banker and borrow a little bit. If we have a surplus of money we can save it for a rainy day. Not so with time. If our factory is capable of producing more than we can use on a daily basis, we can stockpile our merchandise; we can place it in inventory; we can use it later. Not so with time. If we have a great idea we can write it down, save it for the future. Not so with time. If we want to be totally dishonest we can counterfeit money—we can print our own. Not so with time. We can steal merchandise, we can plagiarize written material. Not so with time. Time is the only commodity we deal with which cannot be counterfeited, stolen, plagiarized, obtained by fraud, stockpiled, or placed in inventory. And no force on earth can change that. When we make a deal with the old man with the scythe, he has a little sign right up above his cash register: ALL SALES FINAL—NO EXCHANGES, NO RETURNS, NO REFUNDS. We can't bring our sales slip back and exchange it for anything. If we don't get what we want when we trade that time, there's no way we can change the transaction."

Dan goes on to say that all activity, all work, all productivity is at the same level as the planning and organization which precedes it. *"We can't work at a high level of productivity and a low level of planning.* If we're going to travel that highway of productivity, the highway of planning must lead into it. We've got to plan to use every second that's available to us and use it in the proper proportion." Dan then adds a thought which, if we buy into it, will certainly increase our productivity and effective use of our time:

Why is it we never have time to do it right, but we always have time to do it over?

Dan sums it up beautifully and eloquently when he says, "It appears we must take four building-block steps: (1) realize the true value and perishable nature of time; (2) draw up a plan for the physical handling of our time; (3) understand that a one-shot attack will not work because our attitude regarding time must change, our habits of thinking and doing must change; and (4) for this change to take place, a decision and a commitment must be made.

"Perhaps the most important two words we'll say here and now are those two: *decision* and *commitment*. All of the rules in the world, all of the techniques known to man, all of the tools that were developed, all of the plans ever made, all of the ideas we have suggested for you here—none of these will be worth today's nickel, none of these will produce one fraction of a second in time gained, unless and until we make the decision that *they* will and make the commitment that *we* will. It will be easy in the white heat of inspiration; it will be simple in the desire of the moment, to envision a wealth of time gained, a wealth of time in which we can do all of these things we've always wanted to do, but without a firm, irrevocable decision, without a genuine commitment, nothing can and nothing will happen. The decision must be—the commitment must be—to develop attitudes that will make time serve us, that will get for us every second's worth of living out of every second of life. Such commitment can be made; such an attitude can be developed. The knowledge is ours, the capability is within us—not outside in some magic formula but within us, where rests all potential for our own development.

"The following ad appeared in the want-ad section of a newspaper:

> LOST   Somewhere between sunrise and sunset—
> one golden hour encrusted with sixty silver min-
> utes, each studded with sixty diamond seconds. No
> reward is offered. They are lost and gone forever.

"Did you run that ad? Will you have to run it again tomorrow?"

I don't know how that hits you, but to me it's inspiring and motivating, as well as challenging. Yes, I believe motivation is important. I believe we have to be motivated to clearly accept and understand that tremendously significant advice Dan Bellus is sharing with us.

THE SUCCESSFUL *KNOW* ABOUT ATTITUDE

Allan Cox, author of the widely acclaimed book *Confessions of a Corporate Headhunter*, talks a great deal about attitude and, as a result of a survey of 1,173 executives in 13 corporations, has some strong opinions and factual information. He says, "Attitude determines strength. It determines direction. American executives by and large believe that having a positive attitude is responsible for career advancement." In his survey he asked the question "What was your finding concerning the impact of positive thinking?" Among top executives, 49 percent said it affected their own success very strongly and 46.5 percent said it was a "significant" factor. In a nutshell, 95.5 percent of these men and women said their attitude played a very strong or significant part in their success. The rest were neutral on the question. On the other side, Cox points out that *no one with whom leaders deal is given such short shrift as the negative thinker.*

Mr. Cox points out that positive thinking is not manipulating or being manipulated. It is not being grandiose, it is not being naive. It is not being falsely enthusiastic or optimistic. Most important, perhaps, it is not to deny periodic, normal bouts of discouragement. Thinking positively is not *legislated experience*, either. By this he means you cannot practice it merely because someone tells you to, nor can you extend it selectively, say to life at home, and exclude it from work. He points out that life constantly presents us with obstacles and opportunities. Positive thinking is the means for dealing constructively with both of them.

AN IMPORTANT GIFT YOU CAN GIVE OTHERS

One of the most important and positive things we can give others is *hope* with direction, encouragement, and believability—hope that the future is going to be bright for them, regardless of where they are at the moment. Never will I forget an incident at a hotel on Marco Island, Florida, several years ago. A speaker friend and I were visiting in my room when the maid knocked and asked permission to clean the room. Since this did not present a problem, we invited her to go ahead.

She had been working less than a minute when our conversation stopped and I started watching her in action. Though she was large and substantially overweight, she moved with amazing speed. In three fast movements she stripped the blanket and linens from the bed. With each of her hands working, she removed the pillowcases from both pillows simultaneously. She took the sheet which covers the mattress and quickly put it on one side. Next she put the light blanket on top of that, followed by the cover sheet and the bedspread. Then she put the pillowcase on the pillow and completed that one side of the bed.

At that point she quickly moved to the other side and finished that side of the bed in record time. How she handled the next little maneuver is an absolute mystery to me, but somehow from the opposite side of the bed she flipped the bedspread and the pillow (which she had neatly tucked on the other side) over in the correct spot and, with two more quick movements on her side, the bed was complete.

I don't exaggerate when I say she had made that bed in less than half the time of anyone I have ever seen. Since I served two years in the navy and made a few hundred bunks myself, I consider myself knowledgeable on the subject. But this lady was far and away the best I've ever seen.

Curiosity demanded that I get some information, so I asked her whether she minded if I asked her some questions. She cheerfully responded, "No, go right ahead," but in the meantime she was doing the other things needed to clean the room. First I asked her whether she worked on an hourly basis or if she were paid by the room. She told me she was paid by the room. I smilingly asked, "I'll bet you do all right, don't you?" For the first time she stopped and said, "Well, to tell you the truth, I have a large family and I am the only one to support them so I have to work hard." Then she grinned from ear to ear and said, "And yes, I do all right."

WHERE YOU START IS NOT IMPORTANT

I'd like to complete this story by saying I got her name and address and two years later I wrote to discover she was the manager of the hotel. Unfortunately—and for me, amazingly—I did not even get her address, so I cannot finish her story on that kind of note. However, I'll bet she's still doing "all right."

About a year later I was speaking in Zanesville, Ohio, and had lunch with the manager of a Holiday Inn and the president of the Chamber of Commerce, along with a personal friend. As we visited, I told the story of this lady and the manager of the Holiday Inn said, "Well, obviously that was not me, but it could have been." She pointed out that when she finished high school she got married and had to go to work. The only job available was to serve as the housekeeper at the Holiday Inn and her job was cleaning rooms. However, she determined that she was going to work as hard as possible and be the best at what she did. The net result was that within six months she was manager of that floor of the Holiday Inn. A few months later she was manager of the entire housekeeping department. About a year later they moved her into the restaurant, first as assistant manager and shortly after as manager. A couple of years later she was manager of the Holiday Inn in Zanesville, Ohio, and served in that capacity for several years. This lady, Mrs. Nan Gump, could easily have been immobilized by where she had to start ... instead she realized that *where you finish* is much more important. I remind you, that's in essence what I said about my coauthor at the beginning of this book.

CAN YOU "STAND" MOTIVATED?

Of all the subjects on this earth, surely one of the most exciting and confusing is the subject of motivation. The next example opens the door and deals with just one facet of this intriguing subject.

I don't know how you "stand" when you're waiting in a line

or waiting for something to happen, but I shall never forget a little incident which took place in Washington, D.C. which fairly well describes the average person's concept of what motivation is and what a motivated person does. I had spoken for the National Federation of Parents for Drug-Free Youth, and the response had been very gratifying. The audience laughed at the appropriate places, nodded in agreement at the right spots, applauded at the high spots, and gave me an enthusiastic standing ovation when it was all over. Compliments flowed thick and fast. Had my wife been there, she would have loved everything they said about me! My children would have been a little embarrassed about it, and my mother would have *believed* every word. In short, it was an "up" occasion for me.

The next morning, I was in the restaurant waiting for the host to seat the guest who preceded me. I was quietly standing, awaiting his return. As I stood there, three women who had been present at my talk the night before joined the people behind me who were waiting in line. These three women obviously thought I was out of earshot or would not be tuned in to what they were saying. However, here's the conversation I picked up. First lady: "There is our speaker from last night." Second lady: "Yes, and he is obviously a 'night' person." Third lady: "He must be, because he sure doesn't look motivated to me!"

Now to be real honest, I don't know how you either "look" motivated or "stand" motivated. I suppose the women thought I should have had an ear-to-ear grin on my face, or perhaps I should have been bouncing up and down and waving to the people in the restaurant. If that's their idea of a motivated person, all I can say is they are way, way off base.

The question I am most often asked is, "Are you always so 'up'?" And the answer, of course, is, "No, I'm not always 'up.' " But I am "up" about 95 percent of the time. Usually if I am not "up," it is because I am exhausted as a result of a grueling schedule. Common sense and experience then dictate to me that I either need to take a nap or go jogging—which is exactly what I do if it's humanly possible.

I should explain, however, that there is a vast difference between being "up" and being "on." Anyone who is "on" twenty-four hours a day is "on" something which is deadly. In short order he will suffer from burnout and probably end up as a depressed, perhaps even psychotic, individual. Either that, or efforts to always be "on" could lead to a tragic dependency on drugs, which has claimed far too many (even one is too many) of our young people who are deluded into believing that you must always be "on" and having a marvelous time.

JUST WHO IS MOTIVATED?

Unfortunately, too many people think of the "motivated" person as the loudly enthusiastic, turned-on extrovert who is making noise and is the center of attention, whether he is in a crowd of ten or ten thousand. This is not necessarily motivation, but probably falls under the banner of "hysteria" and hysteria is giving motivation a bad reputation. I'm not saying that the extrovert is not motivated because he *could* be, but being loud certainly doesn't necessarily mean being motivated. Some of the most "up" and motivated people I've ever known are quiet and unassuming. Obvious point: You can be "up" and motivated while quietly jogging, reading, praying, thinking, holding hands with your mate, or even sleeping.

As I wrote that last paragraph, the Redhead was waiting to take a walk in the Botanic Gardens along the Brisbane River in Brisbane, Australia. What an "up" experience it was! The greenery, shrubs, flowers, rocks, plants, birds, boats, water, and people were beautiful, fascinating, and quiet. At no time during the walk would anyone have accused us of being "on," especially when we sat on the bench to watch the ducks and birds in their never-ending quest for food. However, it was definitely an "up" experience and is permanently recorded in my memory bank as a most enjoyable, motivating interlude.

I might also add that this process helps to clean out the garbage and the cobwebs from the yesterdays of life, so that you really are clearing the decks for more effective action today. Another benefit is that this kind of *meditation* will help eliminate lots of *medication*.

Yes, life can be—even *should* be—sprinkled from time to time with "up" experiences. For me, a jog with one of my granddaughters or daughter Cindy, a game of golf with my wife or son, a moving sermon, inspiring semiclassical music, hymns of the faith, or a drama about real life depicting the good guy winning over the bad guy is always an "up" experience. These events turn me on when I need to be turned on to do the speaking and writing which my profession requires.

My guess is you are pretty much the same way, and like me, you have certain things that *do not* get you as motivated as your best performance demands. It may be a certain aspect of your job, such as the paperwork or long and tedious meetings. It might be making cold calls on unmotivated buyers. It might be dealing with and trying to manage other people's frustrations when you feel you have enough of your own aggravations to last a lifetime. The question should be, "Is it possible to be motivated about something that I am *not* motivated about right now?" The answer is a definite YES! Especially if you understand that most small problems, when nourished with procrastination, will grow bigger and bigger.

It will be even easier when you understand a simple formula which I call the *Three-A Formula to develop motivation.* The next three chapters are dedicated to this formula.

Before we really get into this concept of motivation, let me make one more point. You may be as motivated as you ever want to be. The chances are good, however, that there is someone in your life who is not as motivated as you would like for him or her to be. So, as you read the next chapters, don't forget that you are reading from two perspectives: (1) How will this information help me to be a Top Performer? (2) How will this information help me to help others be Top Performers? You will be pleased with the answers you find to both questions—I guarantee it!

PERFORMANCE PRINCIPLES

1. *You must understand motivation to consistently motivate others.*
2. *Management's imperative is to cultivate its human resources.*
3. *What the work force really wants is management leadership whose competence and concern they can trust.*
4. *One of the most important things we can give others is hope, with direction, encouragement, and believability.*
5. *Where you start is not as important as where you finish.*
6. *You can be "up" without being "on."*

Why You Manage...
Why They Follow

> The true motives of our actions, like the real pipes of an organ, are usually concealed. But the gilded and the hollow pretext is pompously placed in the front for show.
>
> Charles Caleb Colton

Awareness
Analysis
Action

13 The first *A* in our Three-*A* Formula stands for *Awareness*. When I am talking about awareness, I am talking about answering the question *Why?* Why are you reading this book? Why are you continuing to work in your job? Why are you continuing to be involved in the day-to-day activities that fill your life? The *honest* answer to the question *Why?* is also the answer to your *personal* motivation. This is not motivation that has been imposed upon you by anyone else; it's your personal motivation. One of the early success writers suggested we take

motiv/ation

the word *motivation* and make a slash between the *v* and the *a*—and if you've got just a little bit of imagination, you can see two words. The word on the left is *motive*, and the word on the right is *action*. People who are motivated have a motive; they have a reason, a purpose, or a cause. And then they take action on that reason, purpose, or cause. Question: *Have you given it any thought at all?*

A friend of mine, attending college, was placed in a 7:30 A.M. English class that met on Saturdays. In his words, "The counselors saw me coming, didn't they? They must have said, 'This guy looks like he just fell off the turnip truck! Let's put him in that 7:30 A.M. Saturday English class and he'll probably show up!' They did—and I did!"

He went on to tell me that the teacher walked to the front of the room and immediately gave an assignment. The class was to write a short theme on "Why I Am Going to College." The students dutifully got down to business, but after about ten minutes, one of them got up and left the room. When the class was over, several of his friends walked out to the quadrangle to find the student who had left early. Sure enough, Ray was sitting in front of the library. "Ray, what are you doing?" his puzzled friends asked.

"Funny, I never thought about it before," Ray said, "but I don't want to go to college! The only reason I'm here is that you guys are here and my other friends are here and my mom and dad wanted me to go to college. I don't want to go to college. I want to go to work at the plant where my dad works, get married, have a family, play slow-pitch softball at night, and spend time with my family on the weekends. I just never thought about it until that teacher asked the question."

The real irony of this true story is that Ray was a straight-*A* high school student, and the chances are good he could have gone on to be whatever he studied to be. However, with that attitude, he would have been a mediocre doctor, lawyer, scientist, teacher, manager, or anything else. He would have been mediocre because he had not identified his own personal reasons, purposes, or causes. If we are to motivate ourselves, we must honestly face up to the real reasons we do the things we do.

If we want to motivate other people, we have got to find out what their reason, purpose, or cause is. People are not going to be motivated for *your* reasons. They are going to be motivated for their own reasons. We must understand that *everyone* listens to the *same* radio station. The station is WII-FM and the call letters stand for *What's In It For Me?* If you want to motivate others, this is the information you need to share. You've got to find out their motive, reason, and cause—and then encourage them to take action.

The first time you attempt to discover what another person's motives are, you will probably get an answer he or she thinks you would like to hear. If you continue to probe, you will get

an answer that someone very close to that person would like to hear. And if you continue to probe, you might get the *truth*. Now, people don't mean to be deceitful. It's just that they haven't given much thought to what really is important to them. You see, money doesn't motivate anyone. If you had a million dollars and stacked it in the shape of a coffee table for your living room, initially you would be excited and invite all your friends and neighbors over to see your "million-dollar coffee table." After about three weeks, you would probably be bored with the "green monstrosity" in the living area. Money is not a motivator ... what we *can do with the money* is what really motivates us and others. Whether it's the biggest home on the street or the largest donation to the orphanage, our motives vary greatly. Honest realization of our motives (or those of others) is the first step in understanding motivation.

FEAR MOTIVATION

Motivation comes in three forms. The first is *fear motivation*. Fear motivation works for some people some of the time. In most cases, it is temporary, but there are occasions when it is effective. When the economy is extremely tight and there are more workers than jobs, many workers will consciously make a much greater effort to be extremely productive, in an effort to ensure their jobs. They will arrive earlier, stay later, and do more while they are there. However, if this is their only motive, the chances are excellent that over a period of time they will grow weary of well-doing and revert back to their old habits and, if the economy is still bad, will ultimately end up losing their jobs. Temporarily, however, it will work and effect an increase in productivity for them.

Fear motivation is also effective on a toddler who continues to reach for things which he can destroy or which might be dangerous to him. A few light slaps of the hand will convince him, in most cases, that it is not in his best interests to pursue that course of action and he will desist. Fear motivation also works for a six-, seven-, or eight-year-old when it comes to acquiring bad habits such as smoking. A threat on the part of the parents to "wear his britches out" if they catch him with a cigarette is very effective and will keep that cigarette out of his mouth. However, the same approach for a fifteen-year-old would be worthless and might even have the opposite effect.

In the marketplace, fear motivation sometimes is temporarily effective to keep workers in line, have them become team players, cooperate with, and on occasion even be subservient to their superiors. But again, the results are temporary and over the long haul can even backfire.

INCENTIVE MOTIVATION

The second kind of motivation is *incentive motivation*. All of us in our business careers have seen the familiar picture of the donkey pulling the cart with a carrot dangling in front of him. The donkey's motivation to pull is obviously to reach and take a bite of that carrot. For this incentive to work, the load has got to be light enough for him to pull; the donkey's got to be hungry enough so that he wants to take a bite of that carrot; and the carrot has got to be desirable enough so that he wants to take a bite. However, if he does not eventually have his bite of carrot, he's going to recognize that it's a "con game" and he will stop pulling.

The only problem is, when you give the donkey a big enough bite of the carrot, he is no longer going to be hungry and, consequently, his motivation to pull is dramatically reduced. At this point, the only way you can get him to pull is to lighten the load, shorten the stick, and sweeten the carrot. The problem here is that in the business world we have a load which is fairly well dictated by market conditions and, if you lighten it too much, or if you give the donkey too big a bite of the carrot (or the profit generated by the free-enterprise system), the operation no longer becomes profitable and we ultimately end up out of business. Remember: Today's fringe benefits are tomorrow's expectations. So what do you do? Answer: Change the donkey to a thoroughbred and make him *want* to run.

CHANGE OR GROWTH MOTIVATION

This brings us to the third kind of motivation, which is *growth motivation*. The primary purpose of growth motivation is to change the thinking, the capacity, and the motivation of the worker. We must make him want to pull that cart (do his job). We must give him reasons for doing what we want him to do *and* which *he* wants to do. In other words, we must work with employees to the degree that we can help them get the things they want in life. That's a major purpose of *Top Performance*: to give specific methods, procedures, and techniques for helping each individual grow and inspiring them so they will want to do a better job—not just for the benefit of the company but for their own benefit as well. As I've said before, in reality we are all "on the same team," and consequently, we have the same objectives. When management and labor both clearly understand that we are on the same side, then both sides will be willing, even anxious, to cooperate.

When I was a small boy my friends and I frequently walked on an abandoned section of the railroad tracks. Each of us attempted to keep our balance and walk the farthest, but inevitably, after a few steps, we would fall. Had we but realized it, two of us could have gotten on opposite rails, reached across and held hands and, together, could have walked indefinitely.

I'm convinced that in the business world, when management and labor, employer and employee, fully understand that they are on the same side and have the same objectives, if they will "hold hands" and work together, all will benefit. Then we are not only developing our maximum potential as individuals but we're also achieving the maximum productivity in our company, which ensures the stability and growth of that company. That's the kind of thinking and motivation which will bring optimum results and permanent benefits for labor and management.

I'm convinced that everyone is motivated at some time in their lives about something. Winners are motivated a high percentage of the time. *Winning leaders* are motivated most of the time and *almost* always when the chips are down. My friend Gene Lewis, one of the great commonsense leaders it has been my privilege to work with, shares this analogy, which clearly points out what happens to entirely too many people:

A glowworm does its fishing not in water, but in the air. It spins and lets down fine glutinous threads. When a gnat or other small insect, attracted by the light, collides with one of these strange fishing lines, it is caught and held. The glowworm reels in the line and consumes the captive. If its hunger is satisfied, the glowworm puts out its light. Otherwise, it drops another line for another tidbit. The soft light that gives the glowworm its unearthly beauty is not produced by the "contented" glowworm. The scintillating lights come from the glowworms that are hungry and indeed earnest about their fishing.

Unique creatures though they are, these glowworms have qualities in common with human beings. With us, as with them, the full stomach too often brings about a state of complacency that dims desire for accomplishment.

The young man starting out in life is spurred on by powerful "bread and butter" incentives. To be sure of eating regularly, he must pass certain tests. He must be able to master the fundamentals of his business, and to adapt himself to the conditions that make for success in that business. Hungry with desire for life's necessities, he "fishes" in that business in dead earnest, and if he has the right qualities, his "glow" attracts success.

But, after he has met with a measure of success, he faces a different kind of test. Is he still impelled by a strong inner drive to fish hard for the really big stakes?

Many who pass the initial tests brilliantly are stopped by this secondary test. They stall at the top of the first hill. They are so eager to enjoy the fruits of their success that they are unwilling to put forth the efforts to augment their education, acquire specialized training, or do whatever else may be necessary to reach still greater heights of service and personal advancement.

226

Obviously, Gene is not talking about *leaders* in that last paragraph. True leaders who are really motivated will use one success to build to an even bigger one. A leader knows that he *is* the example his subordinates look to for guidance and direction. *As a manager, he knows he will be measured and judged by the number of his subordinates who surpass him.* He clearly understands that the mark of greatness is the ability to develop it in others.

A MOST MISUNDERSTOOD INGREDIENT

If you are going to be a consistent Top Performer, it's important that you understand what happiness really is. Many people maintain they'll be happy *when*—they win the trip to Hawaii, New York, or Bermuda. Many people say they'll be happy when they get the new house, but they won't. Then they'll be happy when the landscaping is completed, but they won't. Then they say they'll be happy when the new draperies are up—but that's not true, either. Then they'll be happy when the mortgage is paid off, but again, they're wrong. They'll be happy when they've added the new room to the house, but that's not true. Then they'll be happy when they build that little place out on the lake—but again, it simply is not so.

Happiness is not a when—it is a *NOW!* It is not what you *have* that makes you happy, it is what you *are* that's going to make you happy! Material things are never going to make us happy. As I pointed out earlier, Adam and Eve had the whole world (including, as far as I know, the mineral rights). God gave them everything and authority over it—with the exception of one tree. He carefully instructed them not to eat the fruit of that tree. With all the material possessions they had, what was the one thing they wanted? You guessed it: the fruit of that tree.

MONEY AND POSITION WON'T MAKE YOU HAPPY

Many people say, "When I get a million dollars, then I'll be happy because I'll have security," but that's not necessarily so. Most people who acquire a million dollars want another and then another. Or they could be like a good friend of mine who made and lost every dime of a million dollars. It didn't bother him a bit. He wasn't excited about it, but he explained to me, "Zig, I still know everything necessary to make another million dollars, and I've learned what to do not to lose it. I'll simply go back to work and earn it again." He proceeded to do exactly that—and more. No, security is not based on money. General Douglas MacArthur said that security lies in our ability to produce—and I believe he's right.

Many people say, "I'll be happy when I get to be head of the company, because that represents security—when I'm the person in charge." That's not true. As you well know, you can even get to be the president of the United States and if you don't handle the job properly, you're going to lose it! No, if we are to have happiness, security, and continue to be motivated, we must understand that security comes from within. It lies in our ability to produce. In my mind, one of the best ways to be certain that we will continue to produce even when our needs have long ago been met is to continue to apply these principles and procedures we advocate in *Top Performance*.

HAPPY AND SUCCESSFUL PEOPLE HAVE A REASON FOR WHAT THEY DO

A very wealthy west Texan had a daughter of marriageable age, and he determined to give her a "coming out" party.* This simply meant that he was going to invite all the eligible bachelors in the area over to his home so that he could have a good look at them—you sales folks would call that "group prospecting." His reason was obvious: he wanted the very best for his daughter.

When all the eligible young men arrived from a hundred-mile radius of his two-hundred-thousand-acre ranch (with scores of fully producing oil wells and thousands of head of cattle), he called them all out by the Olympic-size swimming pool, which he had the amazing foresight of stocking with water moccasins, alligators, and other vicious beasts. He told the young men that the first one who jumped into the pool and

* I told this story in *Raising Positive Kids in a Negative World*.

swam the length would be given his choice of three things: one million dollars in cash, ten thousand acres of his best land, or the hand of his beautiful daughter in marriage. He even pointed out that his daughter was his only heir and that when he and his wife passed on, all of this big spread would belong to her and to the man who became her husband.

No sooner were the words spoken than there was a loud splash at one end of the pool, followed almost immediately by the emergence of a dripping wet young man from the other end of the pool. He had set a world's record that would never be approached, much less broken, in swimming the length of that pool.

As the crowd of young men and the girl's father rushed down to the other end of the pool to congratulate the young man, he stood there in eager anticipation. The host excitedly said, "Well, son, you've got your choice. Do you want the million in cash?" The young man responded, "No, sir." Then the host asked, "Do you want the ten thousand acres of my best land?" The young man responded, "No, sir." Finally the host said, "Then I guess you want the hand of my beautiful daughter in marriage!" To this the young man replied, "No, sir." Somewhat puzzled and a little frustrated, the host demanded, "Well, son, what *do* you want?" The young man responded, "What I want is to know the name of the dude that pushed me into the swimming pool!"

Now quite obviously this young man had a reason for what he was doing. It might not be what you originally expected it to be, but he had a reason. Question: Do you have a reason for what you do? Have you clearly identified your *reason, purpose, cause* ... your MOTIVE? Are you willing to take action on that reason, purpose, or cause?

An equally important question: If you are trying to motivate others, have you *clearly* identified *their* reason, purpose, or cause? Or are you trying to get them to take action on *your* motives? Successful people who motivate themselves and others are aware of and *honestly* identify their motives—or those of the ones they would motivate—and then take the action steps necessary for success. Good managers encourage others to take the steps necessary for their personal success!

PERFORMANCE PRINCIPLES

1. *Do you know why you do what you do?*
2. *Motivation = the motives we take action on.*
3. *Happiness is not a where or a when, it is a here and a now.*
4. *To motivate yourself, identify your motives and take action on them; to motivate others, identify their motives and encourage them to take action.*

Education to Overcome Management Paralysis

> **Only the educated are free.**
> **Epictetus**

Awareness
Analysis
Action

14 The second *A* in our Three-*A* Formula is *Analysis*. When I'm talking about analysis, I'm talking about education. There are three great immobilizers that keep you from succeeding and, as a matter of fact, keep all of us from accomplishing what we are capable of. The *only* way to overcome these immobilizers is through analysis and education. The immobilizers are FEAR, DOUBT, and WORRY. These are three negative uses of our imagination.

Let's take a closer look at this concept of FEAR: *False Evidence Appearing Real*. I could take a piece of cloth and my finger and chances are good I could come into your town and rob your bank. I could use the piece of cloth as a handkerchief to cover my face. Then I could put my finger in my coat pocket, giving it the appearance of a gun when I point it at a person. If I aimed it at the teller and said, "Give me your money!" I can guarantee you her palms would get sweaty and her heart would beat fast. At that point, she would give me the money. All the evidence would be false, but because it would appear to be real, the teller would act as if it were real.

You might have read about the young Cuban who hijacked a plane to Cuba with nothing but a bar of soap. He placed the soap in a shoe box, went up to the flight attendant, and said, "Hey, I've got a bomb in here." She said, "Ooooooohhhh, you need to see the pilot!" He went to see the pilot and said, "Hey, I've got a bomb in here and I'd like to go to Cuba." They went to Cuba. All the evidence was false, but because it *appeared* to be real, the captain acted as if it were real.

A CHALLENGE FOR YOU

I want to challenge you to write down in the space provided your ten greatest fears, doubts, and worries. Now some of you might say, "I need more than ten blank spaces!" No, I said your ten *greatest* fears, doubts, and worries. If you have the courage to write them down, here is what you will find: Out of the ten items you listed, seven or eight will already have happened or cannot happen. Of the remaining items, you have absolutely no control over one or two of them. And you will find that only one or two items are within your control.

Question: Does it make sense to dissipate your energies over a long list of things you cannot control instead of focusing your energies on the one or two things you can effectively handle? Since the answer is obviously no, why do we fail to focus our energies on solvable problems? Answer: We refuse to focus our energies only on solvable problems because we are creatures of habit. We have an everyday routine that we are involved in, and if the routine is changed, it upsets us and can even spoil our whole day.

Unfortunately for our society, one of our most destructive habits is the habit of griping, complaining, and moaning. Or, as my associate Bryan Flanagan says, "We become members

My 10 Greatest
Fears, Doubts, & Worries

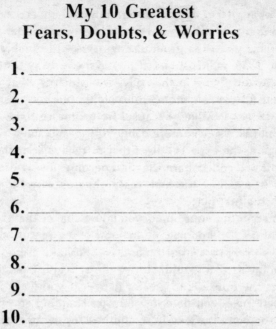

1. _____
2. _____
3. _____
4. _____
5. _____
6. _____
7. _____
8. _____
9. _____
10. _____

of the moan, groan, and carry on club!" Did you realize that some people would rather complain than succeed? If that sounds absurd to you, prove me wrong. Try eliminating the complaining and see if it doesn't help you move toward success more quickly. We live in a society which is used to being negative more than positive. For example, as my speaker friend Don Hutson says, economists have predicted eighteen of the last two recessions! People find fault as if there is a reward for it! Too many people look for the worst in others and never pass up the chance to cut down or criticize others.

NEGATIVE USE OF THE IMAGINATION

As a general rule, I board an airplane from two to ten times each week. Obviously, I know that from time to time there are airplane crashes, so I recognize there is danger for me when I get aboard that aircraft. But realistically, there is even more danger for the airplane, because when airplanes come down faster than they go up, their trade-in value drops to virtually nothing. I mean, you just can't swap them at all!

Interestingly enough, however, though there is danger when the plane leaves the ground, there is even more danger if the plane remains *on* the ground. Engineers will quickly tell you that the plane will rust out sitting on the runway faster than it will wear out flying in the heavens—which is what airplanes are built for. When the ship leaves the harbor, there is certainly danger involved because, from time to time, ships do sink. But there's even more danger if the ship stays in the harbor. Again, the experts tell us that if it stays at anchor in the harbor it will collect barnacles and become unseaworthy faster than if it is sailing the high seas, which is why the ship was built in the first place.

If you rent out your home, you take a chance that the person you rent it to will damage it. In some cases, renters simply do not have pride of ownership and will not take as good care of your home as you would. However, my real estate friends assure me the house is in greater danger if you leave it empty. They tell me it will deteriorate faster standing empty than it will if someone is living in it, and besides, homes are built to be lived in.

Obviously, there is a certain amount of danger in doing anything, but in management there is generally even more danger in doing *nothing*. Man and nature are exact opposites in at least one respect: *We deplete nature's resources by using them up. We deplete man's natural resources by not using them at all.*

Oliver Wendell Holmes was right when he said the great tragedy in America is not the destruction of our natural resources, though that tragedy is great. He said the truly great tragedy is the destruction of our human resources by our failure to fully utilize our abilities, which means most men and women go to their graves with their music still in them. This tragedy is compounded when those of us in leadership positions do not utilize our abilities to properly direct and inspire those in our sphere of influence to become all they are capable of becoming.

The "subtitle" to our company name is "The People Builders," because our corporate purpose, our reason for being in business, is to help people recognize, develop, and use their abilities. One of the vehicles we use to accomplish this is the I CAN course, developed by Mrs. Mamie McCullough. This course is based on the philosophy I espouse in my book *See You at the Top*, and it has positively affected over three million students and teachers all over the United States and Canada.

Several years ago in Rockford, Illinois, a young lady named Marcie Lemaree was taking the I CAN class. I say "taking the class," but actually she literally had to be almost dragged into the classroom, screaming and kicking her feet. She was such a disruption that the teacher finally said, "Marcie, if you will go to the library and listen to the tapes that go along with the I CAN course, I won't turn you in to the principal." Well, that sounded a lot better than sitting in class, so she listened to the tapes and as she listened, some things started to make sense to her. Gradually her attitude changed. Marcie became involved in her school; she became aware of why her attitude was so important; she analyzed and got instruction on how she could be more effective; she became a manager of the basketball team and lettered in girls' track. She also placed fourth out of seven on the rifle team.

Now that might not sound like a big deal to you, but when I share with you (as Paul Harvey would say) "the rest of the story," it might make a difference. Marcie is legally blind. She had difficulty telling darkness from light. When she fired the rifle for the rifle team someone would say, "No, Marcie, you're a little low and to the left, you need to come up and to the right." Did Marcie have reason to FEAR, DOUBT, and WORRY? You bet she did! Did she overcome those FEARS, DOUBTS, and WORRIES? You bet she did! How? The same way you and I overcome our FEARS, DOUBTS, and WOR-RIES . . . through ANALYSIS and EDUCATION! Needless to say, she changed her input, which dramatically changed her output.

IT HAS PROBABLY HAPPENED TO YOU

I think if you will search your memory bank you will be able to identify with this example. The ladies will obviously have a different perspective, but fellows, think back to the time you called a girl for your first date. You remember, you attempted to pick up the telephone and the receiver weighed a ton! You couldn't have lifted it with a crane! So you chickened out for the moment and decided that you would stop by that special person's home the next day after school. Remember how you felt as you sashayed up to that door, and just as you got ready to ring the bell you could feel the confidence draining—so much so that you didn't have the strength to ring that doorbell or knock on the door? Remember how you heard some rustling around inside and ran away because you didn't want the girl or her mother to find some "oddball" out on the porch?

But that series of events really made you *determined!* You charged directly to your home, snatched the phone off the hook, got the right person on the phone . . . and then you couldn't make an intelligible sound!

Now you really were more determined than ever! What embarrassment could be worse than not being able to speak? So you snatched up the phone again, got the special one on the phone, invited her to go out with you, and were told, "No, thank you."

As you hung up the phone you noticed you were still breathing and, to your complete shock and astonishment, your heart was still beating (admittedly faster, but still beating!). Remember saying, "Hey, it didn't kill me to get turned down, so I'll call somebody else"? So you called and called until the law of averages worked in your behalf and you finally persuaded someone to go out with you. Some of you even went on to get married after all that. The reason you were able to make the second and third call was that you overcame your fear, doubt, and worry through learning that it wasn't going to kill you to be turned down.

MANAGING MOTIVATION EDUCATION

Most management books spend some time looking at behavioral scientists' view of motivation, and this can be so technical it is difficult to understand. My approach will seem to some an oversimplification, but as I have often said, some of the greatest truths in life are the simplest. For that reason, I generally speak and write at the seventh-grade, third-month level. I've also found that if I keep it at this level, even college professors will be able to keep up with me. But as my good friend Dr. Steve Franklin, a college professor from Emory University in Atlanta, Georgia, who gave me the preceding line, says, "The great truths in life are the simple ones. You don't need three moving parts or four syllables for something to be significant."

Steve pointed out to me that there are only three pure colors—but look at what Michelangelo did with those three colors! There are only seven notes, but look what Chopin, Beethoven, and Vivaldi did with those seven notes! (For that matter, look what Elvis did with two!) Lincoln's Gettysburg Address contained only 262 words and 202 of them were one syllable. Think of the impact those simple, direct words have had on our society! I know many of our problems are complex, but I believe a simple (not simplistic), direct approach, worded in simple, understandable terms, is the best and most effective way to get results. Now let's look at what three world-renowned behavioral scientists say about three important areas of our life.

MASLOW—McGREGOR—HERZBERG

The three most often quoted behavioral scientists are Abraham Maslow, who dealt with man's *needs* and the order in which they must be met; Douglas McGregor, who dealt with *personalities, values, and assumptions*; and Frederick Herzberg, who dealt with man's *reaction*—or *response*—to what his work is all about.

The truth is that managers and employees are constantly moving in and about these areas, and to understand and successfully complete our tasks, we must have a basic understanding of all three. Let's start with Maslow's theory.

Abraham Maslow believed that motivation is an "inside" job and is not determined by external factors. The internal factors begin with *basic needs* such as food, shelter, water, and air. The net level is the need for *security* or safety—to feel protected from danger. The third level of motivation is *social* in nature and deals with our need to belong to the team and to have the respect of others. The fourth level is the *ego* level where self-esteem, status, and recognition come into the picture. And finally, there is *self-actualization*, which is realizing our personal potential and becoming all we can become.

Maslow said these needs were *hierarchical*, which is just a fancy way of saying they must be met in order, one through five. However, an interesting aspect of his theory stated:

Once the need is satisfied it is no longer a motivator.

How can we help others through Maslow's theory? To meet a person's *basic needs* in the work place, we must: (Now *slow down*. These are to be read and *acted* upon, not just read and agreed with.)

1. Create as pleasant and comfortable a working environment as possible.
2. Provide an adequate income so the person can provide for immediate creature needs, while creating the possibility of increased financial opportunity for additional creature comforts.

To meet a person's *security* or *safety needs* in the work place, we must:

1. Not lose sight of the importance of *basic needs* being met.
2. Provide orderliness and consistency in relationships with superiors.
3. Provide protective rules, regulations, and policies.
4. Provide fringe benefits and seniority protection.
5. Provide clear and consistent Foundational Performance levels.

To meet a person's *belonging needs* in the work place, we must:

1. Not lose sight of the importance of *basic needs* and *safety needs* being met.
2. Provide an opportunity to be a "member of the team."
3. Provide opportunities for developing relationships and being accepted and appreciated by team members.
4. Provide sincere concern for each team member and encourage him or her to do likewise.

To meet a person's *ego-status needs* in the work place, we must:

1. Not lose sight of the importance of *basic needs, safety needs,* and *belonging needs* being met.
2. Provide a Recognition Program which rewards what the company sees as foundational concepts to company success.
3. Provide a Recognition Program which allows the person to be singled out for special recognition.
4. Provide a Recognition Program with different levels of recognition so that different levels of performance are recognized and employees compete with themselves and not always with one another.
5. Provide the opportunity for an employee to move up in areas of responsibility and be placed in "high profile" assignments to show skills.
6. Involve the person in planning activities; get his opinion.

To meet a person's *self-actualization needs* in the work place, we must:

1. Not lose sight of the importance of *basic needs, safety needs, belonging needs,* and *ego-status needs* being met.
2. Allow the person the opportunity for more challenging work, and the freedom to be creative.
3. Reinforce a sense of personal growth in taking action.
4. Allow the work to become an "art" or mission.
5. Grant autonomy.

We looked at Douglas McGregor's Theory X and Theory Y in chapter 4, but let's take another look at how this can specifically apply to motivation. You will remember that Theory X is the basic *negative management assumption.* According to Theory X, workers inherently dislike work and will avoid it if possible, so management must coerce, control, direct every move, and threaten a lack of cooperation with punishment. Workers want to be led, according to this theory, and are without ambition, avoid responsibility, and seek only security. This means that as managers we must:

1. Lay out rigid and inflexible job standards.
2. Determine objectives without employee input.
3. Reward only those who stay within the system and punish those who don't.

Theory Y is the basic *positive management assumption*. According to Theory Y, workers feel that work is as natural as play and recreation. They are committed when properly rewarded, especially when rewarded for areas which promote self-respect and personal growth. Most workers are creative and actually seek more responsibility. This means as managers we must:

1. Provide high expectations and high standards.
2. Be even more reward and recognition conscious.
3. Be firm, fair, and consistent with standards.

Now I want to share something *profound* (just thought it would only be fair to warn you). Obviously, there is some of both of these workers in all of us . . . the key is not the ability in the worker but what the *assumption* does to the manager. Our *assumptions* lead to our *attitudes*, which lead to our *behavior*.

> Management assumptions +
> management attitudes =
> management behavior

The third of our behavioral scientists is Frederick Herzberg, and to understand his concepts we need to understand the difference between dissatisfiers/demotivators and satisfiers/motivators. The motivators include interesting work, challenging work, personal achievement, recognition, and the opportunity for increased responsibility. This level has no ceiling and can continue to grow.

By contrast, the dissatisfiers are working relationships, company policies, working conditions, supervision, and compensation. And here is the key: Although you can achieve satisfaction in those areas, *satisfaction does not increase your motivation.* For example, poor company policies will create dissatisfaction; however, good policies will only create satisfaction, not motivation. Dissatisfiers cause different levels of dissatisfaction, but not different levels of motivation. For example, your idea of a good salary changes over a period of time, making dissatisfaction a reasonable possibility in the future.

Let's translate all this to some specific actions the manager might take and see if we can figure out what motivators are involved:

Action	*Motivator*
• take less control	• opportunity for growth/ responsibility/achievement
• establish more accountability	• responsibility/recognition/ rewards
• give job autonomy	• responsibility/achievement/ recognition
• provide more information	
• assign new and increasingly difficult tasks	• internal recognition/ego satisfaction
	• personal growth/career growth/financial growth

As *Top Performers,* our challenge is to understand all three areas and mix, match, and mold them to meet our personal needs and ambitions.

The next example out of the book of life pretty well sums up what this chapter is all about.

A TOP PERFORMER WITH REAL EDUCATION

After reading this much of *Top Performance,* it might not surprise you that when I think of one of the smartest and most educated people I have ever known, I think of a person with a fifth-grade education. That person is my mother. I want to share a story with you that may seem a little unusual coming on the heels of the likes of Maslow, McGregor, and Herzberg, but I think it combines the best of all these men.

I shall never forget an incident which took place when I was a small boy in Yazoo City, Mississippi. Periodically I was given a chance to do a few odd jobs for an elderly couple who lived several blocks from us. They ran a small dairy and were probably in their late sixties or early seventies. The man was blind. We needed the extra money because things were desperately tight financially in the thirties.

I forget some of the details of the incident, but the bottom line is that something went astray. The lady berated me unmercifully and said I had not done what I had said I was going to do (she apparently subscribed to Theory X) and therefore she was not going to pay me for the considerable amount of work I had done.

When I went home in tears to tell my mother I was not going to be paid for what I had done, she was understandably unhappy. However, my mother was the most loving, wise, and gentle person I've ever known (the epitome of a Top Performer and the symbol of all the positive management skills taught in this book). She also had great faith and was most supportive and loyal. When I finished my story, she calmly took off her apron and said, "Let's go and talk with them, son."

My mother was a small lady. She was nearly fifty years old and all the years of her hard work had taken their toll. When we approached the couple, the lady proceeded to tell my mother in no uncertain terms that I had not done what she'd expected me to do, that I was not dependable, that I had lied to her, and any number of other things. My mother, as all good managers do, patiently heard her out, listening very, very carefully and quietly until the woman had finally finished.

Then my mother said, "Well, let me remind you that I was present when you hired my son to do this work. I remember exactly what you told him you wanted him to do in your yard and garden. Before I knocked on the door I made it a point to come by your garden. I can tell you that not only has my son done everything you hired him to do, but in my opinion he has done a real good job and thrown in some extras as well. My son did not lie to you about this and I want you to know that my son would never lie to you on any occasion about anything." Then my mother summed it up: "You owe my son the money, but whether you pay him or not is entirely up to you. I just wanted to make it very clear to you that my son is honest. If you don't pay him for what he has done, we will be able to live without the money, but are you going to be able to live with the money and the knowledge that you've unjustly accused my son of a wrong which he did not do? I leave it up to you as to whether or not you're going to pay him."

As nearly as I can recall, the lady was still adamant that I had not done what she had hired me to do and my mother closed the conversation by saying, "That's all right. We can get along without the money. You just let your conscience be your guide."

A few days later the lady stopped by the house with the money and apologized to both my mother and to me.

That was a particularly significant event in my life because my mother had stood by me and though it was many, many years ago, I shall never forget how grateful I was for the support she gave me. I believe incidents like this made a dramatic difference in my life. As managers and leaders, the support we give to our people when they are right is extremely important, and even when they are wrong we can defend their integrity while not agreeing with some of their actions.

Two of my mother's favorite sayings were, "It's not *who's* right, but *what's* right" . . . and, "If you've got the right person, what they're going to be doing is going to be right." Yes, my mother was a magna cum laude graduate of the school of life. If you will use the principles we are discussing in *Top Performance*, which she role modeled so effectively, then you, too, will be recognized as a manager who helps employees overcome Fear, Doubt, and Worry, and one who gets Top Performance from your people!

PERFORMANCE PRINCIPLES

1. *Fear, Doubt, and Worry will immobilize you and your associates without the proper education.*
2. *Once a need is satisfied, it is no longer a motivator . . . satisfaction does not increase motivation.*
3. *Management Assumptions plus Management Attitudes equals Management Behavior.*

The Secret to Management Motivation

Action often precedes the feeling.
Anonymous

Awareness

Analysis

Action

15 The third *A* in our Three-*A* Formula is *Action!* You are a person of *action*. It started this morning. You were lying in bed and that "opportunity" clock (negative folks call it an alarm clock!) went off. You reached over and shut it off, and in the process that cool air hit your elbow. And then you did what comes naturally . . . you quickly pulled your elbow back under the covers! Now you have a very basic decision to make: "Am I going to put *all* of me out there in that cold air, or am I going to keep *all* of me right here under these nice warm covers where I belong?" Because you are a responsible person with all the success characteristics we discussed in the first part of this book, the battle between *what you want to do* and *what you are committed to do* is won by the *what you are committed to do,* and you roll out of bed. It's obvious to you and to every other success-oriented person that nothing happens until you take that first step—nothing happens until you get the action habit.

I want to share with you one phrase which I honestly believe is worth the price of this book. Now, just in case you're thinking, *Well, why didn't you put it on the first page and leave the rest out?* the answer is, "I don't want you to just get your money's worth . . . I want you to get a bargain." The reason is partly benevolent and partly selfish. As stated earlier, I firmly believe that you can have everything you want in life if you will just help enough other people get what they want. So why do I want you to get so much from this book? Answer: The more you get, the more people you will tell about the book, which simply means the sale of more books. Now, here's that powerful magic statement:

Logic will not change an emotion, but ACTION will!

Or, phrased another way:

Action often precedes the feeling!

For example, I hate to be the one to break the news to you, but there are going to be days when you won't want to get out of bed and go to work. I know it will surprise some of you, but there really are going to be those days. However, sometimes the best work is done by people who don't want to do the things they have to do, but they have the old-fashioned guts, gumption, and sense of responsibility to get up and go! Who are the successful people? They are the people who do the things unsuccessful people refuse to do! They understand that every task they handle is a self-portrait of the person who performed it, and they have committed themselves to autograph every job with excellence.

As I stated in my book *See You at the Top*, one year I finished second in a national organization which employed over seven thousand salespeople. Later I finished first in another national organization that had over three thousand people in sales. I can state without reservation that there were many days when I did not feel like going to work, but actually started to feel like working after I got into action. Here is a key point: Not once in that year when I was number two of seven thousand did I finish in the top twenty in sales for a single week. Not once in that time did I finish in the top twenty for a single month. Yet at the end of the year I was second in the organization. How did this happen? Simple! I disciplined myself to start *every* day by being in front of a prospect by no later than 9:00 A.M. The net result was *some* business *every* week, so that by the end of the year the cumulative total was enough to put me in second place.

As you well know, big jobs are accomplished by taking lots of small steps. Question: How do you eat an elephant? One bite at a time! How do you lift a cow? By lifting a baby calf every day of its life! How do you lose 37 pounds? By losing 1.9 ounces per day for ten months. How do you effectively lead your people to greater accomplishments and move steadily up the ladder of success? By steadily, on a daily basis, giving your job a "best effort." The only way to coast is downhill, isn't it?

YOU'VE HEARD IT BEFORE—TAKE ONE STEP AT A TIME

My sister-in-law, Eurie Abernathy, has had multiple sclerosis (MS) for many years. In 1985 she spent several days with us over the Christmas holidays. It was her first visit in our new two-story home. Because of the MS, I assumed she could not make it up the stairs to the second floor, so I was surprised when I returned home one day and found the Redhead and her seated in our bedroom, enjoying a chat. After a few minutes, Eurie decided to go back downstairs. As a precaution, I walked in front of her so that if she should start to fall I could catch her. As we made our way downstairs, I expressed surprise that she had been able to go up the stairs, which are relatively steep. She quickly responded with a simple but profound statement: "Yes, I can do anything I want to do, as long as I take it one step at a time." The opportunity for greatness, according to the late sales trainer Charlie Cullen, does not come cascading down like a torrential Niagara Falls. Rather it comes slowly, one drop at a time!

Here is your challenge: Make a list of your ten most important Action Steps to Success. Not what someone else must do to succeed, not what someone else thinks *you* should do to succeed, but what *you know you must do every day!* I fully under-

10 *ACTION* Steps to Success

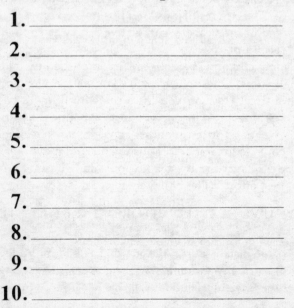

1. _____
2. _____
3. _____
4. _____
5. _____
6. _____
7. _____
8. _____
9. _____
10. _____

stand that you do more than ten things daily, but what are the ten most important activities that translate to success for you?

At the time I set the sales records I spoke of, I was selling cookware. I was conducting demonstration parties, cooking with the heavy-duty waterless cookware I was encouraging people to buy. Many times it would be 1:00 A.M. before the kitchen was cleaned and everyone was gone, but number one on my list was to be face-to-face with a prospect at 9:00 A.M. the next day. Regardless of the fact that the baby kept us up until 3:30; despite the fact that the car had a flat tire or wouldn't start; regardless of any excuses, I was to be face-to-face with a live prospect at 9:00 A.M. *every morning!* When we set our goals and break them into bite-size pieces, there is no limit to what will be accomplished. A commitment to *start* each day at the same time and in the same way is really a commitment to finish, because starting is obviously the first step in arriving. The Chinese were right: A journey of a thousand leagues begins with a single step.

WHAT'S HOLDING YOU BACK?

It is an established fact that the largest and most powerful locomotive in the world can be held in place by a one-inch block of wood. Placed in front of the eight drive wheels of the locomotive, the block will hold it completely motionless. Yet that same locomotive, with a full head of steam, can crash through a steel-reinforced concrete wall that is five feet thick. That is what getting the action habit can do for us! This next example by William Moulton Marston is from the world of sports, but it certainly applies to us in the world of business.

Hitting the Ball

I asked Babe Ruth what was the most exciting moment of his career, and he told me it was during the third game of his last World Series in Chicago. He was in a batting slump, his team was behind, and two strikes had been called on him. The crowd turned against the Babe and began to boo. Ruth's desire to win rose to meet this emergency and he flashed into action. He pointed to a distant spot in the outfield and yelled back at the howling fans, "I'll knock it out there for you!"

Babe smashed the next ball to that precise spot. It was a home run, the longest hit ever made in Wrigley Field. I asked him what he thought about when the ball was pitched.

"What'd I think about?" he snorted. "Why, what I always think about—just hittin' the ball!"

There's your champion, the man who keeps his attention riveted upon his present act and who responds positively to every crisis or desire with all there is in him. With the outcome of a World Series and his own contract for next year hanging in the balance, Ruth thought about hitting the ball. And because he wanted to win more than he ever had before, he hit the ball hard.

The next time you find yourself in a jam, with a string of mistakes behind you and everything hanging on your next move, forget both past and future. Remember Babe Ruth and think about just one thing—hitting the ball.

Let yourself go—give everything you have to your desire to win before the crisis passes. It will be the best performance you ever produced because of the emotional steam behind it. Every crisis offers you extra desired power.

PERSONAL CONVICTION: POSITIVE THINKING AND POSITIVE BELIEVING

When we talk about being people of action, we recognize that action takes courage. Gerhard Gschwandtner of Fredericksburg, Virginia, publishes an excellent sales publication called *Personal Selling Power*, which I highly recommend. One of my favorite parts of Gerhard's format is the interview with action-oriented people. In a recent issue, Mo Siegel was the "interviewee." Now, Mo Siegel is the founder and former owner (he recently sold the business) of Celestial Seasonings, the herbal tea company which captured a major portion of the multimillion-dollar tea industry. He based his organization on a value system he equates with the four legs on a stool. The first leg is *love of product*. Mo Siegel surrounded himself with people who really loved herbal tea and believed it to be valuable to the consumer. The second leg of the stool was *love of customer* (which, in the case of Celestial Seasonings, was distributors). Celestial Seasonings put the customer first in quality-control decisions. The third leg of the stool was *love of art and beauty*, which led Mo Siegel to develop one of the most detailed (and expensive) packaging programs in retail sales. The fourth leg of the stool was *dignity of the individual*. Celestial Seasonings treated everyone (including employees) with the dignity every human being deserves. Any time a serious question arose within the organization, Mo Siegel said the solution would lie within the answers to two more questions: (1) Is the customer happy? (2) Are we making the best possible product?

The answer to that second question led him to commission "blind tea taste tests" in which his product consistently beat the major "black tea" or nonherbal teas which have the major share of the market. Despite overwhelming evidence that Celestial Seasonings had a superior product, Mo Siegel refused to use the concept in an advertising campaign. His personal convictions led him to spend his time and resources in serving the customer better. He stated, "I decided I did not want to make a fortune by bad-mouthing anybody!"

With the current trend in advertising doing exactly that, Mo Siegel's decision was one requiring courage and integrity. Siegel went on to say that "an organization values what it dedicates its time and resources to." In his case it is obvious that he values integrity. He also stated that the reason he was able to grow so big so quickly was his commitment to training. He said that managers need a minimum of thirty hours of training per year and salespeople need even more. I might add I agree with him that training is tremendously important, because it helps change a person from a "positive thinker" to a "positive believer."

Here's the difference: Positive thinking is the optimistic hope—not necessarily based on any facts—that you can move mountains or accomplish other seemingly impossible tasks. I've seen positive thinking and positive thinkers accomplish some incredible things. I've also seen some people get into serious trouble because all they had was positive thinking and enthusiasm. They had no foundations, no skills, no training. Consequently, they let their enthusiasm carry them away and they ended up in serious difficulties. (Someone has said that positive thinking and enthusiasm is like running in the dark—it might get you there, but you might get killed along the way!) Add training to that positive thinking and enthusiasm and you turn on the lights for your trip to the top—which means you will arrive alive.

Positive believing is the same optimistic hope as positive thinking, but it is based on solid reasons for believing you can move mountains or accomplish other seemingly impossible tasks. I've seen positive believers accomplish far more than positive thinkers. Positive believers have even more enthusiasm than positive thinkers because their enthusiasm is based on solid reasons, which gives them the motivation for the long haul, even when things are not going well at the moment.

A good training program—which is obviously what Mo Siegel was talking about—gives the members of his organization solid reasons for believing they can accomplish much with their lives. They believe in their company, they believe in their product, and training enables them to believe in their ability to communicate that belief to others who will, in turn, take action by buying.

I might add this simple example to further illustrate the difference between positive thinking and positive believing: If you are a positive thinker, you probably feel you could set sail for France today and successfully sell your product in that country. If your product is a highly sophisticated one that is sold only in the big cities to successful businesspeople, the odds would be fairly favorable because most of those people would also speak a second language—probably English—and you would be able to communicate with them. However, if your product is one which is sold in the rural areas, the odds are great they would only be able to speak French. With only "positive thinking" on your list of skills, you would have serious difficulty communicating the merits of your product to those prospects. A positive believer, however, would be one who knew the French language and understood something of the culture and the thinking of the people. Consequently, if you were to study the language and the culture and prepare yourself properly to deal with the situations you would encounter in rural France, your chances of being successful would be dramatically increased.

Positive thinking is always important and it certainly will enable you to accompish more than negative thinking will—but positive believing will enable you to do infinitely more than just positive thinking will. That's why in *Top Performance* we give so many steps, procedures, and actions to follow so that, as a leader and as a manager, you move more and more into the positive-believing realm.

A VERY "MOVING" EXPERIENCE

In April and May of 1985, the Zig Ziglar Corporation headquarters was relocated. We had outgrown our building located on Alpha and Omega because in approximately five years we had grown from less than fifteen employees to over sixty employees. About now some of the more astute of you readers are wondering why it took nearly two full months to move a company of less than one hundred employees! To be very honest with you, I had the same question myself!

Due to circumstances beyond our control, we needed to vacate the building we owned and had sold at Alpha and Omega by March 31. However, our new facility wasn't to be ready until May 15. Six to eight weeks without office space is not the best way to run a business. There was every opportunity for "stinkin' thinkin'" to creep into the attitude of our staff. However, due to the excellent leadership of Ron Ezinga, ZZC president, and Den Roossien, ZZC executive vice-president, and our divisional leaders, these two months became the two largest dollar-volume months to that point in the history of our company! Everyone worked from their homes with the exception of a skeleton crew which handled the computer and order-processing station we kept at our old building, and a valiant crew who manned the phones in the new building. I say "valiant" because the only space available in the new building was an area designed to be used for storage that measured approximately ten-by-fourteen feet. Initially there was no electricity or heating in this area.

For about a week these brave ladies answered phones by the natural light of a partially open door. They wrapped themselves in blankets and stocking caps to ward off the cold. After the first week, we got electricity into the room and the door could be kept shut, though there still was no heat except from portable units. There was *never* any grousing or complaining by this group (who, by the way, had volunteered to take care of the phones). They worked the phones and coordinated activities between two locations for offices and approximately forty-five or fifty homes.

Every person in our company *had* to pitch in to make the move work, and frankly most of us would have been glad just to keep from losing a large amount of business. But I am proud to be able to report to you that our "People Building Team" worked together to prove that they are "products of our product" and turned a potentially losing problem into a winning opportunity!

THE "TEAM" CONCEPT

A great deal of emphasis is almost always given to the team concept in superior management books. At the Zig Ziglar Corporation we believe in and stress this concept. As a matter of fact, each leadership unit functions as a team and is given a team name. Our organizational chart looks like this:

The Customer: Everyone's check is ultimately signed by the customer. The customer allows us to stay in business so he belongs at the top of our chart.

The People Building Team: This is the name we give to our staff. The People Building Team works for the customer.

The Leadership Team: This is the name we give our department heads and divisional leaders. Their responsibility is to give leadership and direction to the company, and they work for the People Building Team.

The Development Team: This is the name we give our corporate officers. Their responsibility (in addition to leading their respective areas of the company) lies in long-range planning and development. They work for the Leadership Team.

Zig Ziglar: This is my name. My "title" is Chairman of the Board. My responsibility is to speak and write and give "vision" and "direction" to our organization. I work for all these people!

Most people would say that our triangle is upside down. I think that after getting this far into *Top Performance* you understand that this is the best way for a company to reach its full potential. At a recent People Building Team meeting we shared the following article, "From 9–5." Because it does such a great job of summarizing this team concept, I wanted to share it in full with you.

"Have You Joined the Team?"

Most of us work in departments as part of a network of people who make up our company's team. If our company's service or product is good, there are others to share the credit. If it's poor, there are people to share the blame. But if we believe the old saying that a chain is only as strong as its weakest link, we know that our company's performance is only as good as ours.

Each of us makes a choice as to the role we'll play on the team. We either join it as an actively caring member, or we go through the motions from the sidelines. When we choose to join the team, we have a better, surer shot at work that brings us satisfaction. The choice is ours. Here are the key attitudes that take us off the sideline.

I make a difference here. I know that what I do makes it possible for my office to run smoothly. The effort I put into my job shows up in the quality of my office's services and in my company's earnings.

I'm part of what outsiders see when they judge my organization. With every letter, every phone conversation, every personal contact, I make a statement about the caliber of service we offer. In the course of a year, I make hundreds of valuable business contacts for us.

How I feel on a given day affects the people I work with. I help to set the tone here. I know that when I bring real enthusiasm to the job, I make a contribution few others can equal.

I take responsibility for what bothers me. When a situation is causing me trouble at work, I approach it as my problem. Whether it's a procedure which isn't working, a practice I feel is unfair, or a person I'm having difficulty working with, I do what I can to change the situation. Sometimes it takes patience. More often than not, it takes knowing when to speak up and when to wait, and how to coolly and rationally use my powers of persuasion.

When I can't get a situation changed, I look for ways to minimize its effect on me. Most important, I remember that I've chosen to work here, and so long as I'm here, I'll give my best.

I take an interest in my company. I know that an organization is greater than the sum of its parts; it has a life and personality of its own. I'm interested in how this company got to be what it is today, and how the people in it have grown as it has.

My knowledge of the workings of the company not only helps me in my work, but also makes the work more interesting. It's part of what makes me a valuable employee here; and it helps me set my own career goals and plan my future.

I try to see the big picture—to think beyond my particular job to the kind of product or service I'd like to receive as a customer or client. Because I'm interested in what makes us successful, I notice what's happening in business, politics, or technology that's going to affect us.

I'm proud to be a strong, reliable member of my company's team. I know that *my* success, as well as my company's, depends on it.

Action completes our Three-*A* Formula. Action brings Awareness and Analysis to fruition. Top Performance as a person or as a manager depends on all three. If you will take Action on the concepts we have talked about in this chapter and consciously make a decision to join the team, then you will become even more of a Top Performer.

PERFORMANCE PRINCIPLES

1. More people act their way into thinking than think their way into acting.
2. Logic won't change an emotion, but action will.
3. Action often precedes the feeling.
4. If the first three principles sound a great deal alike, Congratulations! You are catching on!

It Takes Time

There can be no persevering industry without a
deep sense of the value of time.
                                    Lydia H. Sigourney

---

16 The unfortunate truth is that far too many executives are so gung ho and goal-oriented from a
career point of view that they often lose perspective and balance as far as their personal,
family, and social lives are concerned. The prime
reason for this chapter, which I consider the most important
one in the book, is to encourage you to become a Top Performer in your personal, family, and social life as well as in
your business career. Interestingly enough, when you live the
balanced life in your personal, home, and community life, in
the long run you will do better in your business career. Yes, I
know what you're thinking: *But Ziglar, there are only twenty-four
hours in the day.* I agree that it takes time and, as a matter of
fact, that is the title of this chapter, so let's get on with it.

TAKE TIME TO GET STARTED

The chances are better than good that you have fallen victim to that great American habit of sleeping as late as is humanly possible and then, when that "opportunity clock" sounds off, you hop out of bed and go through all the procedures which are so popular in America today.

We generally get up at least thirty minutes too late, turn on the coffee maker, the radio, the television, rush in to shave and shower or apply our makeup. We awaken the kids in a big, big bustle, get them out of bed telling them to "hurry, hurry, or we're going to be late!" It generally takes about two trips, however, to get them up and the second trip is not even as pleasant as the first one. They're sleepy and in most cases slow-moving. We finally get them half-dressed, rush them into the den, plop a bowl of sugar-rich, nutritionless cereal in front of them, encourage them to hurry while we're drinking our coffee and eating our piece of toast or a generally inadequate breakfast.

We hustle to get dressed, quickly put the dishes in the sink or in the dishwasher, make certain the cat has been fed and put outdoors, bundle the kids up, rush out to the car, back out the driveway fighting for every traffic break, silently most of the time but vociferously some of the time, fussing at those people who delay our progress toward our assigned goal. We dump the kids out at school, drive hurriedly or madly on down to the office, where we're in a hurry-hurry environment all day long.

In a nutshell, it's a serious mistake to start your day that way because the way you start your day often determines how that day is going to go and will ultimately play a part in *how many* days you have.

With that in mind, I urge you to start your day in an organized but pleasant and relaxed way. You should do one of three things, and all of them involve getting up earlier.

One option you have is to start the day quietly in one of two ways. Select a quiet nook in your home, such as an office, a library, the den, or someplace away from the flow of traffic. As a leader and manager in your company, you need to start the day refreshed and prepared for the day's activities. From my personal experience, I can tell you that when I rise early and have that quiet time, my day goes better—much better. This excerpt from an article by Eugene Peterson in the November 8, 1985 issue of *Christianity Today* puts it in proper perspective:

> In Herman Melville's *Moby Dick* there is a violent, turbulent scene in which a whaleboat scuds across the frothing ocean in pursuit of the great white whale, Moby Dick. The sailors are laboring fiercely, every muscle taut, all attention and energy concentrated on the task. The cosmic conflict between good and evil is joined: the chaotic sea and demonic sea monster versus the morally outraged man, Captain Ahab.
>
> In this boat there is one man who does nothing. He does not hold an oar; he does not perspire; he does not shout. He is languid in the crash and the cursing. This man is the harpooner, quiet and poised, waiting. And then this sentence: "To insure the greatest efficiency of the dart, the harpooners of this world must start to their feet out of idleness, and not from out of toil."

In the corporate world we might not be faced with the physical danger, nor have a great need for a burst of physical energy, but we are faced with different kinds of "opportunities" which are emotionally and physically draining. To move into these challenges from a time of restful rejuvenation can make a significant difference in our effectiveness.

One of my favorite methods of doing this is to start the day—especially in cold weather—in my office at home with the gas log burning. Sometimes I sit there quietly, thinking through a planned project or agenda, wrestling with the best and most creative way to handle an "opportunity," quoting Scripture or thinking on inspirational thoughts or messages. The first few minutes are the toughest. The temptation to get up and move around is sometimes overwhelming, but I can assure you that if you will quietly sit there, some very creative, inspiring thoughts and ideas will be yours by the time you rise.

You also can, without any notes, quietly work through some situations in which you've been involved. Maybe there's a problem or a puzzle you've been unable to solve. As you are sitting there (in most cases not totally awake), you're still in the "alpha" level of consciousness. At this level your creativity is at its very, very best—a marvelous, extremely productive way to start the day!

The second option you have in starting your day also involves getting up earlier and this option includes reading something of an inspirational nature, such as the Bible or an inspirational book, or listening to recordings which are motivational in nature. Reading or listening are both marvelous ways to get "up" for the day. As a matter of fact, some psychologists have determined that your first encounter of the day has a more direct bearing on your attitude for that day than your next five encounters. Now, I'm not speaking about a "hello" encounter; I'm talking about a significant encounter where you spend time with a person. With this in mind, if you set aside fifteen to thirty minutes early in the morning to "encounter" someone of your choice, either to listen to an inspirational recording or dig into an inspirational book, you will have made a deliberate choice of starting your day with someone who will lift you and inspire you. With that kind of start, it's much easier to keep the momentum going.

The third option for the day, and a very effective way to start it, is with exercise. Later in this chapter I will give you the whys of an exercise program, but it is sufficient to say that one of the most exciting ways to start your day is with physical exercise of some kind. This can involve calisthenics, a swim or bicycle ride, a walk, or it could involve jogging. At any rate, a good exercise program gets the adrenaline flowing and those endorphines to hoppin', and you've got the day off to a flying start.

Yes, I'm absolutely convinced that when you start your day in one of these three ways, and then awaken the other members of the family, your prospects for a productive day are infinitely greater. Your mate will be especially appreciative and you can enhance your family relationship if you awaken him or her with that steaming cup of coffee (or better yet, herbal tea), and a few minutes of getting reacquainted in the morning. Then casually and lovingly awaken the children and while one team member prepares breakfast, the other one can help the kids get ready for school.

Since breakfast is such an important part of the day, both physically and emotionally, husband and wife (and children, if there are any) should sit down and, at a more leisurely pace, have a nutritious breakfast together. It properly starts the kids' day, the family's day, and your day on a high note. It will make an overall difference in your own attitude and your own physical well-being—not to mention what it will do for the kids and your mate. When this happens, more harmony in the family will develop.

One thing that is becoming more and more obvious is that when there is harmony in the family, the effectiveness of the manager on the job is noticeably enhanced. As part of this concept, we know a good, nutritious breakfast enables a person to perform more efficiently and effectively during the day. Eating together establishes bonds between family members that simply cannot be established in any other way. They are most effective. I say it again—take time to get started.

TAKE TIME TO GROW

We have emphasized throughout *Top Performance* the necessity of personal growth for maximum business success. We're all familiar with the story of the woodcutter whose production kept going down because he did not take time to sharpen his axe. As we've indicated throughout the book, the top companies, the ones with the exciting bottom lines, have training and personal growth as major corporate objectives. It's true, the companies "on the go" are also "on the grow." Individually *you* need to take time to grow.

There are many ways to do this, of course, but one of the most effective ways is the utilization of the cassette player in your car. There are literally thousands of hours of recorded material which can be enormously helpful to you while you're going to and from your work. You can learn everything from Chinese art to a foreign language. You can learn how to set goals or close sales. You can learn how to invest in real estate and save on your income tax.

As a matter of fact, a study done several years ago at the University of Southern California revealed that you can acquire the equivalent of two years of college education in just three years while you're going about your normal activities in your automobile. This is assuming you live in a metropolitan area and drive twelve thousand miles each year.

Think about it. By utilizing your time in your car you can become knowledgeable—even expert—in your chosen field and several related ones. That gives you incredible security, regardless of what happens to your company or your relationship with your company. The exciting thing is that to acquire knowledge in that method is one of the fastest, easiest, and certainly one of the most painless ways ever devised.

You also can grow through the utilization of the marvelous books which are available today. The bookstores carry an enormous assortment of books which deal with virtually any subject related to your career and specifically with any aspect of dealing with self and interpersonal relationships. Needless to say, the public library also offers a variety of books if you do not feel inclined to buy them. It is my own personal conviction, however, that as a manager and as a leader, you need to build a substantial library of your own. Personally, I would hesitate to put a price tag on the dollar value of my library, but it would run into thousands of dollars.

Let me offer a couple of suggestions about how you should read and effectively use your books. First—and I realize this sounds selfish—I encourage you to be protective with your books. Keep them for your own personal use or permit others to use them only in your library. In most cases, I encourage you to say no to anyone who wants to borrow a book. (I know for a fact that people often don't return books. For example, I have a number of books in my own library and have no idea how they got there!) If someone cannot afford the book, then do one of two things: encourage him or her to join the library or, if it's a friend, go ahead and buy the book for him. As you build your career and develop your leadership skills, you need to have at your fingertips the resources you accumulate. Needless to say, most doctors and attorneys do not loan their resource material. Your needs are fully as great and your professionalism should certainly be equal to a doctor or lawyer.

When I read a book, or *anything* else, I always have a pen in my hand and I profusely mark the parts which are important to me. I underline, circle, make notes, etc. In the front of the book I jot down page numbers of those things that are particularly important and significant and which I feel will be useful in the future. I then file the books in my library according to the categories of study. This way, when I need information on a particular subject, I go to the correct section, open the book, and find notations in front directing me exactly where to find what I need.

Of all the skills which I have acquired, I believe the ability to read and to enjoy reading is one of the most important things I've ever learned. I encourage you, as a leader, to not only teach your children how to read but also to teach them how to *enjoy* the reading—make it come alive for them and they will be better for having done it. Ditto for your associates and subordinates. As you read the good books and listen to the good tapes, you'll have a daily source of magnificent inspiration.

The third area of growth should be through meetings and seminars. There are many marvelous educational seminars around this country which can help you to hone your skills and develop them to the degree that will enable you to move up the ladder of success and happiness much faster and more effectively. As a practical matter, you should set aside at least one full week each year to go to seminars and personal-growth opportunities which enable you to develop and bring out your inherent abilities. You should also be open to attending half-day and full-day specialized seminars once or twice each month.

I say it again: To really make it big in life—in all areas of your life—you need to take time to grow. It's not a question of whether you do or do not have time. Obviously you do not have that option. You don't have time *not* to grow.

TAKE TIME TO BE HEALTHY

One question I often ask my audiences is if there is a person there who has a thoroughbred horse worth in excess of a million dollars. So far, no one has seriously raised a hand to indicate he has one. I then ask the question "If you *did* have a thoroughbred worth a million dollars, would you keep him up half the night, letting him drink coffee or booze, smoke cigarettes, and eat junk food?" At this everybody laughs, because they realize that not only do thoroughbreds not drink coffee or booze or smoke cigarettes, but the idea of jeopardizing the horse's health—which obviously destroys the performance of the animal—would be so ridiculous as to be beyond discussion.

Then I ask, "Suppose you had a ten-dollar dog? Would you treat him that way?" And again, there's laughter. "What about

a five-dollar cat?" Then I point out that most of us would not treat a five-dollar cat like we treat our own billion-dollar bodies. As far as a million-dollar thoroughbred is concerned, if we had such an animal we would probably keep him in an air-conditioned barn in the summertime and a steam-heated one in the wintertime. We'd hire the best veterinarian money could buy to look after him, and bring in a special nutritionist to make certain he was properly fed. In addition to that, we would get the finest trainer available to develop his potential. You can count on it, you would take care of a million-dollar thoroughbred, and yet we abuse our own billion-dollar bodies.

Actually, to take care of our bodies is a reasonably simple routine. I did not say "easy." There are several factors involved and, since I'm not an expert on any of them, I will simply make some observations and aim you at some of the experts. To begin with, I would encourage you to pick up Dr. Kenneth Cooper's book *The Aerobics Program for Total Well-Being*. This deals not only with exercise but with proper nutrition as well.

One of the things you need to consider is the amount of sleep you get. Some people do quite well on four or five hours. In my own case, I've discovered that it requires seven and one-half hours of sleep for me to achieve Top Performance. Since I know that, I conscientiously work at getting that amount of sleep each evening. Now, I can get by one night with much less sleep and do fairly well the second night, but if it goes three nights in a row, I can guarantee you that by the third day I am at considerably less than my most effective best. For that reason, I work and concentrate on getting a reasonable amount of sleep.

Exercise is the second area which is extremely important. I am a jogger by choice—I literally *love* to jog. However, there are many people who do not like that particular exercise. According to Dr. Cooper, the important thing is that you keep your heartbeat up for at least twenty minutes on about four occasions each week. Fast walking is a marvelous exercise. Riding a stationary bicycle—or, for that matter, one in the streets—is excellent exercise. You might consider those rebounders where you simply bounce up and down—they do a great job. Others prefer swimming, and some experts say that is the most desirable of all exercise programs. Still others enjoy cross-country skiing or racquetball, tennis, etc. The important thing is that you keep that heartbeat up at least twenty minutes on about four days each week. Intelligent adults always begin their exercise programs by seeing their doctors. Please *do not* skip this most important step.

I am often asked, "Well, Zig, with as much as you have to do, when do you have time to exercise? When do you have time to jog?" I often tell people that I've got so much to do, I don't have time *not* to exercise. Incidentally, when I'm on the road and the weather is bad, I jog up and down the corridors of the hotel or motel where I'm staying. On occasion I go into the hotel ballroom or meeting room and run around it. On other occasions, I've jogged in the shopping malls. I am not a hero and therefore do not run around dark streets at night. If the weather's good but it's night and I'm not absolutely certain of the area, I simply run in the parking lot or the parking garage of the facility at which I am staying.

From a time point of view, let me point out that when you jog or exercise, you activate the pituitary gland. The pituitary gland floods the system with endorphines which are over two hundred times more powerful than morphine. The net result is you are on a "natural chemical high" from two to as much as four or even five hours. I have found the best time investment ever to be my time invested in exercise. An hour invested in exercise (counting time to dress, exercise, shower, cool down, etc.) returns two to four times that much high productivity time. The ideal time, according to Dr. Cooper, is in the latter part of the afternoon or early evening. By exercising then, you actually extend your effective work day by several hours.

Number three, in order to be at your healthiest, I encourage you to eat a sensible diet. By that, I mean a well-balanced diet and again, Dr. Cooper's book will be helpful. In my own diet, I concentrate on fresh vegetables, fish, chicken, and whole-grain cereals, and I seek as much roughage as possible. In addition to that, though there is widespread disagreement on this subject, I take and have been taking a natural food supplement for a number of years. Many doctors will tell you that in a well-balanced diet you will get the minimum daily requirements for your health. My point, though, is simply that I am not interested in minimum daily requirements. I am interested in maximum daily performance, and for that reason I do use a natural food supplement.

The fourth step in caring for your health is to eliminate the negatives. Smoking is a tremendous negative. Nineteen deaths out of every one hundred are directly traced to the habit of smoking. Every time you light a cigarette you have chosen to die fourteen minutes earlier. Needless to say, if you smoke cigarettes you're not going to enjoy the maximum health which you could otherwise enjoy.

Booze is another one of those elements in your life which in most cases can be enormously destructive. If you are a "casual" drinker, I would encourage you to read *Dying for a Drink* by Anderson Spickard, M.D., and Barbara R. Thompson, and it might put drinking in a different perspective. I don't pretend to be an authority on the subject, but I've seen a great deal of grief resulting from drinking and I do know that one "casual, social" drinker out of nine will eventually end up with a serious drinking problem. I also know that alcohol is a depressant and that people don't function as effectively when they've had a drink as they do without that drink.

Obviously, the other poisons you want to eliminate are those harmful legal and illegal drugs. The evidence against pot, speed, cocaine, and heroin, as well as many other drugs, is overwhelming. I cannot believe anyone with the intellectual capacity to occupy a leadership or management position would be so foolish as to ignore the overwhelming evidence as to what these substances do to a person and then deliberately "play" with them on a casual, "sometimes" basis.

Thus far in my own career I have never met a single human being who deliberately set out to become an alcoholic or who deliberately had as an objective to become a "pothead" or a drug addict. The question you need to ask yourself is, "Is it worth even a slight risk to experiment with these substances which can destroy me personally, socially, careerwise, and wreck my family all at the same time?" No, when I'm talking about taking time to be healthy, I'm talking about eliminating the poisons which some people choose to put into their systems.

TAKE TIME TO PLAY

Most of the gung ho businessmen and women I know set goals on acquiring new cars, getting promotions, having a certain amount of money in the bank, living at a certain residence, acquiring some educational degree, achieving that plateau of accomplishment, excelling in this area. They set goals in every area of their lives, but often they do not set their objectives properly when it comes to taking time to play. I am absolutely convinced that unless we schedule recreational activities for ourselves and for our families, our own mental, physical, social, and family relationships are going to suffer. When that happens, it's just a question of time before our careers will suffer.

When you check on the top-level executives—those who occupy positions of responsibility—you discover that one of the major problems is executive burnout. This problem can be at least partially alleviated with a willingness to take the time to play. It could be racquetball or tennis or a regularly scheduled round of golf. It could be playing on the company slow-pitch softball team or pickup basketball. My friend Dr. James Dobson, the Christian psychologist who has such an effective work through his radio ministry and through his publications, is one of the busiest men I've ever encountered. Yet he regularly sets aside time for basketball. He and his family go skiing. He takes care of his physical and family well-being by indulging in these forms of exercise.

I believe the capacity to relax and enjoy yourself is an absolute must for those who would climb the ladder and then maintain their position once they have achieved it. You bring a fresh perspective, a fresh excitement, a fresh enthusiasm to what you're doing when you are enjoying life itself. I don't mean just enjoying your job but also enjoying the fact that you are alive and well, and that you are getting more out of life than a paycheck. A move up the corporate ladder and recognition as a community leader can be, even *should* be, your objectives. Financial success and corporate ladder climbing are worthy objectives, but within themselves they do not make you happy if you're not having fun along the way. There is nothing wrong with scheduling your playtime just as enthusiastically as you schedule your work time. I'm assuming you understand that I'm not talking about playing as much as you work, but a regular game of handball or racquetball, a round of golf, or an evening with the family at the movies, theater, church, or community activity on a regular basis can make a difference in your quality of life as well as your accomplishments in life.

TAKE TIME TO BE QUIET

When I handle the next subject in my speeches, I always prepare the audiences by saying, "My next statement is probably going to surprise you, because generally speaking I am quite outgoing." I'm so "loud" from the platform that you might not realize or think in terms of my being quiet, but actually I am by nature a quiet person. Regardless of our natures, *all* of us need to take time to be quiet. I've never known anyone who accomplished major objectives in life who did not take time to be quiet.

As I indicated when I talked about "Take Time to Get Started," we do live in a busy and noisy world and there are those occasions when your batteries are simply going to run down. When that happens, no amount of superficial charging is going to restore those energy cells to their proper level unless you do take that time to be quiet. I dearly love to jog, and my favorite time to jog, particularly in the summer months, is at around nine o'clock in the evening under a bright, moonlit sky. It seems that when those conditions prevail and I'm running in the neighborhood I love so much, I have a renewal of energy that is absolutely incredible. My most productive ideas frequently come as I am doing that jogging. As a matter of fact, much of my contribution to this book was first conceived during my jogging time.

Another of my favorite quiet times is early in the morning when I get up and go into my office. During that period of time some of my most creative ideas are born. In the summer months, late at night, I also love to go out into my swimming pool, which we primarily built for the grandchildren. It's a rare occasion when I actually use it for swimming, but late at night I love to get in, dog-paddle out to the middle of the pool, quietly lay on my back, and put my mind in neutral. The purpose of going into the pool is to get ideas, and it's a rare occasion when I come out of that pool without a creative idea or some thought or concept which is helpful in my personal, business, or family life.

I strongly encourage you to take time to be quiet. There are occasions when you will want to share that quiet time with someone you love—a slow walk (this is not for exercise purposes) with a son or daughter or your mate, when you are in no hurry to do anything except be with that person. It's amazing how close you can draw to that individual as you walk, but it also is amazing how you will develop ideas when you explore with someone you love in a casual, unhurried, completely relaxed manner, a concept or idea you've been wrestling with. When talking in detail to your mate about your business, even though your mate might not have the expertise or specific knowledge you possess, you'll be astonished at how much he or she can contribute with fresh insights. Spouses are generally free of your job-related prejudices and they're not encumbered with a lot of preconceived ideas, so they can look at the overall picture and come up with ideas which are meaningful and helpful. The questions they ask can provoke creative thinking on your part and perhaps force you to take a look from a different perspective.

Take time to be quiet. It might be a few minutes puttering around in your garden, pulling weeds, or looking at great length at some of the miracles of nature which are all around us for the enjoying, if we will but take time to take a peek. Need I remind you that it was during those still, quiet moments at Valley Forge that George Washington found the strength to deal with the problems of winning our freedom and looking after freezing, starving troops? Need I remind you that it was during those still, dark moments, during that great Civil War which threatened to split our nation asunder, that Abraham Lincoln found the strength and the resolve to pull our nation together and see to it that we were reunited as one? It was during those still, quiet moments at Gethsemane that Jesus Christ found the strength to face the awful ordeal which was in front of Him. During still, quiet moments you will find resources which you might never have known existed. Take time to be quiet—and to listen.

TAKE TIME FOR THOSE YOU LOVE

One tragic myth which permeates our society is the belief that you can't be a hard-charging, successful businessman *and* a loving, caring husband and father. That myth was exploded several years ago and reinforced in the January 13, 1986 *U.S. News & World Report* article on the one million "ordinary" millionaires. This article points out that 80 percent of them came from middle- or working-class families and that a stable home life with few outside distractions provides the ordinary millionaire with the stamina to persevere in business. Most of them have lasting marriages, often to their high school or college sweethearts, and are likely to "spoil" (be especially kind to) their spouses and children. They have often suffered adversity. Twice as many salesmen as doctors will be millionaires by age sixty, and fewer than 1 percent of the millionaires are artists, entertainers, writers, and athletes. To me, what this really says is that successful people—including successful managers—have a balanced approach to life. The next example emphasizes this point.

A couple of years ago I stopped by to congratulate the president of a major corporation on his recent promotion. He greeted me with considerable enthusiasm and insisted I sit down so he could share with me the role he said I had played in his promotion. This was entirely unexpected, since my sole purpose was to invest sixty seconds to express my congratulations, but the new president would have none of it.

"You know, Zig," he said, "I honestly believe your talk on 'Courtship After Marriage,' which we use in our video training department, played a substantial role in this promotion." Then he went ahead to tell me the story.

"Our marriage was one of those which was truly out of the book. We both came from the 'right side of the tracks,' both went to marvelous schools, both came from successful family backgrounds. Upon graduation from college we got married and I proceeded to join the 'right' clubs while my wife started serving in the 'right' charities. We were active in our church and had the 'right number' of children." (Meaning they had two. I'm glad my parents didn't feel that was the right number, since I was the tenth of twelve!)

He continued his story: "I want to emphasize, Zig, that our marriage was a good one, but over the years we had gotten a little platonic in our relationship. But as I listened to you talk about your Redhead, I realized that although I had nearly twenty fewer birthdays than you, there seemed to be more excitement in your marriage, so I determined to see if the same thing could happen in mine. I was particularly intrigued with the fact you pointed out that, according to a West German insurance company, when a man kissed his wife good-bye— *really* kissed her good-bye [not like his little sister, but as we'd say down home, really 'stropped one on 'er!'], those men lived 5.6 six years longer than the men who neglected this pleasant little interlude in their lives on a daily basis. [Fellows, your life is at stake!] Not only that, but these men earn from twenty to thirty percent more money than do the men who leave home under their own power.

"With that in mind," he said, "I decided to start really courting my wife. I started picking up the phone and giving her a call for a moment or two during coffee breaks each day. I frequently dropped a little note in the mail or bought her a neat little card or I would take a single flower home. On occasion we had those 'heavy dates' when we really went out for a marvelous time. I went back to opening all doors for her, standing up when she got up to leave the table, holding her chair when she returned—all the little things our ladies so deeply appreciate. Now Zig, I'll have to confess that the changes were not instantaneous, but in a matter of just a few weeks, excitement definitely returned to our marriage. The intriguing thing is, that excitement carried over into the marketplace and made me a happier, more productive executive. I'm absolutely convinced my efforts at the company were recognized and I was promoted to the presidency primarily because of the increase in my effectivenes, which was brought about by the excitement which returned to my marriage. So I just want to say thank you."

I left his office and headed upstairs to congratulate the chairman of the board, whose promotion had created the presidential vacancy. The president called to tell him I was on my way. The chairman was equally enthusiastic and insisted I sit down because he, too, had a story to tell. He pointed to the telephone on the back of his credenza and said, "You know, Zig, for a long time when that phone rang I was tempted to snatch it off the hook and demand to know, 'What have the little monsters done now?' Yes, I'm embarrassed to say my teenage son and teenage daughter were little monsters who were driving me up the wall. It seemed that everything my son ate turned to hair, his room was an absolute disgrace, and his stereo could be heard three blocks away. He was totally void of motivation and, even though (or was it because?) I rode him contantly, nothing was getting done. His fourteen-year-old sister had to be one of the most disrespectful, sassy children anywhere. Frankly, I was at my wits' end and I didn't realize it until later, but I was actually avoiding any kind of contact with them at this point in our lives.

"However," he said, "something you said in one of your talks really got my attention. You pointed out that, from time to time, all of us need to just close our eyes and visualize that everyone and everything we love would suddenly be taken completely out of the picture. [I learned that from my friend and fellow speaker Herb True.] When that really hit me it dawned on me that, should something happen to either of my kids, I really would be a brokenhearted man because, despite all of our communication difficulties, I deeply loved them.

"On impulse one afternoon, I picked up the phone, called my son, and asked him if he would like to go watch the Detroit Tigers play the Texas Rangers. When my son recovered from the shock he said, "Sure, Dad." The next day I took off an hour early, picked up my son, and we arrived at the ball park a solid hour before game time. We were able to get excellent seats behind first base and though we are not 'baseball fans' in the real sense, we really got into the act that evening. We quickly learned that we were to boo the other team and cheer the home team, that we would be wise to question the eyesight and integrity of the umpire, and that our guys were always right and the other guys were always wrong. We took the seventh-inning stretch, ate lots of peanuts, drank lots of pop, and ate numbers of hot dogs. When it was all over, we went out for a snack and it was well past one o'clock when we returned home."

He said, "I actually spent more time with my boy that night than I had spent with him in the last six months. I'm not going to tell you that everything was instantly better, but the walls did start crumbling—the communication barrier was broken. We started talking and building a relationship." With tears in his eyes he said, "You know, Zig, I relearned that not only is my son an unusually bright boy but he is also of high moral character and I'm convinced he's going to do something with his life. Strangely enough, I never said another word about his hair and yet today it is respectable in length. I never mentioned cleaning up his room and, to be honest, if the health inspector were to inspect, it would not qualify for a Grade A restaurant permit, but it is acceptable in our home. And as far as the stereo is concerned, we all now enjoy the fact that his music can be heard clearly and distinctly in his own room, but not at the next-door-neighbor's house.

"Not only that, Zig, but a few days later I called my fourteen-year-old daughter and asked her if she'd like to go out to dinner with me that evening. She was delighted, and so I told her to put on her fanciest party dress because we were going to one of those really nice restaurants where I take my important corporate clients. That evening I picked up a little corsage and she looked so pretty in her dress with that flower! We spent over three hours at dinner that evening. We ordered hors d'oeuvres, the fancy entree, and topped it off with a flaming dessert. What a delightful time we had!

"It's almost the same story as with my son. The barriers came tumbling down. I learned that not only is she a very, very bright girl but she has definite objectives in her life. I believe someday she's going to be a marvelous wife and a good mother, if she decides to go the family route, or she's going to have an outstanding career in her chosen field if she decides to concentrate on a business career. More important, Zig, I can tell you that when I leave home every day I know all I have to concentrate on is my job. I'm convinced I am currently the chairman of the board because of the fact that my family situation has straightened up so much. I can commit all my creative energy to my job when I'm on the job because I know everything is fine on the home front."

Isn't it ironic that these two enormously successful corporate executives, who were spending countless hours on their jobs and, as they often told everybody else, "I'm doing this for my family," discovered that when they neglected their families they were not nearly as effective in the corporate world. Once they got their family lives in balance, their corporate lives also improved. After beating around these old bushes for several years, I'm convinced that regardless of whether you are an athlete or an entertainer, whether you're in business for yourself or work for a major corpoation, if you pay attention to the fires on the home front and keep them properly burning, you will move up faster, more effectively, and far more happily in the corporate world.

YEAH—BUT WHERE DO I GET THE ENERGY?

I've an idea that virtually every reader will agree, at least in principle, with the idea that a good relationship with your family is helpful to your business career. However, you just might be thinking, *Yeah, but where do I get the energy to be a good family person* and *a super manager?* This next illustration should provide you with at least a partial answer.

All of us are motivated about somebody or something in our lives. That's important to understand because motivation literally creates energy. As a matter of fact, in most cases when we claim to be "tired," we are actually mentally or emotionally drained and not physically exhausted. In short, our motivational bucket is running low. Example: Have you ever had one of "those" days? You started with a flat tire which caused you to miss an important engagement. Your office manager called in sick and you had to handle an incredible number of administrative details which you intensely dislike. The air-conditioning unit malfunctioned and made an already boring meeting an impossible one. On top of that, your most productive supervisor resigned. I mean *nothing* went right, and on top of that there is some evidence that you are developing a summer cold. Finally, however, the day mercifully ends and at 5:00 P.M. *sharp* you wearily head for home and some much-needed collapsing time.

A smiling, enthusiastic wife cheerfully welcomes you home and expresses her delight that you did not have to work late because "today is the day." With some dismay you inquire, "The day for what?" Your wife responds, "Why, honey, you remember. Today is the day we've planned for three weeks. Today we're going to clean the garage." Your reaction lies somewhere between exhaustion and anger as you protest that after the trials and tribulations of the day you can't even pick one foot up—much less the four thousand boxes you need to move to clean the garage! Undaunted, your helpmate assures you that she is going to help and it will take only three or four hours.

At that moment the phone rings and, with a tremendous burst of energy, you manage to lift the receiver all the way to your ear and say hello with all the enthusiasm of a kamikaze pilot on his thirty-third mission. The voice on the other end is that of your best golfing buddy with the good news that he has a tee time at the country club in just twenty-three minutes if you feel like getting in a fast nine holes before dark. Guess what? That utterly exhausted, can't-take-another-step body of yours suddenly explodes with energy! Those formerly lifeless legs propel you out to the garage—not to clean it, but to get those golf clubs and hurry out to the country club. You are MOTIVATED!

Now, I'm not about to suggest that your golfing buddy is a better motivator than your wife, but the energy-building motivational appeal (hitting golf balls) was substantially more to your liking than was your wife's inducement ("killing" yourself cleaning that garage!). He was being an effective manager by *channeling the energies* you had in a direction you wanted to go. Effective people managers channel their own energy as well as the energies their people possess at a target they want and need to reach. You've learned how in *Top Performance*. Now do it.

PERFORMANCE PRINCIPLES

1. *Take time to get started.*
2. *Take time to grow.*
3. *Take time to be healthy.*
4. *Take time to play.*
5. *Take time to be quiet.*
6. *Take time for those you love.*

Epilogue
A Unique Opportunity

When I was a small boy in Yazoo City, Mississippi, I worked in a grocery store. Now you must understand that in the late 1930s and early 1940s, things were dramatically different from what they are today. At that time very few kids had money to buy sweets. Molasses candy was one of the delicacies of the day. People would buy molasses and make candy from it. The molasses was kept in a big barrel at the store. When customers brought their jars or jugs in for molasses, we simply filled them from the huge barrel of molasses. From time to time one of the little guys in town who had nothing to do would come into our store to kill time and hope for a handout.

One day a little guy was in the store and thought no one was looking. He carefully took the top off the molasses barrel, stuck his finger in, and put it in his mouth. As he was licking his lips, my boss suddenly appeared and grabbed him by the shoulders, shook him, and said, "Son, don't you ever do that again! That's not sanitary and we won't stand for it!"

The boy was somewhat shaken, but as he left the store I

could tell he was going to survive. A few days later he showed up in the store again. He walked around a few minutes, carefully looked, and when he did not see the owner, he removed the top of the barrel and ran his finger through the molasses. Just as he popped his finger into his mouth, suddenly, out of nowhere, my boss appeared. This time he swatted the little guy across the rear a couple of times and told him to get out of the store and never come back.

You would have thought the kid had learned his lesson, but about ten days later that sweet tooth obviously had gotten to him again and there he was, in the store. Again the owner was nowhere to be seen, so the little guy carefully, cautiously removed the top of the barrel and again ran his finger through the molasses. Just as he was putting it in his mouth, my boss mysteriously reappeared. This time he said nothing as he picked the little guy up and dropped him right into that big barrel of molasses. As he was sinking out of sight you could hear him praying, "Oh, Lord, please give me the tongue to equal this opportunity!"

YOUR CHALLENGE

As I put my thoughts on Top Performance on paper, it has been my prayer *and* my plan to share some information and inspiration which will make a difference in your life. The need for both information and inspiration in our personal and corporate worlds is enormous. The opportunity to benefit many people is great. My prayer is that some idea has struck a responsive chord in you that will enable you to enjoy your life more and be even more effective today than you were yesterday.

The Penalty of Leadership

In every field of human endeavor, he that is first must perpetually live in the white light of publicity.

Whether the leadership be vested in a man or in a manufactured product, emulation and envy are ever at work. In art, in literature, in music, in industry, the reward and the punishment are always the same. The reward is widespread recognition; the punishment, fierce denial and detraction.

When a man's work becomes a standard for the whole world, it also becomes a target for the shafts of the envious few. If his work be merely mediocre, he will be left severely alone—if he achieve a masterpiece, it will set a million tongues a-wagging. Jealousy does not protrude its forked tongue at the artist who produces a commonplace painting.

Whatsoever you write, or paint, or play, or sing, or build, no one will strive to surpass, or to slander you, unless your work be stamped with the seal of genius. Long, long after a great work or a good work has been done, those who are disappointed or envious continue to cry out that it cannot be done. Spiteful little voices in the domain of art were raised against our own Whistler as a mountebank, long after the big world had acclaimed him its greatest artistic genius. Multitudes flocked to Bayreuth to worship at the musical shrine of Wagner, while the little group of those whom he had dethroned and displaced argued angrily that he was no musician at all. The little world continued to protest that Fulton could never build a steamboat, while the big world flocked to the riverbanks to see his boat steam by.

The leader is assailed because he is a leader, and the effort to equal him is merely added proof of that leadership. Failing to equal or to excel, the follower seeks to depreciate and to destroy—but only confirms once more the superiority of that which he strives to supplant.

There is nothing new in this. It is as old as the world and as old as the human passions—envy, fear, greed, ambition, and the desire to surpass. And it all avails nothing. If the leader truly leads, he remains—the leader. Master-poet, master-painter, master-workman, each in his turn is assailed, and each holds his laurels through the ages. That which is good or great makes itself known, no matter how loud the clamor of denial. That which deserves to live—lives.

Yes, leadership has its penalties, but fortunately, it also has its rewards. Here's hoping—and believing—that the principles taught in *Top Performance* will help you reap those rewards.

Recommended Reading

Management and Motivation

Alexander, Scott. *Rhinoceros Success*. Laguna Hills, California: The Rhino's Press, 1980.

Ash, Mary Kay. *Mary Kay on People Management*. New York: Warner Books, 1984.

Blanchard, Kenneth and Spencer Johnson. *The One Minute Manager*. New York: William Morrow and Company, Inc., 1982.

Blanchard, Kenneth and Robert Lorber. *Putting the One Minute Manager to Work*. New York: William Morrow and Company, Inc., 1984.

Bradford, David and Allan R. Cohen. *Managing for Excellence*. New York: John Wiley & Sons, Inc., 1984.

Brown, W. Steven. *13 Fatal Errors Managers Make*. Old Tappan, New Jersey: Fleming H. Revell Company, 1985.

Buck, Lee. *Tapping Your Secret Source of Power*. Old Tappan, New Jersey: Fleming H. Revell Company, 1985.

Carnegie, Dale and Associates. *Managing Through People*. New York: Simon & Schuster, Inc., 1978.

DeBruyn, Robert I. *Causing Others to Want Your Leadership*. Manhattan, Kansas: DeBruyn & Associates, 1976.

Gschwandtner, Gerhard. *Superachievers*. Englewood Cliffs, New Jersey: Prentice-Hall, Inc., 1984.

Hersey, Paul and Kenneth Blanchard. *Management of Organizational Behavior*. Englewood Cliffs, New Jersey: Prentice-Hall, Inc., 1982.

Hickman, Craig and Michael Silva. *Creating Excellence*. New York: New American Library, 1984.

Hunsaker, Phillip L. and Anthony J. Alessandra. *The Art of Managing People*. Englewood Cliffs, New Jersey: Prentice-Hall, Inc., 1980.

Iacocca, Lee. *Iacocca.* New York: Bantam Books, 1984.

King, Patricia. *Performance Planning and Appraisal.* New York: McGraw-Hill Book Company, 1984.

Kirkpatrick, Donald I. *How to Improve Performance Through Appraisal and Coaching.* New York: AMACOM, 1982.

Linking Employee Attitude and Corporate Culture to Corporate Growth and Profitability. Philadelphia: Hay Management Consultants, 1984.

McCormack, Mark H. *What They Don't Teach You at Harvard Business School.* New York: Bantam Books, 1984.

Margerison, Charles. *How to Assess Your Managerial Style.* New York: AMACOM, 1980.

Peters, Thomas J. and Nancy K. Austin. *A Passion for Excellence.* New York: Random House, 1985.

Peters, Thomas J. and Robert H. Waterman, Jr. *In Search of Excellence.* New York: Harper & Row, Publishers, 1982.

Smith, Fred. *Learning to Lead.* Waco, Texas: Word Books, 1986.

Inspiration and Self-Help

Carnegie, Dale. *How to Stop Worrying and Start Living.* New York: Simon & Schuster, Inc., 1975.

Carnegie, Dale. *How to Win Friends and Influence People.* New York: Pocket Books, 1982.

Conwell, Russell. *Acres of Diamonds.* Old Tappan, New Jersey: Fleming H. Revell Company, 1975.

Cooper, Kenneth, M.D. *The Aerobics Program for Total Well-Being.* New York: M. Evans, 1982.

Dobson, James. *What Wives Wish Their Husbands Knew About Women.* Wheaton, Illinois: Tyndale House Publishers, 1975.

Follett, Ken. *On Wings of Eagles.* New York: William Morrow and Company, Inc., 1983.

Glass, Kinder, and Ward. *Positive Power for Successful Salesmen.* Dallas: Crescendo, 1972.

Hayes, Ira. *Yak! Yak! Yak!* Ira M. Hayes, 1978.

Jones, Charlie. *Life Is Tremendous.* Wheaton, Illinois: Tyndale House, 1981.

Maltz, Maxwell. *Psycho-cybernetics.* New York: Pocket Books, 1970.

Mandino, Og. *The Greatest Miracle in the World.* New York: Bantam Books, 1977.

Marshall, Peter and David Manuel. *The Light and the Glory*. Old Tappan, New Jersey: Fleming H. Revell Company, 1977.

Peale, Norman Vincent. *The Power of Positive Thinking*. New York: Fawcett, 1978.

Schuller, Robert H. *Tough Times Never Last, but Tough People Do*. Nashville: Thomas Nelson Publishers, 1983.

Schwartz, David J. *The Magic of Thinking Big*. St. Louis: Cornerstone, 1962.

Smith, Fred. *You and Your Network*. Waco, Texas: Word Books, 1984.

Spickard, Anderson and Barbara R. Thompson. *Dying for a Drink*. Waco, Texas: Word Books, 1985.

Teaff, Grant. *I Believe*. Waco, Texas: Word Books, 1975.

Waitley, Denis. *Seeds of Greatness*. Old Tappan, New Jersey: Fleming H. Revell Company, 1983.

Other Books by Zig Ziglar

Confessions of a Happy Christian. Gretna, Louisiana: Pelican, 1978.

Dear Family. Gretna, Louisiana: Pelican, 1984.

Raising Positive Kids in a Negative World. Nashville: Thomas Nelson Publishers, 1985.

See You at the Top. Gretna, Louisiana: Pelican, 1974.

Steps to the Top. Gretna, Louisiana: Pelican, 1985.

Zig Ziglar's Secrets of Closing the Sale. Old Tappan, New Jersey: Fleming H. Revell Company, 1984.

For Your Continuing Education

Bits & Pieces. Published monthly by Economics Press, Inc., 12 Daniel Road, Fairfield, New Jersey 07006.

Walter V. Clark Associates, Inc., 2 Jackson Walkway, Providence, Rhode Island 02903. 401-421-2008.

Communication Briefings. Published monthly by Encoders, Inc., 860 Westminster Boulevard, Blackwood, New Jersey 08012.

Decker Communications Report. Published monthly by Magna Publications, Inc., 607 N. Sherman Avenue, Madison, Wisconsin 53704.

Front Line Management. Published by Economics Press, Inc., Fairfield, New Jersey 07006.

Guideposts. Published monthly by Norman Vincent Peale and Ruth Stafford Peale, Carmel, New York 10512.

Harvard Business Review. Published bimonthly by the Graduate School of Business Administration, Boston, Massachusetts 02163.

National Speakers Association, 4323 N. 12th Street, Suite 103, Phoenix, Arizona 85014. 602-265-1000.

On the Upbeat. Published monthly by Economics Press, Inc., 12 Daniel Road, Fairfield, New Jersey 07006.

Performax Systems International, Inc. Personal Profile Systems, 3140 Harbor Lane North, Suite 200, Minneapolis, Minnesota 55441. 612-540-5110.

Personal Selling Power. Published monthly by Gerhard Gschwandtner & Associates, P.O. Box 5467, Fredericksburg, Virginia 22403.

Reader's Digest. Published monthly by the Reader's Digest Association, Inc., Pleasantville, New York 10570.

Research Institute Marketing for Sales Executives. Published by the Research Institute of America, Inc., 589 Fifth Avenue, New York, N.Y. 10017.

Selling by Phone. Published by Economics Press, Inc., Fairfield, New Jersey 07006.

Success. Published monthly by Success Unlimited, Inc., P.O. Box 2240, Boulder, Colorado 80322.

Supervisory Management. Published monthly by the American Management Association, 135 West 50th Street, New York, N.Y. 10020.

Working Smart. Published monthly by Learning International, P.O. Box 10211, Stamford, Connecticut 06904.

Working Together. Published by the Dartnell Corporation, 4660 Ravenswood Avenue, Chicago, Illinois 60640.

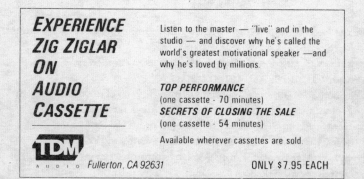